The Christian Family

ANSWER BOOK

The
Christian
Family
ANSWER BOOK

Mike Yorkey

VICTOR BOOKS

A DIVISION OF SCRIPTURE PRESS PUBLICATIONS INC.
USA CANADA ENGLAND

Unless otherwise indicated, all Scripture references are from the *Holy Bible, New International Version®*. Copyright © 1973, 1978, 1984 by International Bible Society. Used by permission of Zondervan Publishing House. All rights reserved; other references are from the *New American Standard Bible* (NASB), © the Lockman Foundation 1960, 1962, 1963, 1968, 1971, 1972, 1973, 1975, 1977.

Editor: Barbara Williams
Design: Andrea Boven
Cover Illustration: Joel Spector
Production: Julianne Marotz
Book Flow/Electronic Production: Elizabeth MacKinney

Library of Congress Cataloging-in-Publication Data

The Christian family answer book / [edited by] Mike Yorkey.
    p. cm.
    ISBN 1-56476-598-9
    1. Family—United States—Religious life—Miscellanea.
2. Parenting—Religious aspects—Christianity—Miscellanea.
I. Yorkey, Mike.
BV4526.2.C442   1996
248.8'45—dc20   96-15976
                                                 CIP

CONTENTS

3—ALL ABOUT KIDS

4—ALL ABOUT SCHOOL ISSUES

5—ALL ABOUT FAMILY ISSUES

6—ALL ABOUT TEEN ISSUES

7—ALL ABOUT MOTHERS

8—ALL ABOUT FATHERS

9—ALL ABOUT MARRIAGE

10—ALL ABOUT THE CIVIL WAR OF VALUES

11—ALL ABOUT DIFFICULT FAMILY PROBLEMS

FOREWORD

In the world we live in, it's not "politically correct" to state there are "answers" to anything. After all, important issues are painted gray, not black and white. And every decision becomes a matter of "personal choice," not biblical principle.

Toss in the constant "double speak" our culture engages in and ending a third-term baby's life becomes a "choice," twelve-year-olds who murder a six-year-old are called "victims," and parents who pray to a personal God are considered on the "fringe" or extremists.

No wonder juries can't convict, teachers are afraid to teach, and parents feel alone and isolated!

If you're tired of where this rudderless society has been taking you and your family, then you've picked up the right book. What my good friend (and award winning editor) Mike Yorkey has done for years at Focus on the Family, is make their magazine the industry standard of excellence and encouragement.

Now your family and mine gets the benefit of dipping into the very best of articles from nearly a dozen years of cutting-edge family counsel. Real-life advice from many of the top family experts in the country, who base their lives and writings on God's unfailing, unchangeable Word.

Let's face it. We all have questions. What we haven't had is a book like this that gives concise, biblical, uplifting "answers" to the issues that hit closest to home. My wife, Cindy, and I keep this book on our shelf, and have turned to it for timely, life-tested, God-honoring advice. I'm sure you and your family will find it a treasure trove of vital information . . . and the answer to many of your parenting questions as well.

John Trent, Ph.D.

INTRODUCTION

As a book author and magazine editor for the last ten years, I've read a lot of great material on how to raise a family and be a better husband. Has this made me a better father to my two children and a better husband to my wife, Nicole? I certainly hope so. Do I still make mistakes? Yes, but I'm making fewer (I hope).

I'm certainly trying to put this knowledge to good use. Thus, when Victor Books approached me and asked if I would be interested in putting together *The Christian Family Answer Book*, the project seemed like a perfect fit. Not only would I benefit from assembling this question-and-answer book, but perhaps God would bless the effort and lives and marriages would be touched.

I've divided *The Christian Family Answer Book* into eleven topical areas. Please note that the questions are designed to move you along while imparting excellent advice. It's written in a breezy, fast-paced style that works for busy parents.

There's a lot of practical information and solid encouragement in the pages of this book. That's why I hope you look at *The Christian Family Answer Book* as a resource you'll want to pick up time and time again.

1

*All About
Raising Kids*

1

What the Bible Says About the Family

....

■ **What does God have to say about the family in His Word? It seems like the only time my pastor talks about this subject is on Mother's Day and Father's Day.**

You need to understand how prominent the family is in the Bible. One superb showing of God's family portrait is inserted in Israel's ancient hymnbook, the Psalms.

> *Unless the Lord builds the house,*
> *They labor in vain who build it;*
> *Unless the Lord guards the city,*
> *The watchman keeps awake in vain.*
> *It is vain for you to rise up early,*
> *To retire late,*
> *To eat the bread of painful labors;*
> *For He gives to His beloved even in his sleep.*
>
> *Behold, children are a gift of the Lord;*
> *The fruit of the womb is a reward.*
> *Like arrows in the hand of a warrior,*
> *So are the children of one's youth.*
> *How blessed is the man whose quiver is full of them;*

They shall not be ashamed,
When they speak with their enemies in the gate.

(PS. 127, NASB)

The home begins with a philosophy, with a personal commitment. It is *not* saying you don't build your home—you do. Rather, it is a warning against the idiocy of trying to build your home alone. You will never pull off the assignment as a Christian parent—as a parent in a dynamic relationship—without the Lord! You will never succeed even if you redouble your efforts by getting up earlier and staying up later. You will only ache, and there is no hurt comparable to the suffering of a failed parent.

■ **My guess is no amount of professional help will compensate either. What is God saying about children in Psalm 127?**

Look at His descriptive terms. He calls children a "heritage" or "gift." One authority says this also could be translated "assignment." Your children are God's assignment of commission, and He does not waste children on parents. He knows the very kind to send to you. Did you think God gave you children for what you could do for them?

■ **Well, that thought did cross my mind.**

No, He gave them because of what they could do for *you.* You can meet your children's particular needs, and they can meet yours in a unique and special way.

The psalmic portrayal also calls children a "reward." Not a curse, not a tragedy, not an accident, but as an expression of God's favor. It is a thrilling sight to see your children through the lens of Scripture as His trophies.

■ **We're childless at the moment. What happens to the couples who don't have children?**

Though children are one obvious reward of the Lord upon a marriage, it does not follow that if you do not have children, He is not rewarding you. God has many creative means of rewarding His children.

If babies are born into your home, you are highly honored. If, in the providence of God, you do not have children, then God has an altogether different and unique plan for you. You may discover the most distinctive ministry you have ever experienced in life—building into the lives of children whose parents couldn't care less. Some of us are here only because somebody else cared for us more than our parents did.

■ **Why are children called "arrows" in Psalm 127? That's quite a word picture.**

That description presupposes that they are to be launched toward a target—and that you know what the target is. One major reason parents fail is they have not sighted the target. Talk to the teens in the average church youth group about their parents. You get a graphic replay of adult activity—often frenzied, directionless, reminiscent of the definition of a fanatic (one who redoubles his efforts *after* he has lost sight of his goal).

Good children don't emerge by accident; they are the fruit of careful cultivation. Make raising good children your clear-cut objective, the specific aim for which you are trusting God.

■ **Our family goes to a large church in the suburbs, and I was scanning the church bulletin recently.** *Every* **night of the week had an activity—from Wednesday night services to Awanas to teen youth groups to prayer meetings. I'm feeling guilty that we don't participate in all these extracurricular activities.**

Don't feel guilty. Hopefully, you are trying to build a home life for your family. If you are in some church thing every night of the week, when are you supposed to spend time with your family? Churches should be engaged in a program of cooperation with the home, not competition. They should be our ally, not our adversary.

When participating in a church activity, two tests should be applied: Does it emphasize the importance of the church? Does it emphasize the importance of the home? In many churches today, the two are almost diametrically opposed. The home simply provides the church with "customers."

In contrast, a church should be primarily committed to training parents to do the work God has called *them* to do, not trying to do their work for them. The chief job of the home, as conceived by God, is to train the family members to live fruitfully in home, church, and society.

■ **I have a neighbor who spends a lot of time in church work, and he's being asked to speak more and more at out-of-town seminars. His kids play at our house all the time; I can tell they are starving for parental love. Is he blowing it?**

God says if you cannot conduct your home life, don't try to lead in public ministry. Think about it: The average church has a child 1 percent of the time; the home has him 83 percent of the time; and the school for the remaining 16 percent. We are too often trying to do in our church on a 1 percent-basis what we cannot accomplish. We are neglecting this choice 83 percent period when children are exposed to parents on a very dynamic interpersonal level. The home marks a child for life.

Columbia University spent $250,000 researching this area, only to corroborate the truth of Scripture. Conclusion: there is no second force in the life of a child that compares with the impact of his home.

SIX THINGS YOU SHOULD NEVER, NEVER DO (WELL, HARDLY EVER)

1. Don't threaten—you decimate your authority.

2. Don't bribe—bargaining usually makes you the loser.

3. Don't lose your temper—a clear demonstration of lack of control.

4. Don't use sarcasm or embarrassment—the fastest way to demolish a relationship.

5. Don't refuse to explain—they'll go elsewhere and you're on the outside.

6. Don't dash their dreams—your ticket into the generation gap.

■ **I'm very concerned about the climate *outside* the home. I know we don't live in a vacuum, and that we breathe the air of a world that is sensual, secular, and incredibly unscrupulous. I know that stuff is rubbing off on my children. In such an atmosphere, how do we train our children? Do we put our heads piously in the sand, hoping everything bad will go away?**

To answer that question, consider this story of two beautiful red cardinals. One spring, these two birds mated, built a nest in a small pyracantha tree, and flourished in the quiet beauty of their secluded home. The female had laid five eggs. She sat on them faithfully every day.

One day, very surreptitiously, a thief came along when the mother had left the eggs free for a short time. A squirrel disheveled the nest and stole the eggs. When the cardinals returned, they sat on a fence near the nest and began, extremely agitated, chirping and chattering as if to sound an SOS. Their home was ruined, and their family aborted.

What a picture of many Christian homes in which the parents look the other way, failing to realize the enemy is at hand.

■ **I understand that the enemy is at hand, so I keep a close eye on the kids. What are some things I can do to build my relationship with my kids? I don't want them to view me as a worrywart.**

Here are some standards for measuring the parent-child relationship:

1. Practice a sincere respect for the child's worth as an individual.
Does he speak to you? He will speak as long as you will listen. Listening far surpasses lecturing as a method of training. If your child does not talk to you, he pushed his "off" button sometime in the past.

2. Provide for your child's basic needs.
Don't provide for all of his *wants*, but rather his needs: privacy, a place to play and study, clean clothes, ownership of his own things, time to be alone, a sensible program of eating and exercise, and an opportunity to make appropriate decisions. Always tell him the truth.

3. Expose children to real-life experiences.
Use births, marriages, deaths, and disasters as teaching times. You will help both to satisfy her curiosity and avoid irrational fears.

4. Help the child set goals by discussing possible objectives.
For example, many children from Christian homes make commitments to Jesus Christ. The parents often comment favorably, but do little to implement the decision. The young person needs to discuss what has happened. He should be exposed to those who've made a similar commitment.

5. Teach the child the how-to of daily life so that she may function without frustration.
Confidence grows in the soil of doing it yourself. We laugh at

the girl who cannot drive a car properly, the boy who can't get his own breakfast, the man who is lost without his wife to match his ties and socks. Seldom do we consider the frustration that hobbles these individuals. Nobody ever took the time to teach them.

A child should be taught to do as much by himself as he can handle. This builds confidence and contributes to safety. The toddler who is taught to use the telephone with serious intent— not as a toy—has been given a tool that will be useful for a lifetime.

6. Fences lend security for emotional development.

Set reasonable limits for the child's behavior. Just as surely as the backyard fence protects in a physical way, behavioral limits shield the young person from the fear of not knowing when to stop.

This material is adapted from Heaven Help the Home *(Victor) by Howard Hendricks.*

2

The Need to Discipline

. . . .

■ **What is discipline? I'm pregnant with my first child, and I'm not sure what this exactly means.**

Discipline is teaching a child the way he should go. Unfortunately, it's one of the most misunderstood words in the English language. Some people think "discipline" means punishment. That's obvious when you hear a parent tell a child, "You better straighten up or I'm going to lay some discipline on you."

However, the English word "discipline" comes from the Latin "disciplina," which means instruction. When we discipline, we teach. But as many young parents have discovered, children are not so easily taught. That's because they have wills of their own. But stick with it, Mom and Dad. When you teach a child discipline, you are giving him one of the most important tools for his future success and happiness. Deep down, children *want* to be disciplined. They *want* parental leadership.

■ **We are parents of a nineteen-month-old boy who is the delight of our lives. Recently, however, he's been a handful. Whenever we ask him not to touch something at a friend's house, he'll look me in the face and then look at the china figurine—and pick it up anyway. When I say "No, Adam, that could break," he ignores me. I**

then have to take it out of his hands and put it away, but it seems like I can't get him to obey. What should I do?

No doubt about it—Adam is challenging you. He's saying, "Are you big enough to handle me or not?" At about eighteen months of age, children will start testing the boundaries. Their little bodies love to explore the new world around them, and that involves touching, bending, shaking, licking, and sometimes throwing everything in sight.

As a parent, you will have to set limits, and when those limits are broken, you will have to follow through and punish your child. He needs to learn what is right and what is wrong, and he also needs to learn to submit to your leadership.

■ **I want Adam to obey me. What are some ways I can control his behavior?**

TEN EASY STEPS FOR DEVELOPING YOUR NORMAL, HEALTHY BABY INTO A DRUG ADDICT OR ALCOHOLIC

1. Spoil him; give him everything he wants if you can afford it.

2. When he does wrong, you may nag him, but never spank him (unless he is showing signs of independence).

3. Foster his dependence on you, so drugs or alcohol can replace you when he is older.

4. Protect him from your husband and from all those mean teachers who threaten to spank him from time to time. Sue them if you wish.

5. Make all of his decisions for him, since you are a lot older and wiser than he. He might make mistakes and learn from them if you don't.

continued next page

If your child is *not* locked in a battle of wills with you, you should first *make* a request. "Adam, can you put that down?" This is the most positive way to control the child's behavior. It is not a statement, it is a question.

But requests do not always work, which means you will then have to *command* your child to obey. While requests are positive, commands give negative nonverbal messages. Therefore, you should issue commands only when a request has been ignored. What you are saying to the child is this: "I don't care what you are feeling. You have to obey me because I know what's best for you."

If he refuses your command, then you have to ask yourself if your toddler is defying you. In those times of open rebellion, the child will need to be punished, usually with a spanking.

■ Should you spank a child for doing something stupid, like spilling her milk?

Of course not. Spankings should be reserved for those occasions when your child is acting defiantly against you or when she has deliberately disobeyed you. If she looks you in the eye and says, "No, I won't clean up my room," then you can repeat your request. If she persists and repeats, "No, I won't," then you can warn her that if she doesn't turn around and march right now to her room, she will receive a spanking.

If she still says no, then she is testing you. Will you follow through on what you said you were going to do? At times like those, you have to give it to her.

■ How should I administer the spanking?

Most child experts agree that two or three swats on the buttocks or back of the legs with a "switch" or neutral object should do the trick. Scripture speaks of using a *rod*, or flexible stick or switch, to discipline children. A very thin switch doesn't cause the child any physical harm, yet the sting is sufficient to convey the desired message.

As for the number of swats to give, some people say that children should be spanked until they cry. This perspective indicates a poor understanding of children. Under this method, they may learn to cry very quickly to manipulate their parents,

6. Criticize his father openly, so your son can lose his own self-respect and confidence.

7. Always bail him out of trouble so he will like you. Besides, he might harm your reputation if he gets a police record. Never let him suffer the consequences of his own behavior.

8. Always step in and solve his problems for him, so he can depend on you and run to you when the going gets tough. Then when he is older and still hasn't learned how to solve his own problems, he can continue to run from them through heroin and alcohol.

9. Just to play it safe, be sure to dominate your husband and drive him to drink too, if you can.

10. Take lots of unnecessary prescription drugs yourself, so that taking nonprescription drugs won't be a major step for him.

or, because they may feel dominated, they may refuse to give their parents the "satisfaction" of seeing them cry. Usually two or three swats is sufficient.

■ **Doesn't spanking create aggression and child abuse? I've had friends say they don't want their children to grow up learning "violence."**

Child abuse occurs when discipline is erratic, or when it is prompted by an attitude of revenge. Without a systematic method of discipline, some parents get so frustrated that they "fly off the handle" and end up whacking their kids. That is not right, nor is it good discipline.

As long as discipline is administered in love and consistency, you need not worry that it will make your child belligerent or aggressive.

HOW TO PRODUCE AN OBSESSIVE CHILD

1. Talk all the time, but don't be very active physically, and never listen to what your child has to say.

2. Expect perfect etiquette and manners from your child from his day of birth on. Don't tolerate any mistakes.

3. Be an introvert. Don't let him see your interaction in a healthy manner with other human beings.

4. Be very critical of the people around you—this includes your minister, your neighbors, your husband, and, most importantly, your child.

5. Be a real snob.

6. Be sure to domineer your husband as well as your children. This is very important.

7. Emphasize instrumental morality as a way of being superior to other children, or of getting to heaven.

continued on next page

■ **My children cry after I spank them, so I often hug them after a spanking. Is that the right thing to do?**

By all means, hug that child and hold him close to your breast! He just wants to be reassured of your love. You will often find that those special moments *after* a spanking is when you and your child will feel the closest to each other.

■ **When my seven-year-old boy started school, he used to throw a terrible temper tantrum every morning. He yelled, screamed, and even bit and clawed me. The problem was beyond my comprehension, so I sought a Christian counselor. His advice was to** make a contract with Josh. I was to tell him that he was going to school no matter what, and that he would get three spankings with the Ping-Pong paddle each time he threw a tantrum.

His advice worked! After only two days, Josh was going to school peacefully, and after two weeks, he was riding his bike to school. Why did this counselor's advice stop Josh's temper tantrums?

Because Josh quickly learned that the certainty of discipline made fussing unprofitable for him. To discipline children properly and consistently, we need to understand the primary purpose of discipline: to warn and to teach.

Discipline effectively *warns* children that their misbehavior will be harmful to themselves and/or others. For example, the consequences of running into the street without looking for cars can be devastating; the discipline for it is minor by comparison.

The second goal of discipline is to *teach* children appropriate behavior. The goals of teaching and correction fall into four main categories:

- ▶ *Correct response to authority.* All of us need to learn to respond to authority with healthy respect, rather than fear or rebellion. If children are disciplined in a loving, consistent way, they can learn to be honest, respectful, and interactive with authority for the rest of their lives.
- ▶ *Self-control.* Appropriate discipline teaches children about acceptable behavior by establishing limits to curtail unac-

8. Don't make any serious commitments to God yourself, and be critical of the religious convictions of your child's grandparents.

9. Tell your child that his father is the boss, but in reality, allow your husband to be nothing but a figurehead.

10. Expect your child to be completely toilet-trained by the time he is twelve months old. Then, when he grows older, he can get even with you by being constipated much of the time.

11. Be a real miser with your money. Always save for the future, and don't let that future ever come.

12. Emphasize the letter of the law rather than the spirit of the law. Make your rules quite rigid, and never allow any exceptions.

13. Practice the Victorian ethic. Shame your child for being a sexual being.

ceptable behavior. As they mature, they will learn to internalize these limits in the form of healthy self-control.

▶ *Love.* Some of us have a tendency to think that love is consistently warm and fun, and that discipline is harsh and bitter. But discipline is (or should be) a strong and active message of love utilized to protect and teach children. Such discipline, given in love, is not always fun, but it is necessary.

▶ *Obedience to God.* The way children are taught to respond to their parents is usually the way they will respond to God. Be sure to communicate to your children that your discipline is designed to teach them what God wants them to learn, and that isn't some arbitrary, self-imposed standard. Also, strive to be a good example of living obediently by obeying God yourself . . . whether you feel like it or not.

This material is adapted from Discipline With Love *(Word/Rapha) by Robert S. McGee,* Parents & Children *(Victor) by Dr. Ross Campbell, and* Christian Child Rearing and Personality Development *(Baker Book House Company, Grand Rapids, Mich.) by Dr. Paul Meier.*

OLD YELLER

Yelling, in the long run, is a lazy and usually ineffective way of disciplining your child. For some children, yelling falls on deaf ears. They shrug it off with a casualness that almost causes the yelling parent to yell even louder. But they're doing that because they want to see if they can get underneath the skin of Mom or Dad.

For other children, particularly those who are shy, yelling can be harmful. A sharp "Stop it right now!" reduces them to tears. Instead of screaming, take the child by the hand. Establish eye contact and tell him what will happen if he doesn't change his behavior, and follow through. If you find yourself yelling at trivial misbehavior, it's time to get a grip on yourself.

3

Hang in There, Mom and Dad

■ I just went toe-to-toe with my two-year-old boy. Like Rocky Balboa's first fight against Apollo Creed, the bout went the distance. It happened last week when I put Jake down for his regular nap. Jake sat right back up in his bed and grinned at me—his mother. *You're not going to get me to sleep,* his face of defiance said.

Oh, yes, I am, I said, as I laid him back down in his crib. *Oh, no, you're not,* he replied, standing back up.

This tug-of-war of wills lasted an hour, with me returning every few minutes to lay him down on his back. I quickly tired of this game, which isn't surprising, since two-year-olds have more energy than a trio of rap dancers. Finally, perseverance prevailed, and Jake fell asleep. Did I handle this right?

You were correct in persevering. Perhaps something inside told you to remain firm. Whether you knew it or not, you were locked in a battle of wills, and you *had* to win—for Jake's sake.

The opposite ends of the discipline spectrum are "ultra-strict" and "Dr. Spock." That's a little joke. Actually, the other end is "ultra-permissive." The goal of Christian parents is to find the middle ground that's best for *each child*. Yes, a hard-nosed method may have worked with the oldest, but that doesn't mean it will be the best approach for your youngest.

Take a long-range view regarding discipline and conflicts. For openers, don't fear it. Sure, there are times when you don't want to come down hard on your child's misbehavior. Other times, you're too *tired* to deal with it.

It's a fact of life that you and your children will butt heads off and on until the day they leave home (and beyond!). Perhaps they won't like your house rules because they're the strictest ones on the block. Maybe you make them do their homework before they can play. Perhaps you enforce a "no-TV-on-school-nights" edict. Maybe their curfew is earlier than their peers'. As you set rules in your house, you will have to decide where to train your big guns and when to hold your fire.

■ **What are some sources of conflict I can expect from my preteens?**

These are the top sources of conflict before the teen years:

- ► wanting to spend time with their friends
- ► fighting with siblings
- ► not doing what they're told
- ► outright disobedience
- ► being selfish
- ► trouble at school
- ► talking back
- ► not listening to directions
- ► breaking rules
- ► temper tantrums
- ► telling lies or half-truths

If your kids are infants or in the cute toddler stage, you've got a few things to anticipate. (And you thought diapers, teething, and ear infections were a pain!)

As kids move into the teen years, they become more responsible (no promises, though). But along with fixing their own breakfasts, cleaning their rooms, and doing homework without being reminded, their ability to cause a parent grief becomes more . . . *sophisticated*.

Teenage conflicts offer whole new worlds for testing parents' patience—and their ability to respond correctly. Instead of moms (or dads) looking down to the child, they're often locked eye-to-eye with them after behaviors such as these:

- ► using bad language
- ► fighting or loud arguments with siblings
- ► talking back
- ► disobeying deliberately the parents' expressed wishes
- ► cleaning room, finishing chores
- ► displaying an attitude of disrespect and defiance
- ► fibbing and telling lies
- ► arriving late without a phone call
- ► breaking curfew
- ► going to church
- ► dealing with girls, girls, girls
- ► dealing with boys, boys, boys (like, duhhh)
- ► shooting at a train with a BB gun (Easily solved: no BB guns.)
- ► wearing makeup after Mom had forbidden it.
- ► drinking or taking drugs (That won't happen to *our* kids, of course.)
- ► hanging out with the wrong crowd of friends.

■ **Whew! Those lists make me wish I could invent a time-warp machine so I can keep my kids at their cutest and most compliant ages. Is it possible for my kids to end up in their twenties as good kids? (And for me to end up still in my right mind?)**

Of course, it is. It's not a bleak situation; it only looks that way. Here's what you key in on. In any era, moms and dads have wanted kids to act with good *behavior*. For many of the parents, behavior is *the* target goal, especially since acting up leads to even worse behavior.

One parent who raised three strong-willed kids who never went through a rebellious stage (hard to believe, isn't it?) articulated it best: "Behavior wasn't the most important issue. Our *relationship* was."

You want kids to be raised not in an *authoritarian* home, but in an *authoritative* home. Permissive parents eventually let their kids take control. A strict home simply means the parents stay in control. Being a strict parent isn't being tough or unreasonable. It means knowing that if you lose the leadership in the home, you're probably going to lose the kids.

Here's what one father did, however, to keep his three kids on his team. As they were growing up, he took the punishment *for them* at least once.

■ **You mean he let the kids spank him when they did something wrong?**

Right. A situation would occur where the kids were obviously guilty. After calmly and clearly establishing that they did deserve the paddle, the father would say something like, "I want to show you what Jesus did for us. Now we agree that what you did was deliberately wrong and deserves punishment. Instead of giving you the paddle, I'll take your punishment for you."

THE TOP TEN WORST WAYS TO DISCIPLINE YOUR GRADE-SCHOOLERS

10. Tell them they can only watch four hours of television per night.

9. Send them to their rooms (where their toys are).

8. Promise them a trip to McDonald's if they stop misbehaving.

7. If they're misbehaving at McDonald's, promise 'em Chuck E. Cheese's.

6. Tell them if they don't shape up, they'll have to go live at the pastor's house.

5. Hit them over the head with one of Dr. Dobson's books.

4. Dangle them over a lawn mower.

3. Threaten to tell Santa what they're like. Or, threaten to tell Santa not to come to your house this year.

2. Bribe them with ice cream. (That's like trying to extinguiush a car fire with a gas pump hose.)

1. Just say yes.

■ **What happened when he said that?**

His two oldest kids couldn't do it. They broke down and cried. His youngest didn't miss his chance. He was tentative, though, perhaps because he was in awe of the moment. It was like he was violating something sacred. After he smacked his father a couple of times, they sat and talked about what Jesus did; what it was like to take their place even though he didn't do anything wrong.

■ **I bet that little episode stuck in the memories of his kids.**

It sure did. Not only will they never forget the sight of their father taking their punishment for them, but it also accomplished at least three other goals:

1. It taught a spiritual lesson: Kids will remember their sinful nature and what God did to initiate a relationship with them

even though they were clearly in the wrong.

2. It allowed each child to see that he's only punished after establishing the guilt of deliberate disobedience or a willful, defiant attitude (as opposed to childish mistakes).

3. It moved the parent/child relationship up another notch toward the *ultimate goal* of mutual respect and friendship.

■ **Explain this "relationship" thing again. Why is it important to work on my relationship with my kids?**

Former Chicago Bears head coach Mike Ditka had some explosive coaching habits. After repeated tirades with his quarterback one year, he was asked by reporters if he was worried about the player's relationship with him. His response?

"Relationship? What do I care about a relationship? I'm the head coach."

When you're coaching forty-seven professional athletes, you can get away with that type of strategy. But when you're coaching precious sons or daughters to be lifelong followers of Jesus Christ, the quality of your relationship is a strong determiner of whether they'll respond to your faith the way you'd like . . . or resentfully pull away from you for a lifetime.

That's why "relationship" is so important. It's what keeps you and your children close for the long haul.

This material is adapted from Faithful Parents, Faithful Kids *by Greg Johnson and Mike Yorkey,* © *1993. Used by permission of Tyndale House Publishers, Inc. All rights reserved.*

4

Four Ways to Become a Listening Parent

. . . .

■ **I know it's important for parents to listen to their kids. Can you give some tips to keep in mind?**

Here's Listening Tip #1: Simply shut up and let your children talk.

■ **Whoa! That's pretty crude.**

Sorry for the direct language, but it's true. You can't listen if you're talking. Zip it! Close your mouth and force yourself to let your children talk. Listen to their words. Examine the expressions on their faces as they convey their thoughts. By listening regularly and repeatedly, you will begin to get to *know* your child. Keep this thought in mind: Talk and you say what you already know, but listen and you can learn something new.

■ **You know, you may be right. Recently, I met with a very important person. As I waited in his executive secretary's office, I was a little nervous. When I was ushered into his presence, I became more nervous. Why? Because this learned, successful man barely said a word. He kept asking me questions, saying he wanted to know as much about me as he possibly could. I learned something that day: Let the other person do the talking!**

The smartest people you'll meet in the fields of business or parenting are usually the best listeners. Conversely, the dumbest individuals are the blabbermouths.

Here's Listening Tip #2: Structure the time and place to listen. It's hard to talk next to a passing freight train! There is a time and place most appropriate to listen to your child. Find out where that place is. It may be fishing, eating lunch at McDonald's, riding a ski lift, going grocery shopping, walking in the mall, watching a football game, sitting on the back porch, or tucking your child in at night.

Do you know the best places to get your child to talk? If you don't, pay attention the next time your child opens up. What are you doing? Where are you?

Obviously, it would be ideal if there were a regular pattern to your listening time with your child. Generally, it is better if just one parent is present. There are times when both Mom and Dad can listen together. However, kids have a tendency to open up more with just one parent.

Find the best time and place, and regularly establish an opportunity of listening to your child. You will fall in love with those moments.

■ **It seems like each time I get into a good conversation with my children, the phone rings or I have to run off to an appointment. What can I do?**

Listen to Listening Tip #3: Squelch all interruptions. Think for a moment . . . what or who is interrupting the listening time with your son or daughter? Identify those interrupters and make a commitment to stop them.

When you're at home, keep telephone conversations as short as possible, turn the TV off, keep the radio low, and get ready to start listening to your kids.

Also think through any decisions that take you away from your kids.

■ **What do you mean?**

One time, a teenage son came home and with great dismay told his father how one of his friends was not going to the Kansas City Chiefs football game with his dad.

"Why's that?" the father asked.

"His dad is going to take one of his business associates instead."

"I can't believe it!"

"You would never do that to me, Dad!"

Yes, there are times when we need enjoyment with friends, but can you imagine choosing a friend over your son for the football game? Don't do it, Dad! Your time with him is limited. Some day he will be gone, and all you will have left is memories.

■ I'm starting to get the message—LOUD AND CLEAR. What's the fourth tip?

Listening Tip #4: Inhibit an explosive response. In other words, hear the full story before jumping to conclusions. When we become good listeners with our kids, we can learn some things that might have provoked a quick-tempered response on other occasions. Although it can be trying at times and extremely difficult to accomplish, hold your response until the right time.

That doesn't mean our parenting relationship is a "one way, our way" type of arrangement. The role of parents is to discipline, correct, disagree, and con-

> **QUOTEBOOK**
>
> "People who fly into a rage always make a bad landing."
>
> —WILL ROGERS

front. Sequentially, this should happen *after* we have listened and heard all the facts and sentiments our children are attempting to express.

The malady of our day is the alarming number of teens who commit suicide each year. Teen suicide leaves a parent dizzy with grief and despair. Suicidologists make it clear that the majority of young people who take their lives emit warning signs prior to their fatal death wish. Listening can prevent this tragedy.

Consider this heartrending letter from Dawn, a mother:

As you have probably guessed, I'm yet another mother trying to pick up the pieces after my daughter Leslie's suicide on December 14. Indeed, Leslie had gone through a lot of classic signs—a loner period, involvement in drugs, etc. It all terminated when my house was raided for drugs because her boyfriend was selling pot out of Leslie's room. The case was dismissed because the narcotics agents said they didn't have enough evidence to issue a warrant.

That was a turning point in our lives. I wanted to distance

Leslie from her boyfriend and other peer influences, so I sent her to live with our other daughter in Portland, Maine. Leslie came off drugs and alcohol and threw herself into her studies. I kept as close as I could to her via phone and periodic visits. Last May, she returned home for Mother's Day. Our plan was to let her put her toe "back in the water" and see if she thought she could return home for good. It was not to be. She could see that she would cave in to peer pressure again, so she returned to Portland. It was very hard for us, as we missed each other terribly. To be honest, I wanted her home.

Kelly, her sister, said she was quiet for a while after she returned to Portland, but then she soon bounced back and picked up her studies and projects at school, including gardening and Sober Support groups.

Her grandmother, my mom, died in November, and she and Leslie were very close. Then Leslie got a letter that her boyfriend was getting married. A slight tiff with her sister completed the scenario for the day. That afternoon, her sister found her on the floor of her bedroom, dead of a gunshot wound to the head.

Like all parents, I'm shattered. I'll heal, but I'll never quit crying.

Apparently, Leslie didn't have anyone to talk to the time she needed it most. Parents, take heed. Start listening. In fact, start listening today!

This material is adapted from How to Save Your Kids from Ruin *(Victor) by Jerry Johnston.*

5

Showing Love through Physical Contact

. . . .

■ **My parents never touched me when I was growing up, so consequently I have trouble kissing my daughter when she goes to bed or giving my son's hair a tousle. I think it was because my dad felt children should grow up to "be strong," but I have an ache in my heart. Is my problem common?**

Indeed, it is. Surprisingly, studies show that most parents touch their children only when they have to—helping them dress, take off clothes, or perhaps a boost into the car. Otherwise, few parents take advantage of a pleasant, effortless way of helping give their children that unconditional love they so desperately need. You seldom see a parent take an opportunity to touch his child out of the blue.

■ **Do you mean hugging, kissing, that sort of thing?**

We're talking about *any* physical contact. It is such a simple thing to touch a child on a shoulder, gently poke him in the ribs, run your fingers through her hair. When you closely watch parents with their children, many actually attempt to make the least possible contact. It's as if these poor parents have the notion their children are like mechanical walking dolls, the object being to get them walking and behaving correctly with the least assistance.

These parents don't know the fantastic opportunities they are missing.

■ Has any research been done on the importance of physical touching?

Tons. Scientists have discovered that touch plays a surprising role in our physical and mental well-being, and it begins at birth. Researchers at the University of Miami Medical School's Touch Research Institute showed that premature babies who received three, fifteen-minute periods of slow, firm massage strokes each day showed 47 percent greater weight gain than their ward mates who did not get this attention. Eight months later, these babies displayed greater mental and physical skills.

■ So you mean "A hug a day will keep the doctor away"?

It's more than a hug. We're also talking about eye contact as part of our everyday dealings with our children. A child growing up in a home where parents use eye and physical contact will be comfortable with himself and other people. He will have an easy time communicating with others, and consequently be well liked and have good self-esteem. Appropriate and frequent eye and physical contact are two of the most precious gifts we can give our children.

■ Can you give me some examples of what we're talking about here?

Infants need to be held, cuddled, hugged, and kissed—the "ooey-gooey love stuff." This type of physical affection is *crucial* from birth until the boy reaches seven or eight years old. It's crucial because research shows that infant girls receive five times as much physical attention as boy infants.

As a boy grows and becomes older, his need for physical affection such as hugging and kissing lessens, but his need for physical contact does not. Instead of baby "love stuff," he needs "boy-style" physical contact, such as bear hugs, "give-me-five" hand slaps, and old-fashioned roughhousing.

Keep this thought in mind about giving physical affection to boys: It is far easier to give affection to a boy when he is younger, especially around twelve to eighteen months of age. As he grows older, it becomes more difficult. Why? One reason, as hinted at in an earlier question, is the false assumption that the physical display of affection is feminine.

■ We've discussed boys. What about the affection needs of girls?

Girls generally do not display as much directness as boys to emotional deprivation during their first seven or eight years. In other words, they do not make their affectional needs so evident. But don't let this fool you. Although girls don't show their misery as much when they are younger, they suffer intensely when not properly cared for emotionally.

With girls, physical contact (especially the affectionate type) *increases* in importance as she becomes older and reaches a zenith at round the age of eleven. What a critical time!

■ Why is affectionate love so important to girls at that age?

The answer: preparation for adolescence. Every girl enters adolescence with some degree of readiness. Some are well prepared, while others are poorly prepared.

The two most important aspects of this preparation for girls are self-image and sexual identity. If she is comfortable as a "woman" when she enters adolescence (usually around thirteen to fifteen), her adolescence will be relatively smooth, pleasant, and comfortable with only the usual ups and downs. The

---

THE TOP TEN WORST WAYS TO DISCIPLINE YOUR TEENAGERS

10. Tell 'em you *really* mean it this time.

9. Only *threaten* to take away their MTV.

8. Shame them with stories of how your parents never let *you* get away with all the stuff you let them do.

7. Tell them you'll make them get jobs if they don't agree to stop terrorizing you.

6. Ask your spouse to do it.

5. Make them get really goofy haircuts.

4. Sic the dog on them.

3. Burn their music CDs. (Careful: the fumes could take several years off your life.)

2. Change the locks on the house.

1. Send them to *your* parents' house for the weekend.

more stable and healthy her sexual identity, the better she will be able to withstand peer pressure. The less she thinks of herself as an "OK female," the less stable she will be. She will then be more susceptible to pressure of peers (especially males) and less able to hold on to the values you've taught.

■ **As a father, what can I do to make sure my daughter feels "OK female" when she hits adolescence?**

A girl gets her sexual identity at that age primarily from her father. If the father is dead or otherwise removed from relating to his daughter, a girl must find other parental figures to fill these needs. But when a father has a viable relationship with his daughter, he is the primary person who can help her be prepared in this particular way for adolescence. What a responsibility!

A father helps his daughter approve of herself by showing her that he approves of her. He does this by applying the principles we have discussed thus far—unconditional love, eye contact, and physical contact, as well as focused attention. A daughter's need for her father to do this begins as early as two years of age. This need, although important at younger ages, becomes greater as the girl grows older and approaches that magic age of thirteen.

One problem in our society is that as a girl grows older, a father usually feels increasingly uncomfortable about giving his daughter the affection she needs. This is extremely unfortunate. Yes, fathers, we must ignore our discomfort and give our daughters what is vital to them for their entire lives.

This material is adapted from How to Really Love Your Child *(Victor) by Dr. Ross Campbell and* Faithful Parents, Faithful Kids *by Greg Johnson and Mike Yorkey © 1993. Used by permission of Tyndale House Publishers, Inc. All rights reserved.*

2

All About
Transmitting
Spiritual Values

6

Every Home Is a Stage

■ Teaching our children a saving knowledge of Jesus Christ is the most important task parents have set before them. If, at the end of my life, I haven't transmitted my belief in Christ to my children, then I haven't been faithful to the calling God has given to me. How can I make sure I don't mess up?

You can do everything you can to lead them to a decision for Christ, but you can't *force* them to do it. You have to keep modeling Christian behavior to set the stage for your children. You do that by saying a blessing before meals and talking to them about how Jesus is always with them. Some children have their own spiritual awakening timetable, and all a parent can do is be there and listen.

■ My nineteen-year-old daughter, Beth Ann, is in her second year at a college in New England. Recently, I called the school administration and asked to speak to the person in charge of the spiritual nurturing of the students. The administrator didn't know how to answer. She said no parent had ever asked that question.

I'm worried about Beth Ann's salvation. Before she left for New England, I took her out for dinner—just the two of us. After a pleasant dinner and warm conversation, I gently asked her, "What do you believe about God?"

"Well, Dad," she replied, "I really believe all that you and Mom have talked about." That's all Beth Ann would say—or could say. Now my wife and I are upset, feeling like we have blown it. Have we?

Perhaps Beth Ann wasn't ready to talk about her faith. You need to tell her that you accepw her right where she is, and remind her that you love her unconditionally. We can coach our kids on faith, but we can't *make* them believe what we believe. We can't argue them into the kingdom/ and that's hard for many parents since we're used to making things happen in life.

■ **One time my eight-year-old daughter, Teri, was asked to clean up the toys in the basement. She wasn't getting any cooperation, however, from Jeff, her five-year-old brother. So Teri decided to get her brother in trouble by telling me that Jeff had hit her. I knew this was a lie, since I had been watching from afar all the time. When I asked her about it, she didn't want to admit that she made up the story. What should I do if I catch my child in a bold lie?**

Ask her to come to the living room couch. Then take out a Bible and show her 1 John 1:8-9: "If we claim to be without sin, we deceive ourselves and the truth is not in us. If we confess our sins, He is faithful and just and will forgive us our sins and purify us from all unrighteousness."

Then lovingly point out the need to ask God for forgiveness. If she accepts your leadership, lead her in prayer and ask her to confess her sin. It will still be a hard lesson for her to learn.

■ **To make my faith real to my kids, I often look for time when I can crack open my Bible when they're around. A good idea? Or is it too forced?**

Great idea. Kids, even if they won't appear to notice those things, *do* notice. Also, make sure church attendance isn't a helter-skelter thing. It's not a good witness to drop the kids off at church and drive off, which some parents have been known to do. Children are perceptive, and they are watching you like hawks, and they start watching awfully early.

continued on page 50

DON'T BE AFRAID TO FESS UP!

It helps to admit mistakes to your children. If you do mess up, ask your child to forgive you—they do it so easily.

I (Mike Yorkey) learned that lesson during the summer of 1991, when Focus on the Family moved from its Pomona headquarters in Southern California to Colorado Springs. A moving van packed our belongings, and we jumped into the family car for the trip east.

The first night at 10 P.M., we pulled into Las Vegas and checked into the Excalibur Hotel, then the world's largest with 4,200 rooms. The place is so huge that finding our room was a chore; we entered a wrong door from the parking lot and had to drag our heavy luggage past thousands of slot machines and gaming tables.

Tired, cranky, and out of sorts, we never thought we'd find the elevator to our room on the 24th floor. The next day at check-out time, I told Nicole I was making a "first trip" to the car with a couple of bags. I took my seven-year-old son, Patrick, with me. Leaving the hotel, the mid-August heat—it was 110 degrees that day—hit us like a sledge hammer. We trudged our way to the far reaches of the parking lot.

Wouldn't you know it? When we arrived at the car, I had forgotten the blasted keys. The last thing I wanted to do was lug that luggage all the way back to the hotel room. So I asked Patrick if he could "guard" the bags while I ran back to the hotel room for the keys.

I felt a little funny leaving Patrick in the middle of a Las Vegas parking lot, but it was midday. I would only be gone five minutes. Ten minutes max.

When I got back to the room, Nicole asked me where Patrick was. I pointed to the window.

"He's down with the car and luggage," I said.

"What?"

I repeated what I said.

"You stupid jerk!" Nicole screamed.

I bolted back to the elevator, fearing the worst. My only son. Kidnapped. Never to be seen again. When I got to the car, Patrick was standing there, hands in his pockets.

I hugged him, put the bags in the car, and walked him back to the hotel room. Then I sat him down on the queen bed.

"Patrick, Daddy just did a really stupid thing. I left you out with the car all alone, and I shouldn't have done that. I made a big mistake. I'm sorry, and I won't let it happen again. Can you forgive me?"

Patrick cast his eyes downward and whispered, "Sure, Dad. It's OK." I

continued next page

couldn't believe he wasn't mad at me.

I never felt so thankful in my life. Patrick was safe, and I had just experienced the unconditional love of a child. I felt humbled inside, but thankful I had learned such an important lesson.

That's right, Mom and Dad. When you're home, you're on stage one—front and center. You're the star of the show, and your audience is soaking in everything you say and do.

■ I've often heard Christian family experts say that values are caught by children, rather than taught. What does that mean?

You can't sit down a thirteen-year-old boy and say, "Jimmy, we're going to learn a little something about lying today." No, Jimmy learned that lesson a long time ago when he overheard you tell the pastor that you were going to be out of town during the church workday (but you never left the city limits that weekend).

Or how about the time you mentioned to your wife that you were thinking of buying a radar detector for your Saturn. Since you were racking up the miles on the freeway during the commute, you thought a Fuzzbuster was just the ticket to outwit the highway patrol.

What kind of lesson were you teaching your kids? Do you want to tell them that if you have enough money you can speed and evade the police?

■ I don't think my son will comprehend a real relationship with God until he's in his teens. His sister is spiritually immature too. Will they tune me out if I started talking about Christ all the time?

No, they won't. Not if you talk in your own words and at their level. Realize too that you set—or should set—the spiritual temperature around the house. You might organize a time of family prayer each month. Or keep a list of prayers in a loose-leaf notebook, and every now and then you can look back and see how God has answered your prayers. Maybe one time you can go around the dinner table and have everyone write something nice about their brother or sister in the notebook.

Although they might write something simple like "I like the way Willie shared with me," or "Julia played real nice with me," the main idea is that kids remember *something*. By writing them down, they can go back and read their comments any time and be encouraged.

The earlier you start these little rituals—such as genuine communication, a prayer notebook, or devotional time—the easier they'll be accepted by your children. Any counselor will tell you that values taught early in life have a better chance of sticking. If we put our relationship with God above sports, TV, work, and hobbies, then our children's attitude about loving God will be enhanced. Guaranteed.

■ **Daily or weekly "family devotions" are one of those ideas that sounds great on paper, but putting them into practice is easier said than done. I've found trying to be a spiritual leader in our home to be very difficult. Sometimes I lose my patience trying to meet my kids' spiritual needs. How can I get over this frustration?**

As for family devotions, you'll find the shorter the better. Many parents say they have learned to be sensitive about doing anything structured with their kids. Children can resent being "force-fed" spiritual doctrine. Keep modeling spiritual discipline to your kids. Let them see your praying when they walk into your bedroom in the morning. Let them hear normal, everyday conversation about eternal lives of others. Even sharing a couple of Bible

THE TOP TEN WORST EXCUSES HEARD FOR NOT GOING TO CHURCH

10. "If I went *every* Sunday, Christmas and Easter wouldn't seem quite as special."

9. "The people there are too friendly. They must be up to something."

8. "The NFL on FOX."

7. "I always feel guilty when I go."

6. "The time change is coming soon, and I'm afraid I'll go to church on the day I could have slept in an extra hour, and I'll be the only one there."

5. "Sunday is a day of rest. Need I say more?"

4. "If God had meant for us to go to church every Sunday, He never would have given us golf courses, Saturday nights, the NBA's Game of the Week, ten-course brunches, and cozy beds to sleep in."

3. "Why, those lying, cheating, hypocritical televangelists! They make me so mad."

2. "I always like to stay up late on Saturday nights, and I know that if I went to church the next morning, I would probably nod off during the pastor's sermon."

1. "I went last month when a friend got married."

verses at the breakfast table can be a good beginning. Reading a Bible story to the kids as they go down at night will work too, especially if they get to "stay up" to hear you read. In fact, you may find that the best time to have devotions is when you tuck the kids in bed. Lots of questions pop into their minds, and that's what makes it a special time. They will often talk about things that are bugging them, and when that happens, you can talk about what the Word says about it.

■ Sometimes I feel stupid praying about the "little things" with my kids. Should I feel that way?

Not at all. Even praying for stuff lost around the house—items you think God isn't concerned about—can turn into a spiritual lesson when the kids find that toy in a miraculous way.

■ I have to admit that I haven't been much of a spiritual model for my kids. How can I change things?

While radical changes may be in order, you should have a one-step-at-a-time strategy. Don't try to become "Joe Onfire" overnight. Here's a sample strategy to move forward:

- ▶ *Get rid of the past.* The Scripture from 1 John 1:9 quoted earlier in this chapter wasn't just a trite verse that applies to kids. It's *the* answer to starting fresh with God. No matter how far away we've walked from Him, all it takes is a quick turnarouod, and He's right there with us.
- ▶ *Examine the present.* In a journal, or perhaps just on a piece of paper, take inventory of your walk with God. If you haven't spent any meaningful time with Him for several months, write it down. If you haven't prayed for—or with—your kids in weeks, make a note of it too. Then resolve to improve.
- ▶ *Set a goal for tomorrow.* The fastest way to get discouraged is to make lofty goals for sweeping changes. Take a realistic look at your time and ask yourself where you could find five to fifteen minutes to get one-on-one with God. (Many working parents say it's best to do this before breakfast. Don't think you can pick it up at night. You'll be too tired.)
- ▶ *Start each quiet time with a prayer like this:* "Lord, I don't

want to spend time with You because I have to; I want to do this because no one loves me, accepts me, or understands me as You do. I need You. Guide me and speak loudly to my heart, and make me long for You."

Don't start a detailed prayer list if you've never had one before, and don't give yourself chapter and verse reading requirements. The key is getting thirsty for God again. Drowning yourself with major changes will not last.

► *Choose a few close friends for your team.* Tell your spouse, a friend at church, even your pastor that you're trying to make some big changes through some small steps. Tell them you would covet their prayers. No real friend would turn down that invitation for help.

Finally . . .

► *Realize that your schedule will probably not be "God friendly."* Satan works against us by keeping us away from things that will benefit us the most. His strategy is to keep us off balance and too busy to muster much spiritual hunger for God. He's successfully torpedoed generations, convincing them to reject—or neglect—Christ as their leader and authority. Most of the time we don't even realize Satan's been at work until it's too late.

Once we've lost the motivation to keep plugging along, he's succeeded. Many people will throw up their hands and complain that there's no hope.

■ **That's hardly the way to end a chapter, telling us there's no hope.**

Of course, there's always hope! No rut is too deep, no trench is too wide, no schedule is too hectic, and no heart is too cold for God. He will graciously allow you to start all over. God is a miracle-worker who delights in shedding light into the darkness of "hopeless" situatioos— like us. If your heart truly desires change, pray diligently. Don't give up until you're where you want to be. Then, by the Lord's mercy, you'll take one step toward Him . . . and another.

This material is adapted from Daddy's Home © *1992 and* Faithful Parents, Faithful Kids *by Greg Johnson and Mike Yorkey,* © *1993. Used by permission of Tyndale House Publishers, Inc. All rights reserved.*

7

Focusing on Family Prayer

◼ **Every morning, our family dresses quickly, grabs a bowl of cereal, and makes a mad dash to get to work or school on time. Lost in the rush, however, is prayer before the start of the day. How can I turn that situation around?**

If we try to live on the spiritual nourishment gained from just the Sunday worship service, we become like the Israelites who attempted to gather manna for several days. Since God had told them to pick up the manna each morning, those who disobeyed found their "left-overs" spoiled. We too must fetch our spiritual food daily and teach our children to do the same.

Many parents believe prayer time must be for a certain duration or culled from a specific outline or study. That doesn't have to be the case at all. Each family's personality and schedule is unique and should be considered as they're setting aside time to pray. Why not just call it "time with Jesus" and do it every day?

◼ **One obstacle we've found with family prayer is the limited attention span of our small children. How do we overcome that hurdle?**

Since the familiar adage "Children learn what they live" is true, we can painlessly give them good habits to emulate. Here are a few ways to get started:

- ▶ *Set the day's mood.* Since most families wake up in shifts, the easiest way to start the day with prayer is to make it the last thing the family does before piling into the car or before the first person leaves. Even with everyone in coats and holding books or car keys, this is an opportune moment to concentrate on the Lord as you ask Him to lead the day, to provide opportunities to share His love and Word, and to surround each one with His protection.
- ▶ *Be flexible.* If daily family prayer takes on a military stringency, it's not likely the children will look forward to it. Discipline is not the immediate goal. As you come to the prayer circle with lighthearted joy and anticipation, the children will see that God is approachable and accepting.

  In addition, you want to:
- ▶ *Occasionally take extra time.* Sunday morning at the breakfast table, for example, is a good time for the family to join hands and pray. Take a few minutes to greet the Lord together, thank Him for your blessings, and pray for the pastor and the congregation.
- ▶ *Make prayer a natural part of your routine.* Just as brushing teeth, feeding the dog, and making peanut-butter sandwiches quickly become part of our morning schedule, prayer can become an important habit too. This daily practice will never trivialize God or make prayer seem too familiar, but it will impress the importance of His presence upon each family member. Prayer builds families and encourages closeness, while honoring God as the ultimate head of the home.

■ **I need some parenting advice. I've only been a Christian for a year, and that's when I started taking our family to church. We have our teens involved in a youth group, but I sense that's not enough. How do I go about this?**

Do you want your children to run well in life rather than stumble through it? Would you like to see them among the increasing number of teens who are making pledges of virginity, praying around school flagpoles, sharing Christ on the sidelines of football games, starting anti-drug and alcohol accountability pacts, and participating in Bible study teams?

Sure, you do, and it's happening because moms and dads all across the country are exchanging their Just-a-Parent membership cards for invisible coaching jackets with two bright words stitched across the shoulder: FAITH TRAINER.

■ **Faith Trainer. So you mean I should be a spiritual coach to my kids?**

Yes, but it's more than that. You're running the "good race" as well. Ask any relay runners about "the zone," and they'll tell you it's the one place on the track where everything must come together. If the baton pass is not completed within that allotted space, the team is disqualified and the race is lost.

Moms and dads have a passing zone to contend with too. It's about one inch wide and eighteen years long. From the moment our children are born to the time they go out on their own, we have the awesome responsibility of training them to run on life's narrowest path—one that leads to godliness.

■ **How can I make a good pass to my children that will carry the baton of faith into the next generation?**

A DOZEN WAYS TO TELL YOUR CHILD "I LOVE YOU" (WITHOUT SAYING THE WORDS)

1. When your child is participating in an athletic event or musical performance, be there watching.

2. Find a new way to trust your child by granting a new area of responsibility.

3. Have a family picnic on Sunday afternoon.

4. Walk in the rain and jump puddles together.

5. Listen to your child with all your attention.

6. Sit down together and watch your child's favorite TV show.

7. Skim rocks together on a lake, pond, or river.

8. Say, "I'm proud of you."

9. After your teenage son or daughter comes in from a date, have popcorn together by the fireplace.

10. Tell your child about the things you appreciated most about your own parents.

11. Have a family water-balloon fight (with you as the prime target).

12. Take an evening walk together.

There is no set pattern for the perfect faith trainer. The baton can be passed by any Christian with a willing heart and a relentless spirit. A good example was the Apostle Paul, who was a master at passing the baton of faith to a young person. That is what he was doing when he wrote 2 Timothy. That book of the Bible is an excellent guide to train our children.

■ **What's the make-it or break-it phase of baton passing?**

It's being an example, modeling, and *practicing* what you preach in front of your kids. Christianity, like kindness, is more caught than taught.

If you and your spouse gladly submit to each other, your kids will learn to be submissive. If you have a passion for God and His Word, they will too. If they see you on your knees a lot, they will pray a lot. If you ask for forgiveness when you fail, they'll be more humble.

On the other hand, if you're harsh, your kids will be harsh. If you drive too fast, they'll be lax on the laws of the land. If you buy porno magazines, they'll sneak pornography into their lives.

Faith training hinges on this point: Sons and daughters take their cues from their fathers and mothers. If you live with clear consciences, they will too. Faith training requires a parent to run with integrity.

Integrity was the key to Paul's success with Timothy, because Timothy knew that his trainer set a standard that Timothy could aspire to without reservation. Paul dared to say, "Follow my example, as I follow the example of Christ" (1 Cor. 11:1).

■ **I often say yes to other people without checking with my family first. How can I get my priorities right?**

We all lead crazy lives, but buying a calendar and watch can do wonders for you. Start by putting the calendar on the refrigerator. When something comes up, learn to check for family events first.

An ideal goal is to schedule at least a day and three nights per week to do *only* family things. Plan fun family vacations, including long weekends just for family. Keep in mind that you need time with each of your children regularly. Perhaps your golf game and social friends will have to wait until your last child goes to college. Until then, the home calendar rules.

The wristwatch can be your other priority provider. The bedtime hour is your time with the kids, to visit one on one and memorize a Bible verse with them. The Dallas Cowboys might be playing the San Francisco 49ers on "Monday Night Football," but they'll have to play without you during that precious time.

■ **My parents left me on my own when I was growing up, so I have a hard time seeing myself as a "faith trainer." What advice do you have for me?**

Some parents have been tricked into thinking that children arrive in this world with all the information they'll ever need to become productive members of society. These parents believe their job is to just stay out of the way and watch the beautiful process unfold. Under that plan, society should be flourishing by now.

That hasn't been the case, has it? If we look at Paul's mentoring of Timothy, we see an abundance of directives found in the text of 2 Timothy.

- ► Retain the standard of sound words (1:13).
- ► Remember Jesus Christ (2:8).
- ► Flee the evil desires of youth (2:22).
- ► Pursue righteousness (2:22).

Paul didn't ask, "Does Timothy want to do these things?" Of course not. And no effective faith

THE TOP TEN WORST REASONS FOR NOT READING THE BIBLE

10. There aren't enough action photos.

9. Once you've read the blood-and-guts box scores in the Old Testament, loaves and fishes aren't too exciting.

8. Anything they can make a kids' version out of can't be too important.

7. If I start studying the Bible, it won't be long before I'm not learning from my pastor's sermons anymore.

6. The New Testament is all Greek—even to the best of seminary students.

5. I can wait for the movie version.

4. If I act as though I know what I'm talking about, someone might ask me to lead a Sunday School class.

3. The book has been seen in a lot of seedy motel rooms.

2. It was written in code—if you don't have the ring, you can't understand it.

1. It was written by a bunch of foreigners.

trainer will, either. Trainers must give clear instructions—or the baton will be dropped along the way.

■ How can I impart God's Word as a faith trainer?

Without a doubt, the single most important command in Scripture is Deuteronomy 6:5–9. It spells out our duty for all of us who think, *There's just not enough time in the day:*

> *And you shall love the Lord your God with all your heart and with all your soul and with all your might. And these words, which I am commanding you today, shall be on your heart; and you shall teach them diligently to your sons and shall talk of them when you sit in your house and when you walk by the way and when you lie down and when you rise up. And you shall bind them as a sign on your hand and they shall be as frontals on your forehead. And you shall write them on the doorposts of your house and on your gates* (NASB).

Keep that Scripture in mind, and try, Mom and Dad, that today is the day for us to become better, more-committed faith trainers. Today is the day for our children to grow closer to the Lord.

This chapter is adapted from writings by Stephanie Bennett of Brick, New Jersey; Faith Trainer *(Focus on the Family Books) by Joe White; and* Daddy's Home *by Greg Johnson and Mike Yorkey, © 1992. Used by permission of Tyndale House Publishers, Inc. All rights reserved.*

8

Passing on the Baton of Faith

. . . .

■ **Joe White, in the previous chapter, said parents should strive to "pass the baton" of faith on to their children. Can you amplify on that?**

In a relay race, runners must hand the baton to the next runner in a passing zone. Dropping the baton or failing to pass it in the zone results in disqualification.

When parents pass along their faith, the baton must be passed during the childhood years. Keep three points in mind about passing the baton of faith to your children:

1. It's God's job to bring your children to faith, not yours.
He offers His free gift of salvation and then waits patiently until they receive it with a whole heart.

2. All children have free wills, and that plays a big part in whether they'll choose to follow what they've been taught.

3. The parents' role is to instill spiritual values and point their children toward Christ.
While we don't shoulder the entire load, we do have the responsibility to be faithful stewards of those little lives God's given us.

■ **So how can I make sure I don't blow it?**

First, you have to take the long view. Ask yourself: What type of Christian do I want my children to be when they're twenty-five?

■ **Hey, that's a tough question. We're busy just trying to get through the week!**

But think about that question again. Then ask yourself this easy follow-up: Do you want your children to have a faith like yours? You have to realize that the quality of their Christian lives and how active they are in their faith may be determined by what they see in you.

Do you want your children to have your love and compassion for those in need? Your attitude about church? Your desire to reach out to those who don't know Him? Your ability to resist temptation? Your understanding of the Holy Spirit's work? Your love and obedience to Jesus? Your . . . OK, we'll stop.

While the goal here isn't to produce unwarranted guilt, you should realize that you are a *major* player in your children's lives. You have just one chance to run around the track of life as a parent; that's why passing the baton of faith is so crucial. You want your kids to stay on the spiritual track and hand the baton to *their* kids.

Remember too that passing

STAGES OF FAITH

Researchers have discovered common stages in our faith development. Jay Kesler outlines them in his book *Energizing Your Teenager's Faith* (Group).

1. Children in grade school who talk about God and Jesus are echoing the words they have heard from adults. It is an "experienced faith." Important patterns of spiritual development can be formed during these years.

2. Junior highers have an "affiliated faith" that sees their beliefs in terms of a relationship. Jesus is their "best friend." Their faith grows mainly through church and youth group interaction.

3. High schoolers develop a "searching faith." Tough questions are asked to help them sort out whether to personally accept what they've experienced. This is the time parents need to spend hours discussing those questions.

4. Young adults begin to develop an "owned faith." Having freely accepted Christian beliefs, these adults incorporate biblical values as their own.

the baton of faith is more than a hand-off. Indeed, the Christian life has been accurately compared to a marathon, not a sprint. And we can't leave the coaching job primarily to others. We don't just put our children in Sunday School at age seven, sit back, and let the church do the rest. We have to be in this marathon relay race as a team—for life.

Kids, even adult kids, need to know that if they fall, we'll be there to help pick them up, pat them on their backsides, and send them on their way again. If they run too slow, we'll remind them to pick up the pace. If they run off the track, we'll point them back to the right lane. If they're discouraged, we're the first to encourage. If they quit the race, we'll tell them we still love them.

■ **My parents used to fall back on negative attitudes when they were raising us. How do I keep from doing the same thing?**

Parents *can* go through periods when they are overly critical, always yelling that their children's efforts aren't good enough. Count on this: If children feel they can never please their parents—or God—they'll quit trying.

■ **My parents were hung up on how well I behaved, thinking if I was a good little boy, then for sure I'd be a good little Christian. Was that a good idea?**

That wasn't a bad target for your parents to shoot for, but it wasn't the bull's-eye—a good relationship with your children is. In a similar fashion, our relationship with God is His greatest concern. But being a nice person, doing good works, and knowing the right "Christian lingo" isn't what God wants. He prefers that we zero in on following Him because He created us and loved us enough to die for us. And what He wants parents to do is pass on their *relationship* with Jesus Christ—not a code of conduct—to their offspring.

■ **What process do children and young adults go through before they're ready to follow Jesus Christ?**

Most take these steps:
1. They hear about God and His love for them through Jesus Christ.
2. They learn more about the Person who was born, died on the

THE TOP TEN WAYS TO HIDE YOUR FAITH FROM YOUR KIDS

10. Don't blow the dust off your Bible—let alone pick it up!

9. Limit their spiritual training to "Now I lay me down . . . and "Romper Room" grace.

8. Leave child evangelism to the trained professionals.

7. If they catch you kneeling by your bed, pretend you're looking for a missing sock.

6. Always have your spouse say grace (or eat dinner in shifts so that everybody's on his own).

5. Offer simplistic answers to their heartfelt questions about life.

4. When the preacher says something that touches your heart and you start getting misty-eyed, pretend your contacts are bothering you again.

3. If they catch you with your Bible open, tell them you're doing research for the crosswords.

2. If the pastor calls during the week and asks if you'd mind reading Scripture or giving your testimony for the Sunday service, say, "Oh, uh, I think we'll be out of town that Sunday. In fact, we may be out of town for the next few months."

1. If the pastor starts talking about your thought life, tell the kids that you think you might have left the motor running in the car and you'd better go outside and check.

cross, and raised from the dead on the third day.

3. They count the costs involved in following Him.

4. They accept (or reject) His payment on the cross for their sins, and begin building a relationship with Him.

5. They continue to learn more about Him and what He requires.

For some, the first four steps can take less than an hour. But for many of us, they take much longer. For all of us, number five is a lifetime proposition.

If you're tracking, you can see that this process parallels the one we went through for marriage:

1. We met our future spouse or heard about him or her from someone we trusted.

2. We started to spend time with him or her, with the goal of getting to know the person better.

3. We wondered if this was "the one." Deep down, we asked ourselves if we wanted to make a lifetime commitment.

4. We made the choice to be married, and later we recited vows to love and cherish our spouse for the rest of our lives.

5. We're now spending our days finding out new and wonderful (and not-so-wonderful) things about our spouse.

■ **That's a rough comparison. Can you explain it better?**

All relationships move. In a similar fashion, we need to keep our children moving forward toward Jesus Christ. Remember, picture what type of Christian you want your children to be when they've left the nest. See if these parents' stories strike a chord with you:

▶ "We lit Advent candles, celebrated the church seasons, made a big deal about Holy Week, and sang a lot too," said one Philadelphia father. "The kids I see without any traditions won't have anything to pass on to their children."

  Some other things you can do as a family: Sing Christmas carols to neighbors, eat lamb and bitter herbs at a Passover meal, attend Christian concerts together, give up a special treat for Lent, watch Christian videos together, or spend a week at a Christian summer camp. The ideas are limitless!

▶ "Dad prayed for us every morning," one Oregon woman remembers. "We'd get out of bed and see him on his knees. Then when we left for school, Mom would put her hands on all of the kids together and pray over us before we'd walk out the door. It was an incredible feeling knowing we were under God's protection. I had a secure feeling that the day would go fine. I do the same now with my kids."

▶ "Dad was always calling us to be men," a Washington minister relayed. "I remember standing in the garden with a hoe in my hand and Dad holding another in his hand. That afternoon, he told me a man stands up for what he believes and thinks his own thoughts. I learned to trust my dad with the deep things of my heart."

▶ "My parents were never the type of people who acted one way on Sunday and different on Tuesdays and Thursdays. They were the same at home and at work," said a Los Angeles mother.

■ **I've been in some churches that don't bring up the subject of sin. I'm wondering what I should say about it to my kids.**

Many Christian families are insulated from the darkness of sin. Consequently, it's easier for children to grow up without an appreciation for their own sin, and the wonder of God's grace. One key to keeping children faithful is making sure they understood what sin is.

In a sense, sin is an authority issue: wanting to be your own boss and be independent from others. You should teach your kids to evaluate their own relationship with Christ by discerning whether they are complying with God's agenda and pleasing Him. If they have stepped away from the Lord, tell them the reason is that they want to run their own lives.

Some other points you want to get across are:

- ▶ God knows we're going to make mistakes and isn't surprised at anything we do.
- ▶ God's more sad than angry when we disobey Him.
- ▶ He's quick to forgive when we ask Him to.
- ▶ Above anything else, He wants a clean relationship with us.

The earlier your children "own" their relationship with God, the better. From an early age, emphasize how personal God wants to be. Help them see that God is the greatest friend they could ever have. Give them responsibility for maintaining a close relationship with Christ by showing them how important yours is with Him.

■ **What happens if you become a Christian after your kids are in their teen years? That's my story.**

Don't despair. It's never too late to present Christ to your children, even when they're older and don't seem interested in your faith. The key is to admit your mistakes and not give up. They can *turn* to faith. The only time we are ever allowed to give up on our kids is when God gives up on us. And that isn't going to happen.

This material is adapted from Faithful Parents, Faithful Kids *by Greg Johnson and Mike Yorkey,* © 1993. Used by permission of Tyndale House Publishers, Inc. All rights reserved.

9

Preparing Your Children for Intimacy with God

- -

■ **My children came into this world issuing an all-points bulletin: "Hear ye! Hear ye! I have needs—lots of them—and I expect you to meet them!" Why do they burst on the scene believing that the world revolves around them?**

It's part of our fallen nature. We all made our entrances into this world in the same fashion. But when we become parents, one of our jobs is to gently redirect their narcissism.

■ **Can you explain this further?**

The diagram on the following page illustrates what this fallenness looks like.

The "closed system" that you see is ineffective because it takes God out of the picture, and it's impossible to have true emotional health without spiritual health. What you have here are two mutually needy humans taking from one another. It won't work.

■ **Why's that?**

Suppose your gas tank was running low, so you siphon gas from your spouse's car. Later in the day, your spouse comes out and finds her gas

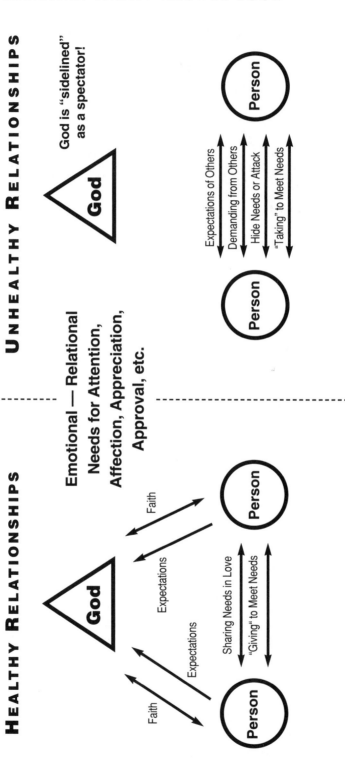

From David and Teresa Ferguson, Paul and Vicki Warren, and Terri Ferguson, Parenting with Intimacy (Wheaton, Ill. Victor, 1995), 186. Used by permission.

tank is low, so she siphons some from your tank. At that rate, eventually both tanks will be empty—and so will two mutually needy people. Healthy relationships need a never-ending source. The system on the left side of the diagram illustrates an "open system," drawing from an unlimited supply of love and comfort. The source? God.

■ So what's my goal here with this diagram?

Parenting with intimacy is a call and commitment to move your child from right to left. In effect, you're called to help "drive out their fallenness."

■ That sounds awfully severe.

On the contrary! It's the most moving thing you can do for them. Your goal is to drive it out—not with the rod but with your approachability. Let's look at three specific dimensions of this process. (You may want to refer back to the diagram from time to time.)

■ What's the number one dimension?

Number one is: Expectations and faith in God versus expecting and demanding from people.

Fundamental to healthy/unhealthy relationships is the issue over expectations. *Who* am I expecting to meet my need? Healthy relationships look to God as the One who promises abundance. Unhealthy relationships expect another person to be the source of provision, which eventually becomes demanding and manipulative. This is clearly seen in the Genesis 3 account of the Fall as Adam and Eve are tempted to look outside of God's provision.

As you seek to redirect your child's expectations toward God, you will find that times of confession and forgiveness are quite possibly the most life-impacting times you will share together.

■ What's the second dimension?

Number two is: Sharing needs in love versus hiding needs or attacking.

Since our fallenness has its roots in the Garden of Eden, it's natural to return there to discover the origin of our tendency to hide our needs or attack. When God went looking for Adam and Eve, they hid from Him because of their sin. When they were finally pinned down, they resorted to attacking and blaming. Children display this same type of behavior too.

■ So how can we turn this around?

One of the exciting things that we have as parents is the opportunity to live out the reality of Ephesians 4:15 before our children: "Instead, speaking the truth in love, we will in all things grow up into Him who is the Head, that is, Christ."

Sharing the truth in love is pivotal in developing healthy relatiooships as vulnerability and mutual trust are deepened. Provide a safe atmosphere in which they can share openly and model for them the appropriate sharing of your own needs. Let them experience your home as a secure place to share needs in a loving way. This is essential for the development of a sense of security. In this environment, they have the freedom to be a kid . . . as well as the freedom to grow up.

■ And I do that by . . .

Depending on the age of your child, you may need to help him develop a "needs" vocabulary. Many adults have difficulty placing names on their needs. A child shouldn't be expected to do this on his own. Train him in how to

---

A SERMON WE'D LIKE TO HEAR

I'd rather see a sermon than hear one any day;

I'd rather one should walk with me than merely tell the way.

The eye's a better pupil and more willing than the ear,

Fine counsel is confusing, but example's always clear.

And the best of all the preachers are men who live their creeds,

For to see God put in action is what everybody needs.

I soon can learn to do it if you'll let me see it done;

I can watch your hands in action, but your tongue too fast may run.

And the lecture you deliver may be very wise and true,

But I'd rather get my lessons by observing what you do.

For I might misunderstand you and the high advice you give,

But there's no misunderstanding how you act and how you live.

continued next page

ask for his needs to be met appropriately. For example, say "I can't hear you when you whine. Can you tell me what it is you need?" Or "Let's talk about it. I really do care."

■ **It was nearing nap time for our four-year-old daughter, Susie, and she was showing telltale signs of a hard day at play. Then she picked a fight with her brother. I was at my wit's end. What should I have done?**

You had a "teachable moment" there, Mom. You should have kneeled down next to her, taken her face in your hands and said, "It looks and sounds to me like you might be needing a little lap time—and maybe a hug. Would you like Mommy to hold you?"

Expect your little girl to smile and leap into your arms. By taking this route, Susie will experience a home that provides a secure environment where people love her and care for her and want to know her needs and respond to those needs. Even at the tender age of four, Susie was learning to say what she needed. And on this occasion, it was a hug!

■ **I have teenagers. Do you mean I have to hug them?**

Yes. You can get your teen thinking about that if you always say to your spouse—in front of your teen—"Honey, I've had a hard day. I need a hug." Then your youngster will see that he's part of a family that has needs and *meets* those needs.

> When I see a deed of kindness, I am eager to be kind.
> When a weaker brother stumbles and a strong man stays behind
> Just to see if he can help him, then the wish grows strong in me,
> To become as big and thoughtful as I know that friend to be.
> And all the travelers can witness that the best of guides today
> Is not the one who tells them, but the one who shows the way.
>
> One good man teaches many, men believe what they behold;
> One deed of kindness noticed is worth forty that are told.
> He who stands with men of honor learns to hold his honor dear,
> For right living speaks a language which to everyone is clear.
> Though an able speaker charms me with his eloquence, I say,
> I'd rather see a sermon than to hear one any day.
>
> *Author unknown*

■ **And what is the final dimension?**

The third is: "Giving to meet needs" versus "taking to meet needs."

Each of us comes into life with a huge fear that our needs will not be met. Therefore, we make demands—we "take" from others. Your role as a parent is to help cast out that fear. Take the initiative to model what God did on our behalf: He left His world to enter ours. We didn't seek Him—He sought us.

Mutual giving is key to healthy relatiooships . . . two people giving to meet important emotional needs; neither person "taking" from the other. Giving rather than selfishly taking is the crucial ingredient that brings joy and grateful appreciation. "It is more blessed to give than to receive," says Acts 20:35.

■ **But our household is more "take" than "give." What can I do about that?**

Nothing chokes intimacy faster than feeling "taken" from. "Taking" is characterized by a very conditional love: *I'll love you if. . . . I'll love you when. . . .* This performance cycle is never-ending and never satisfies!

For example, Cory always bugged his dad to take him to the park. Each time his dad reluctantly agreed, but Saturday after Saturday went by, each bringing a new excuse why they couldn't go. Cory could barely hide his disappointment. Finally, Cory's mom took her husband aside one Saturday morning and said a bit melodramatically, "Either you take him to the park this morning, or he's scarred for life. And it will be your fault!"

"C'mon, Cory, let's go," muttered his dad unenthusiastically.

After spending a half hour watching Cory play on the swings and climb the monkey bars, the father and son slowly walked back to the car. On the way home, Cory said, "Dad, thanks for taking me to the park. Maybe next time you'll want to go."

■ **That's quite an insight from a little guy.**

Indeed, and what contribution did this outing make to Cory's growing concept of God? An opportunity missed! Contrast this with the parent who proactively looks for ways to meet his child's intimacy needs and nurtures his concept of God as one of a Heavenly

Father who delights in meeting the needs of His children. Know your child and take the initiative to enter his world to meet those needs.

This material is adapted from Parenting with Intimacy *(Victor) by Dr. David and Teresa Ferguson, and Dr. Paul and Vicky Warren, and Terri Ferguson.*

10

Talking to Your Kids About God

. . . .

■ **I'm one of those parents who can't seem to put two sentences together about God without stammering or clearing my throat. How can I get over this hurdle with my kids?**

Before you can freely discuss spiritual concepts with your children, you must first *disciple* your children.

■ **Disciple them? What does that mean?**

You yourself must have a growing relationship with Jesus Christ, and your kids need to *see* that relationship. The reason is children are usually quick to notice inconsistencies between "do as I say" and "do as I do."

After that, you should never *bore* your kids with the Gospel. What do you think goes through a child's mind when he is doing something with his parents that he enjoys, and suddenly Dad becomes serious and says, "Why don't we talk about God for a while?" The child is likely to say, "Hey, this is no fun." So the key is to connect "discipling" and "having fun."

■ **How do I do that?**

Here are some ideas:

1. Let your life be an example to your children. If you want them to memorize Scripture, then *you* better memorize with them.

2. Set aside a time for discipling each week—say Wednesday night after dinner.

3. Make plans together. Decide how you want to spend your time.

4. Get into your child's world. If your small son loves looking for frogs, go look for frogs with him.

5. Make sure to "build in" fun. Go out for ice cream, go shopping, play ball, or take an evening walk.

6. Talk on a feeling level. Go beyond questions like, "How was school?" Instead, ask, "How do you feel about . . . ?"

7. Let your children know that during the time you have set aside for them, there is nothing you would rather be doing.

■ **I've read that parents should "model" Christ to their children. I think I know what this means, but I would like a better definition.**

Parents become excellent models for Christ when they show their kids they really love the Lord Jesus and practice that love in their daily lives. Or, to put it in simpler terms: Don't act like legalistic hypocrites.

More young adults have been turned off to Christianity by legalistic parents. These parents said all the right things in front of their friends and church members, but acted totally different behind closed doors. It is a tragedy for parents to profess something they do not live, because their children can only conclude that Christianity is just another religion, a game, a crutch needed by weak people. Legalism is a curse. It has turned so many people away from the Gospel!

■ **What are some ways that I can make sure I am modeling Christ without being a hypocrite?**

Besides watching how you act when outsiders aren't around, you should bring other vital Christians into your home to serve as secondary models for your children. This could be college students or adults who are on fire for the Lord. If a missionary family comes home on furlough, invite them over for dinner and hear their testimonies. Your children should be around vital people who are living rich and meaning-ful lives for Christ, which will make Christianity more attractive to them.

■ How can I create a desire for God's Word within my kids?

You're keen to notice that you have to create a desire. But it doesn't help when many churches have killed excitement for the Bible because they treat it like a dull book. We create excitement by being genuinely excited ourselves. Here are three ways you can do that:

1. Surround your kids from an early age with good books.
Not preachy books, but good books that have some scriptural content. When they're young, read to them. Talk about what you're reading. Let them *see* you reading.
2. Share what you're learning.
One simple way you can do this is by pointing out things that have happened in your life.
3. Consistently show your appreciation for God's Word.
Read 1 Thessalonians 2:13 to your children. This will show that you are treating Scripture not like a regular book but as the Word of God.

■ Our son Kurt has his SAT college entrance tests next week. He asked us to pray for him, and I said I would be praying that God's will would be done in his life. Kurt replied, "Oh boy, it's just my luck that it will be God's will that I flunk." I was dumbfounded. What should I have said to him?

You should have reminded him that God opens *and* closes doors. If college was for him, then we want God to help him get the test scores he needs.

To us, it's a positive answer if our teen gets strong SAT scores and a negative answer if he gets bottom-rung results. But that's not how God sees it. God's closed doors are probably more important than His open doors because they are God's way of keeping us from going in the wrong direction.

This material is adapted from Parents & Teenagers *(Victor) and several authors: Bill Bright, Barry St. Clair, Warren Wiersbe, and Evelyn Christenson.*

3

....

All About Kids

11

Take a Play Break!

■ **My children are pulling me in six different directions. I'm so busy juggling schedules that I'm starting to define "family" as a group of assorted kids and a parent or two who share the same house, sit down occasionally for a quick meal, and mostly run off in all directions to pursue different activities. At any rate, what has happened to quality family life?**

Mom, you need to slow down. You need to . . . *play.*

■ **What? Play with my kids?**

Certainly. Remember your old grade school art room? All the shelves were filled with colored construction paper, balsa wood, colorful pipe cleaners, clay, colored pencils of every hue, ribbons and crepe paper, old magazine pictures, chalk and paint, water colors—even those goopy finger paints.

That cluttered room was every kid's dream. With your dad's old dress shirts as artist smocks, you concocted all sorts of wonderful things. So why not make your own "Playful Place" at home?

■ **Where do I start?**

Set aside one night a week for your family. Figuring that your children are still in the preteen years, bring a box of clay to the kitchen table after dinner. Start by rolling the bright colors into a family of snakes. Then get out the paste and the construction paper and whatever else you have and for one glorious evening, see what happens. No set lessons or directions. Mix and match. Follow a whim. Go with the flow.

■ **Having a "Playful Place" would be a major departure for our family. If we're going to give it a try, what should we keep in mind?**

YOUR HOME CAN BE DRY GROUND IN A MUDDY WORLD

By Dr. Tony Evans

There are some good reasons for building a home where the kids will feel encouraged to bring their friends and where their friends will always feel welcome. But I can hear some of you moms saying, "Oh, that's just what I need, a lot of kids traipsing through the house all the time. How will we ever get anything done? Besides that, the house will always be torn apart."

I understand your concerns; they're legitimate. So let's see if I can ease your mind a little. Realize first that I'm not talking about a twenty-four-hour-a-day free-for-all. Don't be afraid to enforce your normal family rules about how much roughhousing is permitted indoors, where food may be eaten, what language is acceptable, and so on. Let kids be kids, but also mark off the boundaries.

Continued next page

▶ *You'll need a healthy respect for each family member as a creative individual.* Criticism is strictly out. The goal is to have fun. Start out small; your play evenings shouldn't mean a major expenditure for craft materials. Get out those old magazines and scissors. Paste pictures of your favorite things on mats cut from brown shopping bags. Decorate shoe boxes like log cabins. Find interesting junk in the garage. Watch for fun items at garage sales.

▶ *Remember we always have time for the things that are really important to us.* Brainstorm this wild idea with the kids and ask them to help you figure out ways to fit a play evening into your already tight schedule. Their enthusiasm usually gets the ball rolling.

▶ *Free yourself from having to maintain an immaculate home.* Why should the fear of clutter dictate what's best for you and your family? Your children are young only once. Who knows what wonderful memories you'll create in the midst of that mess on the floor?

▶ *Have fun.* If you don't know where to begin, start with clay. Squish and smash. Make a bust of the family dog. Roll out a clan of fearsome snakes. Build baskets and fill them with dozens of brightly colored eggs. Make tiny furniture and fill it with a family made out of round balls.

■ **I have to admit that I'm still not convinced this will work for our family.**

How about kite-making so you'll be ready for a windy weekend this spring? Have you ever tried soap carving? Had a good bubble-blowing session lately? Did you miss out on tie-dyeing when it was the rage in the sixties? What about getting a variety of wafers and turning everyone loose to create their own cookie houses?

If you'll allow yourself to get a little wild, you'll discover many interesting things to do with assorted fabrics, paints, glue, and odds and ends. Your daughter's penchant for combining weird colors and textures might produce a treasured wall hanging. A holiday wreath might result from Mom's tying ribbons around a bent coat hanger.

The important thing isn't the

As you consider making your home into a haven for children, a place where your kids and their friends *want* to come, what pictures come to mind? Are you excited about the potential ministry, or are you worried about spilled soft drinks and dirty bathrooms?

I'm reminded of a story told by a former major league baseball superstar. One day when he was a boy, he and his friends and his father were out in the yard playing ball. They played there regularly, so the grass took a beating.

One day, as the kids and the father were playing in the yard and having a great time, the boy's mother leaned out of one of the windows and yelled, "Can't you guys find someplace else to play? You're killing the grass."

The man looked at his wife and answered, "Honey, we aren't raising grass. We're raising kids!"

finished product, but the fun you have together during the evening. The benefit from this acwivity lies in the *doing* and in the free-wheeling creativity that's unleashed—even if your creation doesn't turn out the way you expected.

If the "Playful Place" sounds intriguiog, maybe you've rediscovered hope. Maybe you aren't so old that hardening of the attitudes has set in. Your only problem might be deciding what to do first.

This article is adapted from writings by Elaine Hardt of Phoenix, Arizona, and Guiding Your Family in a Misguided World *by Dr. Tony Evans. Copyright © 1991 Dr. Tony Evans. Used by permission of Focus on the Family.*

12

Toying with Trouble

■ My son, Eric, turned seven a few months ago, and like millions of youngsters his age, he's really looking forward to Christmas. What shall I buy him? The radical yo-yo with skull and crossbones? Or should I opt for the "Flushomatic High Tech Toilet Torture Trap with real ooze flushing action"? Perhaps I could purchase Really Rude Bart, whose specialty is making flatulence noises.

It's lucky I don't have a young daughter, or I would have to take out a second mortgage just to keep Barbie in pumps and party dresses. How have we gotten to this point? And—more important—where is it taking our children?

When shopping for toys during the holiday season, parents should keep several points in mind: *The toy industry is big business.* One hot item—such as Mighty Morphin Power Rangers—can reap a cool $100 million, while a bust—such as Pocahontas dolls—can push a company toward Chapter 11.

One standard guides the $13-billion toy industry: If it sells, it must be good. The values we hold as Christians—honesty, purity, goodness, innocence—are not the measuring sticks for a toy company's new line. It's up to us to find items that uphold our standards/

■ **We know the toy industry is powered by movies and Saturday morning cartoons—not to mention the tie-in at McDonald's. We try to shield our children to the magnetic allure of the entertainment world.**

Good for you! Toys focus more on violent themes and the occult than ever before. Children who watch violence on television (the average is four hours a day) often reenact the violence in their play and then become more aggressive in their behavior. Youngsters imitate without realizing they may hurt their playmates.

Be wary of toys that are tied into the occult. Stroll down the aisles of a major toy store, and you'll discover many occult-based toys. Example: A modern "ghost" decked out in a black-and-white suit, with blackened eyes and wild white hair, can spin his head 360 degrees. Upon pulling the string, your child will hear such treasured phrases as "I'm the ghost with the most" and "It's really dead around here."

■ **OK, I know there's junk out there. So, what kind of toys should I look for?**

The best toys allow a wide margin for the child's imagination. Yes, some "test laboratories" say that "the more batteries a toy needs, the better kids like it." But psychologist Dr. Lee Salk finds that the appeal of such toys is short-lived. "While children may be initially fascinated by some highly structured toys that do very specific things, they remain interested far longer if the toys are more flexible and can be used in different ways," said Dr. Salk.

You can't go wrong with building toys such as Legos, Lincoln Logs, and Bristle Blocks. They never fail to involve children because the end product is always different. Dolls, stuffed animals, and puppets do not have to be elaborate to fire a child's imagination. Board games and puzzles bring families closer together. They teach kids to take turns, relish a challenge, enjoy successes, and graciously admit defeat.

And those are values worth giving your children any Christmas, birthday, or special occasion.

This material is adapted from writings by Sandra Doran of Attleboro, Massachusetts.

13

"But I Don't Want to Go to Bed!"

■ **We have the toughest time getting our two-year-old daughter to bed. What should we do?**

Infants and toddlers need bedtime rituals to provide an atmosphere of security. You might start putting your two-year-old in bed, and then repeating the familiar rhyme: "This little piggy went to market, this little piggy stayed home. . . ."

Then let your child kiss her teddy bear on its fuzzy cheek while you rub her back. After a good-night prayer and a quiet song, you pull the blanket over her shoulders while you kiss her goodnight. Then you turn out the lights and leave the room.

■ **So you're saying that I should be playing out this little ceremony the same way each and every night, right?**

Exactly. Bedtime rituals are a comforting transition from the busy day to a restful night. Some children go to bed willingly, but all too many do not. Creating the idea that sleep is a delightful retreat takes a well-planned approach to keep bedtime from becoming a hassle.

■ **I know. Last night, my daughter asked for a drink, another song, another kiss. . . .**

Simple rituals can make the difference. You can help bedtimes run smoother by starting with a warm bath to soothe and relax your daughter. Dress her in comfy pajamas and get her brushing her teeth and swishing her mouth.

Then let her choose a beloved stuffed animal before getting into bed. Read a favorite bedtime or Bible story, then cuddle with a back rub or a recounting of the fingers and toes. Finish with a loving prayer, and then whisper "I love you" as you leave the room.

Both boys and girls enjoy bedtime rituals. Don't toss your son a businesslike "Good night, see you in the morning," after having hugged and kissed his sister in the next room.

■ What about night lights? Are they a good idea?

Certainly. Night lights, as well as "security" blankets, teddy bears, and other stuffed animals, are reassuring to children of both genders. The idea is to nurture a bedtime ritual of your own. Both you and your children will benefit.

■ When I announce "Bedtime!" all I hear are groans and pleas to stay up "just a little longer." Foot-dragging and time wasting have become art forms in our house. It seems like it takes a whole hour from the first "Bedtime!" to lights out. What can I do?

A surefire way to end the day is by telling bedtime stories. Weaving verbal images isn't as difficult as you might think. Simply starting with "I want to tell you about . . ." will do the trick. Telling stories the last fifteen minutes of the day is one of the best things we can do for our children.

Bedtime stories also give us wonderful opportunities to share "teachable moments" with children—explaining family situations and giving opportunities to observe our sense of right and wrong. Stories can help children ponder great thoughts, dream impossible dreams, and strive for ideals honoring to God.

■ Great, but I'm not a good storyteller. So where do I start?

Don't worry about your children's reaction—it'll be positive. What child wouldn't want to stay up longer? If they associate bedtime stories with extra time up—even if you start the whole process fifteen minutes earlier than their normal bedtime—you're still ahead of the game. Your children will be willing to drop a lot of things if they hear, "Kids, it's time for a story!"

■ But what happens if I don't get the story "just right"?

Don't worry about it. Just enjoy talking to your children about the things in this world. Jesus sometimes began His stories with "A certain man"—an example that readily carries over into our more recent "Once upon a time."

Besides, children love stories—especially ones about what it was like in the "old days" when we were growing up. Many of today's young people can't imagine a world before VCRs and microwave ovens, so if you describe the first time you watched a video, you'll get some big eyes.

■ OK, let's say I try to tell a few stories. But what happens if I get stuck and run out of ideas?

Then turn "story time" into "conversation time." Your children will be more receptive if they have a chance to unwind and talk about their day. But you may have to initiate the conversation at first. If you start with a question like, "How was your day?" you might get a grunt or an "OK." To get the conversation rolling, ask, "What was the most important thing that happened to you today?" or "What made you happy today?" After they talk about the events, you can build stories around them.

■ I've found that I don't have to come up with new stories. Instead, it seems like my kids want me to repeat their old favorites.

Children love repetition, so don't be surprised if they ask you to repeat the same story you told last week or even last night. In the retelling, your children will mentally add more details to the scene they're creating in their heads, often picturing themselves as the main characters. Every time they hear the story, their imaginations fill in more details. Not only do they enjoy often-repeated stories, but they actually increase their visualization skills and become more creative.

■ **Should I have a certain goal when I tell a story?**

Yes, by all means. What do you want to accomplish with your story? Entertainment? Calming after an intense day? Teaching a value? Don't feel every story *has* to have a moral, however. You might use the time to instruct—such as telling how a caterpillar becomes a butterfly. You can pass your love for the night skies by giving detailed accounts of ancient sailors following only the stars.

Be sure to keep the story on the children's level. Look at the events in your story from the children's perspective. How would they tell this story to their friends? What words would they use? Which details would be most important to them?

■ **I had a good story going the other night when one of my children fell asleep. Does that mean I'm a lousy storyteller?**

Just the opposite: Your child was so relaxed that he could no longer fight off sleepy eyelids. To the young child, your presence means more than the content or even quality of the story. Your hand rubbing his back and the steady cadence of your voice will put his mind at ease, allowing him to close his eyes and slip into dream world.

So, if you aren't in the habit of telling bedtime stories, begin tonight. Not only will you share a special rapport, but you'll have opportunities to pass on your beliefs, solve problems together, and dispel fears—all important aspects of parenting.

This article is adapted from writings by Beverly Lewis of Colorado Springs, Colorado, and Joel Coppieters of Farnham, Quebec.

14

How Can I Get My Kids to Read?

. . . .

■ **When the kids come home from school, they are not allowed to plop themselves in front of the TV, staring blankly at Looney Tunes and recycled sitcoms. If they have finished their homework and can't "find anything to do," then they read. But I have to be honest—it's a struggle to get them to crack open a book. What are some things I can do to keep their reading interest up?**

Even though your children are not voracious readers, you are far from the typical U.S. family. In fact, a recent study by the U.S. Department of Education's Commission on Reading reports that the average fifth-grader reads less than four minutes each day—but watches TV for more than two hours!

Those are frightening statistics, but with a little encouragement from you, your children can love to read. The first thing they should understand is that reading is the foundation of all learning. At school, the common thread in class is reading. Even math courses require it for word problems. Education experts tell us what every parent has long known: without the basic tools of reading, children inevitably fall behind in other subjects.

Reading opens children's eyes to people and places they would otherwise never see. Even the poorest child can travel around the world through words. A child living in a large city can envision soaring mountains and mighty rivers—with the help of a favorite book. In a few paragraphs, a farmer's child can "hear" the sounds of racing engines and bustling crowds. Books can take children back in time or into the future.

Reading also opens a great treasure—the Bible. The printed Word clarifies the way of salvation, gives guidance for our daily lives, and provides access to our Father's heart. And all are just a turn-of-the-page away.

■ **Besides my child's report card, what are some other indications of reading ability?**

Here are five signs to look for:

▶ *A good reader enjoys being read to and reading to others.* Does your child eagerly request nighttime stories? Or does he pretend he's sleeping to avoid the ritual? The parent's attitude plays an important role. If your child senses that you dread reading to him, he'll conclude that reading is something to be endured rather than enjoyed.

Research shows that adult involvement influences the child's reading activities. Educator Dorothy Petty is convinced too. "Those who are read to regularly have their own collections of books, go to libraries, and participate in family reading activities. Not only do they make good progress in school, but they also develop a lifelong love of reading," says Mrs. Petty.

Another sign of a good young reader is one who requests stories throughout the day—not just at bedtime. A wise parent will heed such requests.

▶ *A good reader finds time for reading every day.* Children, like adults, can always find time for hobbies they enjoy. If your child offers a dozen excuses for not reading, a little parental encouragement is in order. By the time your child is in fourth grade, he should devote two hours each week to reading.

▶ *A good reader can summarize the stories he reads.* One of TV's side effects is passivity. Besides that, who can remember what they watched two days ago? In contrast, reading requires active involvement for maximum comprehension. To ensure that your child is reading carefully, ask questions. Encourage him to talk about whatever book he is reading.

► *A good reader shows continuing improvement.* Your child's teacher can provide valuable insight here. You also can monitor your child's reading level by encouraging him to read aloud. He should be able to read increasingly difficult words and sentences. The U.S. Commission on Reading concluded that the most important step in assuring your child's success in school is to read aloud to him.

► *Good readers enjoy visiting bookstores and the library.* If all you hear are moans and groans from a child reluctant to enter bookstores and libraries, then reading is not a top priority for him. Unless you take action now, reading may never be an important part of his life.

■ **Well, my child is not a good reader. Justin, who is in fourth grade, has never finished a book. What do we do?**

What does Justin like to do? If he loves baseball, take him to the library or bookstore and get him several books on baseball. Discuss what he's read at dinnertime, and keep encouraging him to read on his own. At bedtime, you could read one of those baseball books to him too.

■ **I agree that reading aloud is very important. When should I start reading to my young son? He's ten months old.**

TIPS ON READING ALOUD

1. Reading aloud does not come naturally. To be successful, you must practice.

2. Be expressive when you read. Change your tone of voice to fit the scene and character.

3. Adjust your pace to fit the story. Slow down during suspenseful parts and help build the suspense.

4. Read slowly enough for your child to build mental images of the story.

5. Allow time for discussion after reading.

6. Don't use the book as a reward for being good. Withholding the book then becomes a punishment and may build negative feelings toward reading.

7. Listening is a skill that must be learned and practiced. It takes time.

8. Show your love for books by telling how much pleasure you get from reading them.

Believe it or not, you can start reading *now* to your infant. Language skills are being built at this moment. Your son will also associate books with the comfort of sitting on someone's lap. You can start family traditions, like the ever-popular bedtime story.

As your children start school, begin a "reading hour" in your home. No, that doesn't mean sixty minutes of reading, but it does mean a special time when the TV and telephone are off-limits. The children could read for fifteen minutes before the lights go out. Building a home library is also important, since a comprehensive study of early readers concluded that the availability of books played a central role in their success.

■ **I'm very concerned about what my child reads, although I know some parents who believe that as long as the child reads, it doesn't matter what's in his hands.**

Kevin Washburn, a Christian educator and expert on motivating children to read, says you should be concerned with what your child reads. He compares reading "junk books" with eating junk food.

"Children may prefer cookies and ice cream," says Washburn, "but parents know the importance of solid food. The same is true with books."

■ **So, how can I tell a good book from a bad one?**

One way, of course, is to read the book. Does it have an interesting plot? Are the characters true-to-life and memorable? Is the story line consistent with your Christian beliefs? If you don't have time to read the book, at least scan the first few chapters.

Whether your child is six months or sixteen years, now is the time to encourage him or her to read. It may take some creativity and effort on your part, but the reward of giving your child a gift that lasts for a lifetime—a love for reading and learning—is well worth it.

This material is adapted from writings by Donna Partow of Mesa, Arizona, and Charting Your Family's Course *(Victor) by Eric Buehrer.*

15

Teaching Them How to Apologize

. . . .

■ I saw my third-grade son, Jeffrey, stick out his foot and trip his younger sister, Kim. After scolding Jeffrey, I asked him to apologize. He mumbled "Sorry," but I was left with the sinking feeling that Jeffrey had no idea of what it means to apologize.

Most children don't have a clue what it means to apologize. A faint "sorry" is usually standard.

Perhaps we adults need to teach our children how to apologize. Accidents and misunderstandings will arise from time to time; courtesy dictates that caring people of any age know how to verbalize their concern and ask for forgiveness.

A sincere apology should state what we did that was wrong. It must convey our sadness that we have caused the other person harm. It should state our desire to be forgiven. And it should mention that we will be more careful in the future.

■ What's the best way to teach a youngster how to make an apology?

Role play. Describe some circumstance, then say what you think would be an adequate and kind apology. Discuss the matter, then invent another situation and let your child go through the steps of asking for forgiveness.

The person to whom an apology is being directed also needs to know how to accept the apology. He or she needs to say something on the order of, "I forgive you."

Learning how to be responsible for one's words and actions is part of growing up. There is no substitute for these lessons.

When a situation comes up at home and you need to ask forgiveness from your child, you can demonstrate and experience the real essence of Christian caring. God will wonderfully bless our families when we learn the honesty and humility of apologies.

This material is adapted from writings by Elaine Hardt of Phoenix, Arizona.

16

Little Lies

. . . .

■ My hand closed over the small chunks of onion I had chopped. I blinked back stinging tears as my son Josh yelled into the kitchen.

"What's for dinner, Mom?"

"Spaghetti."

"You're not putting onions in the sauce, are you?"

I hesitated only a moment, then firmly replied, "No. I know you don't like them."

I felt a twinge of guilt as I opened my hand and the onions fell into the pot. *Picky eaters make little lies a necessity,* I told myself. *Josh wouldn't touch the spaghetti if he knew the truth. He'll never tell the difference.*

Ah, but God will. You can chuckle away any guilt you may have, but what would you say if your nine-year-old son brought home a safety pamphlet from school that started with this advice for when your son is home alone: "Have your child tell the stranger you are taking a bath, taking a nap, or lying down because you don't feel well."

An authoritative source has just taught your child to lie—albeit for a very good reason. The next time you remind your son that Jesus said we shouldn't lie, think of that pamphlet—or the thought of dropping the onions into the spaghetti sauce.

■ **OK, I see your point, but what should I tell my child to say when he's home alone?**

Suggest that he say, "Mom can't come to the phone right now. Please call back."

But that question is easy compared to the lying going on all around us. If your child attends a public university, don't be surprised if one of his professors teaches that lies are necessary for success.

■ **How can I establish truth as a value in our home when society actually rewards lying? Are there ever *good* reasons for lying?**

In Proverbs 6:16-17, you'll learn that the Lord *hates* lying. Jerry White's book, *Honesty, Morality and Conscience*, explains this concept further.

"Lies destroy trust, yet the habit of lying can develop so subtly that it goes unnoticed. We begin by lying about 'small' things that 'don't matter.' Then we develop a pattern. Soon valuable credibility and friendship are lost."

As you consider your relationship with God, you'll discover that the reason you can always trust Him is because you know His Word is always true. The psalmist wrote, "All Your words are true; all Your righteous laws are eternal" (119:160). It isn't just in *some* areas that God speaks the truth, but in every single thing He says. By being able to trust His Word, you'll know His truth doesn't leave room for doubt.

■ **I admit it. I've lied in the past. How can I change?**

As a first step, confess them to the Lord, and then confess your "little" lies to your family and ask their forgiveness. Then promise that no matter what, you will tell the truth in the future.

That will be difficult to do, but if you take this important step, you will notice an important result: As you instruct your children on bigger issues—sex, drugs, the importance of working hard in school— they will know they can believe you. You will win their trust.

■ **How can I then teach my children to tell the truth?**

The most effective way you can teach them is by your own example. If it's all right for you to tell lies, they'll feel the same freedom.

Little lies lead to big lies. If you make it clear that *no* lie is right to tell, then the importance of truth in your household will be understood.

If you catch your children making a mistake and lying, your role is to help them confess the lie and ask for and receive forgiveness. Sometimes, however, they aren't too eager to confess. Kids have a way of coming up with more "excuses" than there are fleas on a long-haired cat. Sometimes you might find their little lies are just as difficult to pick out!

■ **My son has been giving me some evasive answers lately. A friend told me that to get at the truth, I shouod let him think I knew more than I did. That seemed dishonest, and when I tried it, my son was smart enough to force my hand.**

You must realize that the Lord Himself has given you a resource you need to determine truth. "And I will ask the Father, and He will give you another Counselor to be with you forever—the Spirit of truth. The world cannot accept Him, because it neither sees Him nor knows Him. But you know Him, for He lives with you and will be in you" (John 14:16-17).

You can tell your children, "Even if I don't know the truth about this situation, you need to remember that God does." You can carry that a step further by praying and asking God to guide you to the truth. And He does that in as many different ways as there are situations—school notices, a teacher's phone call, or a crumpled paper that tells a story different than your son's.

Your son will learn that when Mom starts to pray, he might as well confess. He will also learn that even if the truth doesn't immediately come to light, it will eventually.

This material is adapted from writings by Patti Covert of Ontario, California.

17

Please Pass the Manners

■ **Strolling through our local supermarket recently, I asked myself, "Where have all the manners gone?" It seemed more mixed nuts were in the aisles than on the shelves. Shoppers cut into the checkout line, nibbled unpurchased fruit, and snapped at clerks. Finally, we stood at the service counter behind a mother and her unruly child. The store manager, wanting to defuse the little "time bomb," gave the boy a balloon. The mother asked her son, "Well, what do you say?"**

"Blow it up," the child replied.

Is it just me, or have we lost our manners?

We've lost our manners. Although our society is much ruder and cruder than past generations, that doesn't mean we can't do our little bit to stem the tide. Actually, good manners are more than just knowing which fork to use; it's showing consideration for others. The best description of manners comes from 1 Corinthians 13:4-5: "Love is patient, love is kind. It does not envy, it does not boast, it is not proud. It is not rude, it is not self-seeking, it is not easily angered, it keeps no record of wrongs." Thus, true manners are more than a veneer of rules we employ when company arrives. They are principles that work in our day-to-day world.

■ **Good speech. So what are some of the principles of good etiquette?**

They are graciousness, courteousness, consideration, and respect. When we are *gracious*, we show kindness and warmth. When we are *courteous*, we show good manners toward others. When we are *considerate*, we are thoughtful and attentive. When we are *respectful*, we admire and appreciate others.

■ **Can you give me some examples?**

We're gracious when we:

► Ask, "May I, please?" and respond with "Thank you."
► Say, "Excuse me," or "Sir?" or "Ma'am?" when we haven't heard what was said.
► Say, "Excuse me" when we walk in front of someone.

We're courteous when we:

► Open and hold doors for others.
► Assist others with coats or packages.
► Walk nearest the outside, or curb, of the sidewalk.
► Carry an open umbrella for another.
► Stand aside and permit women to enter an elevator first.
► Give up our seat to an older person or a woman in a subway or bus.

We're considerate when we:

► Don't whisper in front of others.
► Don't tell secrets confided to us.
► Don't gossip or tattle.
► Don't annoy others with a loud voice or radio.
► Don't crack knuckles, pop gum, or crunch ice publicly.
► Promptly return what we borrow—and in good condition.
► Are prompt for appointments.
► Never draw attention to those who are different.
► Pick up things that don't belong on the floor.

- Don't slam doors.
- Go up and down stairs quietly.

We're respectful when we:

- Never contradict our spouse (or parents) in public.
- Show proper respect for elders and all those in authority.
- Give others the same respect we appreciate from them.
- Make everyone in our presence comfortable.

■ **How can I remember to do all this? You've outlined a huge list.**

Don't worry about memorizing anything. If you can remember the Golden Rule from Luke 6:31, you'll do just fine: "Do to others as you would have them do to you." Actually, that's all you need to know about good manners.

As for children, however, you'll have to be more proactive. Don't forget that manners courses are no longer part of most school curriculums, so children need to learn them at home. And they do—they study their parents. Unfortunately, within a generation, we've gone from "I'm sorry" and "Thank you" to "Shut up" and "Don't have a cow, man."

■ **Well, we don't watch the "The Simpsons" in our home. So where do we begin?**

Let's start at the dinner table. In an age when so many pick up their food at a drive-up window, it seems that table manners have become a dying art. We should learn how to use a knife and fork properly. We should learn now to keep our elbows off the table. We should learn how not to talk with food in our mouths. We should remember to end the meal by expressing appreciation for the one who produced it.

Carl Amann, a high school counselor in Michigan, has worked with teens for nearly three decades. When asked what he sees as the biggest problem in today's families, he said, "No one answers to anyone. Once I asked my students, 'How many of you have a seat at the dinner table that you call your own?' Only a couple of kids raised their hands. They go home, grab something for supper, and eat while they watch TV.

"The family doesn't talk—even if they're home together. So where can the teen go to ask questions about moral issues? Parents need to be available. And kids need to know they can ask questions. They talk to me because there's very little communication in the home."

■ **One of my pet peeves is calling a friend and hearing her young child answer the phone—rudely. ("Hello? Who do you want?") That's why telephone manners are a big deal in our household. What should I emphasize with my first-grader?**

Children should be taught to answer the phone politely. For example, "Hello, this is the Anderson residence" or "Hello, this is Megan," is correct. We want to make the best impression we can since people can't "see" us over the phone.

■ **How should my children introduce or be introduced?**

Say the woman's or the older person's name first. "Grandpa, I'd like you to meet my friend, Peter. Peter, this my grandfather, Taylor Johnson." (At which point, Peter would say, "I'm glad to meet you, Mr. Johnson.")

The most important thing is to put people at ease; help them to relax so they can remember the folks they're meeting. Speak clearly, be warm, get the names right, make a good impression and smile. Few people will remember if you forget the order of introduction. But they will remember if you mumble, mispronounce their name, or act awkwardly.

■ **I can't stand it when people don't respond to invitations. Last month I mailed invitations to my Sunday School class for a get-together at our home. I heard back from only one mom!**

People have forgotten that when an invitation arrives by mail or phone, a prompt reply is always considerate. Formal, written invitations may say, "RSVP," an abbreviation of French for *Reply If You Please.* A reply is expected whether or not you can attend. If the invitation says, "Regrets only," a reply is necessary only if you *cannot* attend. If you accept an invitation and later discover that you cannot attend, notify the hostess as soon as possible.

■ **At social functions, a hostess will serve beverages and hors d'oeu-vres (appetizers) before dinner to give guests time to gather and introduce themselves to one another. What are some do's and don'ts?**

Don't set a glass down on a table without using a coaster. With dips, only dip once per chip or vegetable slice. You'd be amazed at the number of people who keep dipping the same carrot into the sour cream dip. And don't overeat. Save room for dinner—no matter how good the appetizers are.

■ **I feel awkward when my wife and I sit down to eat in the formal dining room of our good friends. For instance, I get confused which fork or knife I'm supposed to use. What should I do?**

It can be a little daunting if you're not sure of yourself in social settings. But using the right silverware is not that difficult. Silverware is used from the outside in, with the first fork on the left being used first, and the first spoon on the right being used first. A spoon or fork placed above the dinner plate is used for dessert.

If the setting is confusing, watch the hostess and use what she uses. If you begin with the wrong utensil, don't worry about it—just continue to use it for that course.

Use the glass to the right of the plate. Large stemmed glasses should be held by the bowl, not the stem, to avoid spills. Glasses without a stem should be held in the middle. When passing a glass or cup to someone, never touch the rim with your fingers. Ever seen someone do that to you? It's gross!

After the blessing has been said, wait for the hostess to lift her fork—or asks you to begin—before you eat. As dishes are passed, use the serving utensil provided—never your own—and return that utensil to the serving dish before passing it on.

When taking your portion, leave enough for other guests. Take a little of everything, and refrain from asking, "What is this?"

■ **What should I do after the meal? I'm never sure if I should offer to help clean up.**

It's certainly all right to offer taking the dishes to the kitchen, but don't insist. At any rate, you should always thank the hostess and compliment the meal. Upon leaving the table, place your napkin at the side of the plate (don't refold it), and push the chair under the table.

This material is adapted from writings by Hermine Harley, author of The Family Book of Manners, *(Barbour). Mrs. Harley lives in Ft. Myers, Florida.*

18

Conversation: The Best Part of Dinner

. . . .

■ **I am an elementary school principal, and I can really notice the difference in our kindergartners over the years—their lack of vocabulary. They aren't able to carry on a conversation. I think it's because they sit in front of the TV so much and aren't talked to by their parents at home, especially at mealtime. When I was their age, I could recite all the American Presidents because my parents made a game of learning at the dinner table. Whatever happened to old-fashioned dinner conversation?**

Children learn conversational skills in the course of family discussions. When conversation doesn't happen in the home, children have difficulty conversing with adults, and sometimes even with their peers. When conversation does happen, they learn skills that carry over into school and into life. A recent national poll on factors contributing to happiness and high marks in school included these findings: Religious students with strong family support are the most likely to succeed in school. A remated factor is that the most successful students were also those most likely to eat dinner regunarly with the whole family.

■ **I can certainly see it in our classrooms. We often are able to identify students who come from such families. These students** seem confident that their opinions are respected, even if they aren't shared. The give-and-take of good family discussion is valuable for another reason: It gives children practice in articulating their thoughts at home so that eventually they'll feel confident outside the home.

Each of us needs a forum where we can express our dreams, our irrational fears, and our crazy ideas. We need a place where people bear with our jokes, even if they've heard them many times or if they're not funny. We need a place where we don't have to be the smartest or the funniest, where what we have to say is of value.

A friend reminisced about her son's days in kindergarten: "I loved those days when Rob thought he could do anything, and the world hadn't yet taught him he couldn't." The world will, indeed, tell each of us that we can't always accomplish our dreams. We don't need to learn that at the dinner table. Rather, we need the reinforcement to keep trying!

TALKING ABOUT GOD AT THE DINNER TABLE

In his extensive travels over thirty years, Dr. Harold Westing, associate professor of pastoral ministries at Denver Seminary, has stayed in homes instead of hotels whenever possible. During his visits in hundreds of homes, he has learned there are basically two ways families teach children about Christianity: as a system, or as a relationship.

Teaching spiritual principles is most effective when they are delivered in the warp and woof of life, in the course of everyday conversation—like answering the question, "Where did you see God working in your life today?"

Don't exclude God talk from the

continued next page

■ **We're a family of five, and the characters and chemistry are unique. Is there some formula we can use to get everybody talking?**

A few tips will help ensure success:

1. *Sit down together at the table* and keep distractions, especially the television and telephone, at a minimum.

2. *Treat each family member with respect.* Establish ground rules regarding monopolizing the conversation. If you have someone who loves center stage, jump in when he or she pauses for a breath and ask someone

else to comment.

Too often we listen with our minds preoccupied with our own response. But when communication—the real connection—takes place, it's awesome. And it's worth wading through many other family discussions to get there!

3. Establish some basic rules concerning acceptable table language, behavior, and topics.

4. Children should ask to be excused and should learn to sit at the table for a reasonable length of time, according to their age and personality, after they have finished eating. For young children, coloring books at the table can help keep their minds and hands occupied.

5. Steer the conversation away from criticizing other people, whether present or absent. Although we don't condone everyone's behavior, we should uphold each person's worth. If this is the general attitude displayed toward people through the talk around the table, children will feel safe expressing their own feelings. If a child or adult expresses strong feelings—for example, disappointment over failing a test—empathize rather than criticize. Don't make light of it, think of excuses, or blame the teacher for being unreasonable.

6. Ask questions at the table for which anyone seated will have an answer; and which cannot be answered with a simple yes or no. Set the tone by being honest and vulnerable. For example, if a child is experiencing a rough ride through puberty, reminisce about your own experiences at that age. Let your child know you didn't feel secure about yourself, or that you didn't

fun talk you have at the table. Don't relegate it to only a set apart, solemn time. If you read a family devotional or passages of Scripture at the table, or perhaps memorize Bible verses, keep the time brief, the focus relevant, your prayers genuine, and don't be afraid to have fun.

Use object lessons. Place a jar of yeast and water in the center of the table and ask, "What does this have to do with the Bible?" As you use the salt shaker ask, "Who can think of ways salt is mentioned in the Bible?" (Let your speech always be seasoned with salt. You are the salt of the earth. Lot's wife became a pillar of salt.)

Don't keep God in a box; include Him at the table.

make it to adulthood without suffering some scrapes along the way.

7. *Remember what Colossians 4:6 says:*

"Let your speech always be with grace, seasoned, as it were, with salt, so that you may know how you should respond to each person." Using just the right amount of salt doesn't call attention to the saltiness or the lack of saltiness in food, but it enhances natural flavors. Let your conversation bring out the best in others. Be animated, but not sharp. Participate, but don't dominate.

■ **Those are great tips, but what is there to talk about in our home?**

Plenty! You can plan a discussion question or two, or just let it flow. Chances are over time you'll use a good mix of both. Encourage children to participate at their own levels of understanding.

Planned discussions are the same as "putting a subject on the table." When you do this, remember the objective is to get everyone thinking and sharing from his or her own experiences and insights. The point is not to reach a consensus or the "correct" answer.

Good topic ideas can surface from other conversations, books, newspaper or magazine articles, movies or TV shows, political speeches, or neighborhood issues. When a good idea comes to mind, write it on the calendar or a chalkboard in the kitchen. Or put it on a Post-it note at your place at the table so you won't forget it. Sometimes assign other family members to come up with the questions.

Read excerpts from a letter addressed to the family and reminisce about those particular relatives or friends. Pray for them. Compose a round-robin reply, with each person adding a few lines. Bring a cartoon, riddle, joke, or poem to the table.

If a child is studying a foreign language, or if a parent knows another language, learn as a family some common words and expresskons. Discuss how that language differs from English. Learn the gracious words: *thank you; please; excuse me; good morning.*

■ **What happens if a conversation falls flat?**

Try another one. Discuss movies the whole family has seen, musical performances, or books. Encourage family members to think, analyze, and articulate with the goal of discerning the precious and recogoizing the worthless.

Children oust learn that not everything in print is worth reading. Not everything on television is worth watching. Not everything seen and heard in the various media is true or healthy. Not all adults are trustworthy, nor their conduct worth emulating.

Define words and concepts: urban vs. suburban, civil rights, abortion, freedom of speech, freedom of religion, salvation by works or by grace. Katie Couric of the "Today Show" says she grew up in a home where her dad asked each of his four children to bring a new word to the table each night.

Discuss a child's writing assignment with questions like, "How do you think you'll approach that?" "What have you learned on this topic?" "What do you want your readers to learn?" Verbalizing the main idea will help a child write more clearly.

■ **We have some friends who use mealtime for a periodic family meeting. What's that?**

Family meetings are helpful to discuss a problem the family needs to handle collectively, such as family rules regarding homework, bedtimes, and television. At the beginning of summer, hold a family meeting to plan a vacation or discuss how you want to take advantage of the long days.

Family meetings can help you decide on an appropriate gift the family will give at an upcoming wedding, birthday, or gradua-

CONVERSATION STARTERS

When famine and civil war gripped Somalia several years ago and the United Nations sent troops and food, one family pulled out the family atlas—a good resource to keep near the table. Where is Somalia anyway? Perhaps a child knows and an adult doesn't. What countries does it border? What are its climate and topography? One six-year-old girl reflected at her family dinner table: "Too bad Somalia doesn't have a Joseph. He prepared for famine."

Put a globe in the center of the table and make a game of finding particular countries, oceans, seas, large cities, or continents. Study a chart of the constellations visible at that time of year. Choose three or four in particular and then search the sky for them later that night. Curiosity is contagious; pass it on.

The world is shrinking rapidly through advances in communication and travel. Our children are likely to venture farther into the world than we have, at the least by linking electronically with people of other cultures. At the table, families can share knowledge and skills that will help prepare children for life in their world.

tion celebration. Think of a neighbor, relative, or friend who could use some encouragement and in what ways you as a family could help. Fix a meal, watch pets, baby-sit, mow the lawn, give flowers, and so on. Soon after Christmas, hold a family meeting for the purpose of writing thank-you notes.

Parents set the tone at the table. They must forge an undercurrent of respect, and they must be willing to listen. While parents may have the final say, it's important that children feel their ideas are valued and that they participate in family decisions. When they do, the family is richer, the family's sense of identity is stronger, and the children are better equipped to participate with confidence in the classroom and in their world.

This material is adapted from Table Talk *by Mimi Wilson and Mary Beth Lagerborg. Copyright © 1994 Mary Beth Lagerborg and Mimi Wilson. Used by permission of Focus on the Family.*

19

Teaching Children to Work

. . . .

■ **All I do around the house is work, work, work. How can I get my children to clean up after themselves and take the load off me?**

Mom, you're working too hard on your chores and not enough on your kids! All parents know that it's harder to teach children to pick up their socks than to pick up the socks for them. This is true of almost any job we ask our children to do, at least at first. But to do everything for them is to teach them to be irresponsible and prepare them for disaster in adult life. Children must be taught to work if they are going to achieve anything in life.

In our world, there is a strong connection between work and reward. We're not doing our children any favors when we give them everything.

■ **I agree. I have two children about to enter the teen years, and I want them to learn the value of a buck. What's a good way to get my point across?**

Robert Smith, a Southern California schoolteacher, once taught a fellow named Carl. All through school, Carl was a fair student, but he was capable of a great deal more than he ever produced. He glided through high school taking the easiest courses. Following graduation, he never kept a steady job that paid much more than the mini-

THE CHRISTIAN FAMILY ANSWER BOOK

TWENTY-ONE JOBS FOR THE ENTREPRENEUR

1. Washing cars. All you need are sponges, a pail, a chamois, and a good supply of elbow grease.

2. Windows. Many people would gladly pay an enterprising youngster to do this chore.

3. Have spade, will dig. Have you tried lately to hire a workman to dig anything? It's a lost art. A strong boy or girl can dig holes to plant flowers or dig up weeded areas.

4. Garage sale assistant. People need help carrying boxes and setting up garage sales.

5. Fence painting. Where's Tom Sawyer when you need him? The situation is that bad. Fences take time and patience with a brush and roller, and they're a good place for a child to learn how to paint.

6. Baby-sitting. Once, teens usually baby-sat at night, but today, there is a crying need for daytime or afternoon child care.

7. Reader. Many senior citizens with diminished vision are unable to read. They tire of the fare on radio and television and would be pleased to find a good young reader with a pleasant voice to read their favorite books to them.

8. Mobile shoeshine boy. Have your child set up his own shoeshine stand—on a skateboard. He can load his polishes and brushes on his board and be in business!

continued next page

mum wage. One time, Carl looked up his old schoolteacher. "Every employer wants experience," he complained. "How do you get experience if you can't get a job in the first place? Besides, they all seem to want proof that you'll be a good worker."

"What kind of jobs did you do growing up?" Robert asked. "How did you earn your spending money?"

"Oh, Dad gave me plenty of money. I didn't have time to get a job. I played football," he said. "Besides, Dad wouldn't have let me work anyway. He said he made enough money so I could spend my good years without having to sweat."

■ **So by not making Carl get some kind of job during his teen years, he ended up harming the young man.**

Correct. It's a pity Carl never learned the value of hard work. Carl is one of an army of young people who don't know *how* to work. He's had none of the experiences his father's generation acquired when they worked for spending (and saving) money as youngsters.

All children need working experiences as a part of their maturation process, just as much as they need the formal education of the schoolroom. And those who don't acquire that experience in their teenage years often play "catch-up."

■ Why is that?

It's not the *specific* skills one learns while baby-sitting or mowing the lawn or sweeping up, it's the *behavioral* attitudes one learns in getting and keeping a job that are absolutely critical. These are virtues such as reliability, honesty, neatness, punctuality, attentiveness to detail, simple courtesy to a customer, realistic expectations, persistence, and sweat.

These virtues don't spring full-bloom overnight. A good personnel officer can tell, almost unconsciously, whether the applicant in front of him has done his time and learned his lessons on the job. Teens who have outside means of making their own money are nearly always the hardest-working students in the classroom. They are the most successful when they graduate. Indisputably, good work attitudes at home serve to reinforce appropriate school behavior, and vice versa.

■ So why didn't Carl's father want his son to work?

Carl's father expressed a common attitude in our modern

9. Dog walker. Dogs need exercise. For reasons of time pressure or illness, many people can't give their pets their daily constitutional. The elderly often need a reliable person to walk or feed their pets.

10. Artist. If your budding artist is good, cheap, and traditional, a few patrons will be found, especially if he does children's portraits.

11. Letter writer. A senior citizen with arthritis will use this service occasionally. Tact, discretion, and neatness are musts.

12. Worm farming. Mealworms are easy to raise in a small area. Earthworms are popular with gardeners and fishermen.

13. Vacuuming. A careful child will find plenty of people willing to pay him to push a vacuum.

14. Trash can patrol. Some men hate this job. Single mothers have trouble wrestling the cans to the curb. In either case, this can be a source of earnings for a strong boy or girl.

15. Mowing lawns. Many an enterprising teen has mowed lawns for pocket money. And young people are much cheaper than professional gardeners. Some people just need extra help to trim hedges and weed gardens every now and then.

16. Neighborhood produce stand. If you live in a rural or spacious suburban area, this is still a popular source of spending money. Raising and marketing
continued next page

vegetables and fruits teaches concepts about math, business, and life that no text can equal.

17. Typist. If your child knows how to type well and is a careful worker, he will find plenty of people who need word processing. This could be a good way of putting that home computer to use!

18. Attic and garage organizer. Who has time for spring-cleaning these days? If your child is neat and has a knack for organization, he'll find neighbors ready to hire him.

19. Home maintenance expert. Every family has a multitude of chores begging for attention. Pay your kids to do them. It's better than an allowance. Your children will earn money and acquire valuable work experience.

20. Gofer. Minor errands to local stores and other neighborhood locations give your child a chance to ride his bike and earn some cash at the same time.

21. Paperboy. Some newspapers, especially small town dailies, are still delivered to homes. Being a paperboy or papergirl provides good business experience and develops responsibility.

society. He didn't want work to put a dent in the boy's social life, and he was certain that earning pocket money was meaningless. But he, like many parents, was upset when Carl took his car for granted and acted nonchalantly about the high cost of insuring it. He couldn't understand why the boy wasn't more appreciative. Carl couldn't have cared less.

That's why the *values* learned by earning and spending our own money help us recognize work as a unit of energy expended, measured by our own effort and toil. Children learn to use money wisely when it's their own money they're spending.

We all know full-grown adults who are hopelessly immature when it comes to responsibility, promptness, diligence, and attention to detail. These virtues are learned. They don't just develop during puberty. Children need to be nurtured by parents who care enough to encourage their offspring to work at home or around the neighborhood.

Neighborhood jobs are fine for those too young to hold a part-time job at a fast-food restaurant or supermarket. Many elderly people need someone to perform minor jobs around the house. Homeowners, especially two-income couples, can't find time to keep up the yard or other routine household tasks. They are more than willing to pay an enterprising teen to do them.

Parents, of course, must ensure that their children don't work *too much*. Balance is the key word. If you really want your child to have an edge when he reaches the work market, no skill is as valuable as the knack for hard work. Give your child this knack. At the same time, watch your child develop a stronger sense of his own self-worth, greater self-confidence, more responsible behavior and appropriate personal habits. As sweat glistens on his forehead, your child will discover the unique joy that accompanies the phrase "Well done." That's a joy you owe him.

■ **I'm worried that my teen might work *too* much. We have kids in the neighborhood who are working twenty, thirty hours a week at McDonald's, and I don't think that's right.**

It's not. In those cases, the modest paychecks are tossed into a sinkhole of car payments, lavish dates, designer clothes, stereos, and TVs. In addition, high school students in California and Wisconsin who worked more than twenty-one hours a week did much poorer in school than teens who worked ten or less hours a

WHAT ABOUT ALLOWANCES?

Teaching children the wise stewardship of resources is essential for Christian parents, and training them how to handle money is a good place to start. One of the best ways for children to learn about money is to have an allowance.

Many parents do not give formal allowances, but instead give their children money on an irregular, unplanned basis as it is requested. This method doesn't teach them how to manage money. A regular allowance avoids these problems, but there are widely divergent opinions about which type of allowance is best. Some parents pay children only for chores around the house. Others give a regular allowance but withhold it if chores are left undone or as punishment for misbehavior.

Many parents, however, think these methods encourage children to be good only for the money, and to see household chores as paid labor instead of natural responsibilities as members of the family. At the same time, the irregularity of payments makes it impossible for children to learn how to budget or save their income.

Other parents pay allowances regularly and at a fixed amount with no conditions attached. This systems seems best for helping children learn how to budget, but it fails to teach the connection

continued next page

between work and rewards.

The best approach, perhaps, is a combination of these two methods. Give each child a regular, fixed allowance that must be budgeted for specific basic needs, plus a little more to spend at his or her discretion. This allowance is simply the child's share of the income as a family member.

At the same time, basic responsibilities around the house are expected to be fulfilled; if they aren't, take disciplinary measures other than withholding allowance. In addition, extra chores you might normally pay someone else to do—like washing the windows—can be done by your child for additional earnings. This extra income will teach the connection between work and wages, and will be available to the child for "fun things" that aren't basic needs.

week. The students working long hours were so tired (many high schools start at 7:15 A.M. these days) that they struggled to keep their eyes open during class.

■ **So what questions should I be asking about teen employment?**

Try these out: *Why* is my teen working? It is to learn *how* to work? To learn responsibility? To pay for necessities I can't afford? To augment the child's college fund? Or is it make payments on that gleaming Z-28 sitting in the driveway?

Adding work to a teen's regular school day doesn't leave time to pursue outside interests such as football, track, drama, and the French club. And what about church activities? Does your teen have time to invest in his or her youth group? Parents need to count all the costs before allowing their children to join the work force while their values are still forming.

■ **But didn't you say that Carl's father made a mistake by allowing his son to play football and not get a job?**

Right, which means you should follow the old rule—everything in moderation. Here are some guidelines to consider regarding teens and work:

► Keep the hours to under ten a week. Studies show that grades suffer when you go past the ten-per-week mark.
► Let them work during vacation periods. Employers desperately need help between Thanksgiving and Christmas and during summer vacation.

▶ No work after 6 o'clock. A full school day and three hours of work is enough for anybody, even for energetic teens. If your teens are not home for dinner, you're also losing an important time to reconnect. Be on the guard for burnout. Check with teachers to see if your kids are catching up on sleep during class.

▶ Remind them that a portion of their earnings should go back to the Lord. The Lord delights in our offerings.

▶ Finally, force them to save. Yes, it is their money, but tell them the money will come in handy one day for a car or college-related expenses.

This material is adapted from writings by Robert Smith of Whittier, California, and 40 Ways to Teach Your Child Values *(Living Books) by Paul Lewis.*

20

How to Debt-Proof Your Kids

. . . .

■ Faced with the huge task of mothering two boys, I set out to be the perfect parent. Before they were even out of diapers, I found myself doing what comes naturally to most moms and dads: making sure they had everything I didn't have when I was a kid.

In the beginning it was gratifying to pump anything money and credit could buy into their little worlds. I would spend hours in the toy and department stores picking out that perfect game for Jeremy or that cute outfit for Josh. And I soon learned I didn't have to leave the comfort of my living room to give them more: I could create Christmas anytime of the year by using our new bank card and a few home shopping catalogs.

But the more I bought for my sons, the more they wanted. The more I gave in to their desires, the less appreciation they showed. In my heart, I knew the day was fast approaching when nothing would satisfy them and more would never be enough—neither for them nor for me.

Your story sounds like Mary Hunt's, founder of the *Cheapskate Monthly* newsletter. It wasn't until Mary's husband lost his job and they found themselves $100,000 in debt that she realized the silent message she had been sending her boys: We have a bottomless container of money to which you are automatically entitled.

That was about as far from the truth as their income was from meeting their expenses, but because Mary never stopped spending, her sons were oblivious to that fact. The last thing in the world she wanted was for her boys to turn out as financially irresponsible as she was.

THE MIRACLE OF COMPOUNDING INTEREST

Here's a story you can use to help your kids understand compound interest:

In 1492, Christopher Columbus decided to save for retirement. He had one penny, and he knew he could earn 6 percent on his money every year. He put the penny in his left pocket and placed the interest [$0.01(the original penny) X 6 percent = $0.0006 (the amouot of interest he earned after each year)] into his right pocket for safekeeping. He never added anything to the original penny in his left pocket. Yet the interest in his right pocket accumulated year after year.

Chris, who has always been a healthy guy, is now 503 years old. He decided to retire this year, so he took the one penny from his left pocket and added it to the simple interest in his right pocket. Do you know how much Chris had?

Well, the interest in his right pocket added up to only 30 cents [503 years X $0.0006 (the interest he earned after each year) = 30 cents (after 503 years)]. Along with the original penny from his left pocket, he had 31 cents with which to retire. Not good planning!

continued next page

■ **How did Mary instill some sound financial principles in the still-wet cement of her kids' minds?**

Mary created her own kid-sized money system: the Hunt Kid Financial Plan.

Rather than drop this bomb on the boys unannounced, she began talking in general terms about a wonderful thing that would happen to each of them on the first day of their sixth-grade year. In fact, she raved about the plan so much that the kids were beside themselves with anticipation. So the day Jeremy entered the sixth grade, she led him first through the Hunt rite of passage—an introduction to the plan.

The plan's premise was this: Children must be allowed to experience real-life money conflicts while still in the safety net of parental protection. To never allow a child to make an independent financial decision prior to leaving home is to set that child up for financial failure as an adult. After spending a lot of time thinking about and designing the plan, she was certain that starting sooner rather than later was best:

First, she told her boys that each would receive a monthly cash salary. She chose the word "salary" because it sounds more businesslike and respectable than the word "allowance." They explained that at the start of each school year, their salaries would be reviewed for a possible increase based on their needs and how well they managed their money the year before.

To determine the amount of their salaries, she and her husband, Harold, figured out how much money they were willing to spend on their optionals—things above and beyond shelter, food, and clothing. Their kids, of course, didn't realize their salaries were the money they would have spent on them anyway. Instead, they figured they had just arrived in the land of unbelievable wealth. And to their advantage, the salary they gave them was considerably less than the sum total they had been forking out. They had been allowing their boys to $5 and $10 them to death.

■ **Did the Hunts require the boys to tithe their salary?**

Without exception, they required Jeremy and Josh to give away 10 percent of their monthly salary. They could give to a needy stranger, a friend whose parent might be out of work, a charitable organization, or the church offering. They wanted them to experience the joy of giving and to make wise choices

What could Chris have done differently? Let's assume Chris was much more astute about investing. Instead of putting the interest in his right pocket, he put it into his left pocket with the original penny—the principal. Over the years, he would earn the same 6 percent interest on the original penny *and* the compounding interest in his left pocket.

At the end of the first year, he had $0.0106 in his left pocket [0.01 X 0.06 (interest earned on the original penny) + $0.01 (the original penny) = $0.0106)]. At the end of the second year, he had $0.011236 [0.0106 (total earned after first year) X 0.06 (interest earned on original penny) + $0.0106 (first year's interest earned on original penny) = $0.011236]. This is called compounding interest, and it continued for 503 years. How much did Chris finally accumulate for retirement?

The answer is more to his liking. At the end of 503 years of compounding the original penny at 6 percent interest, Chris was a billionaire: He had $53,561,191,327! None of us may live 503 years, but all of us have more than one penny to save.

in selecting the recipients.

Also, they were so convinced that giving back to God invites His supernatural intervention in their lives that they wanted their boys to catch the spirit of His command: " 'Bring the whole tithe into the storehouse, that there may be food in thy house. Test Me in this,' says the Lord Almighty, 'and see if I will not open the floodgates of heaven and pour out so much blessing that you will not have room enough for it' " (Mal. 3:10).

■ **Could the boys spend it all, or were they forced to put some of the salaries into savings accounts?**

Each of their children had to save 10 percent of his monthly salary in a school savings account at the neighborhood bank. Most banks offer this type of account, which has no minimums or service fees. Their rule was simple: savings without withdrawal. This eliminated any questions about long-term versus short-term savings. Also, they likened compounding interest to fertilizer that makes money grow—a concept any sixth-grader can understand.

To prep them on the rules of bank etiquette, they made a few runs to the bank together, held deposit-slip training sessions, laid down the law about courtesy in line, and took them by the teller counter. They felt like real men because they were doing "grown-up" things, which was exactly their goal: The Hunts wanted them to develop a habit of saving that would follow them through their adult lives.

■ **After tithing and savings, the boys were free to spend as they pleased, right?**

Along with each son's first salary, the Hunts presented him with a "Things-I-have-to-pay-for" list. That list reflected the optionals Harold and Mary were releasing into their sons' hands. They made sure their guidelines were clear: "If you want these things, you are responsible to pay for them using your salary. If you don't want them or want something else instead (that we approve of), that's your choice, and we will trust your judgment." As a parent who struggles with the desire to control, this was the scariest part of the plan for Mary. But she took a deep breath and asked God to help her let go a little at a time.

The parents made sure the boys' lists, which grew each year, were always commensurate with their ages. When Jeremy was ten years old, for example, his list included movies, food outside the home, school supplies, clothing upgrades (the parents established an amount they would pay for items of clothing, shoes, etc.), hobbies, spending money or birthday party gifts; when Jeremy reached high school, he had to pay for more of the extras: his admission to football games, fast-food items, any dates he went on, and his yearbook. The goal was for their lists to include the optionals and essentials by the time each graduated from high school. The Hunts wanted their boys to leave the nest prepared to face a world fraught with the many financial traps that could ruin their lives.

■ Were the boys still required to do chores around the house as part of their contribution to the family?

Yes, Jeremy and Josh performed household tasks, but their parents did not make their salaries dependent upon their performances, since they wanted their plan to emulate real life. (While job performance is important to financial success, most people in the business world don't have their salary slashed because of an occasional mistake or shortcoming.) Instead, Harold and Mary let them know that they expected a certain level of performance, and if they did not deliver, they disciplined them appropriately.

■ Looking back, was the Hunts' plan a success?

Ten years have passed since they introduced the plan to their sons. Jeremy is twenty-one, and Josh is twenty. Both attend college and live at home. Though the parents are hesitant to declare the plan a complete success until more time has passed, a progress report is in order.

- ▶ *First, Harold and Mary weren't the "bad guys"* when their boys couldn't buy or do something for lack of funds. The boys knew it wasn't their parents' fault and easily concluded *they* just couldn't afford it.
- ▶ *Second, eliminating the stress that money*—or lack of it—can bring between parent and teen freed the family to enjoy each other and grow together in how they managed their money.

Harold and Mary agree that their sons' adolescent years were among the best.

► *Third, not once since they started the plan has either child asked them for a loan.* That doesn't mean the boys always had money: They discovered what it meant to be broke early in the month. But while they all recall times when each made foolish purchases, neither ever experienced more than a little discomfort as a result of their unwise spending.

► *Fourth, both boys independently elected to save far more than the minimum required* and often lived on 10 percent rather than 80 percent. Each purchased his own car with cash. Both found part-time jobs after finishing high school, because under the plan, salary from the parents ceased after graduation.

► *Finally, Jeremy and Josh learned to feel comfortable with their personal financial management skills.* Both manage their own checking accounts and automatic teller machine privileges. Neither has ever bounced a check and can't understand how anyone else could (or as Jeremy remarked a few years ago in reaction to the House of Representatives banking scandal, "You'd have to be pretty stupid to write a check for more money than you have in your account!"). They've learned to wait for the best deals and not to buy new if used will do. They stand in awe of the magic of compounding interest. Best of all, the boys have followed their parents' lead in consistently giving part of their money back to God in some form.

The Hunts are confident their boys are prepared to enter a world filled with preapproved credit card applications, pressure to have now and pay later, and all other forms of financial temptation. Though it will be hard to send them off to fly solo soon, that day would certainly be more difficult if Harold and Mary hadn't started letting them go ten years ago.

Giving their children some personal financial control at such a young age conveyed to them how much they were trusted. That trust, in turn, developed their confidence, maturity, and decision-making abilities. But that's not the end of the story.

Despite their mistakes as parents, Mary is sure God had His hand on their efforts, because He *promises* to bless those who obey His laws:

"Great peace have they who love Your law, and nothing can make them stumble" (Ps. 119:165). With His help, they have guided their children around the pit of debt and onto the road of financial freedom.

This material is adapted from writings by Mary Hunt of Cheapskate Monthly *(P.O. Box 2135, Paramount, CA 90723), (310) 630-8845 and* 21 1/2 Easy Steps to Financial Security *by Alvin H. Danenberg.*

21

Raising Sports-Minded Kids

. . . .

■ **My young children, Ryan and Caitlin, love their gymnastics lessons. In the last year, Ryan has also played in organized soccer and T-ball leagues, coached by his dad. Often, when I'm driving the kids to another practice, I wonder if Charlie and I will be able to raise them with the right attitudes about sports and competition. How can we keep the fun in sports without going overboard on winning and losing? If one of our children becomes a standout athlete, how can we nurture that talent without ignoring the needs of the other child? How can sports bolster their faith in Christ?**

These are important questions, ones often asked by parents whose children are heavily involved in swimming, soccer, gymnastics, baseball, basketball, football, tennis, or taekwondo, to name a few. If sports play a big part in your family, remember that your ultimate goal is to encourage the development of godly character.

If your daughter is heavily into gymnastics, tell her that you support her, not because she wins meets or comes home with trophies, but because her character has been strengthened by the challenges she faced. Keep your children on an even keel by occasionally placing Bible verses on humility next to their corn flakes. An excellent verse to memorize is God's promise in Romans 8:28: "And we know that in all things God works for the good of those who love him, who have been called according to his purpose."

■ How can I keep sports from becoming more important than church in my household?

Besides being a parent who makes church a priority and family devotions a regular occurrence, prod your child to take part in youth group activities. Yes, that's difficult when practice and competition takes place after school and in the early evenings, but it's important for your child to make friends with peers outside the gym.

■ We feel like we are doing a good job honoring God in our home, but if anything falls by the wayside, it's usually schoolwork. Is that wrong?

Schoolwork not only balances the rigors of athletics and broadens a child's perspective, but it's also more important in the long run. One day, one year, you're going to have to back off basketball or tennis a bit and have your youngster concentrate on his studies. It also helps to establish a rapport with the teachers, so when the busy sports season arrives, they will be flexible with your teen's game and travel schedule. You're going to have to work extra hard to keep the homework from faltering.

Be sure to have an "off-season" in the home. Sports psychologists agree that athletes who keep the pressures of competition in balance are those who have purposely scheduled "downtime" in their training. Our children need some time off, too—a period to goof off and have fun away from their sport.

■ Our oldest daughter is quite a volleyball player, but her younger sister has no interest in sports. All my husband talks about at the dinner table is Valerie's volleyball—will her team finish first, will she play in college? I sometimes wonder if my husband is placing too much attention on Valerie's volleyball at the expense of Lindsay. Is there a danger?

You're going to have to watch out for sibling rivalry, Mom, by being on the lookout for signs of discord. Dinnertime conversation shouldn't be monopolized by Valerie's kill shots and blocking strategies, but should also include current events, church activities, and upcoming plans.

If Lindsay is a talented piano player, organize "sing-along" nights so she will be the spotlight. By strengthening family ties, you'll be keeping sibling rivalries to a minimum.

■ **My husband is positive that our twelve-year-old son, Ricky, will be the next Barry Bonds. How can I bring him and his expectations down to earth?**

Through cold, hard numbers. There are a little more than 650 major league baseball players in the country, but several million youngsters play the game in various leagues each year. In gymnastics alone, there are 40,000 girls competing in sanctioned meets, but only *six* will make the U.S. Olympic team!

Thus, the odds of your son or daughter playing in Yankee Stadium or going to the Olympics are, quite frankly, infinitesimal. Some parents see their child excel at the local level, and all of a sudden the pressure is on. Visions of million-dollar contracts and huge endorsement fees dance around their heads. Goals are good, but it's even more important to see your child's involvement in sports as part of a broader picture. Sports can help your children mature and become a responsible adult. Any successes they enjoy on the playing field are a bonus.

■ **At my son's Little League games, we have a dad with a bull-horn voice who constantly rides the umpire—especially when his son is pitching. I also know a mom who constantly compoains to sports administrators within earshot of the children. Why do we have these pushy "sports moms" or "sports dads"?**

Some parents get so wrapped up in their kids' sporting events that reason and civility get left behind at home. Kids see that, too. Talk about it at the dinner table with your children, and explain why you don't bait umpires or go overboard with league administrators. But most of all, yell encouragement—not derisive putdowns—from the stands. That will elevate the competition.

■ **Last week, my daughter Molly lost a close tennis match in a third-set tiebreaker—a match that kept her team from winning state. She was in tears afterward, and I didn't know what to do. Should I have tried to say something?**

There wasn't much you *could* say. Molly was hurting, and about all you could do was sympathize with her. A lot of parents mumble, "Better luck next time," but it's more important for a mom or dad to say, "I'm sorry you lost. I hurt with you. Tell me what you're feeling."

When you're having your discussion, don't talk *at* her, but *with* her. Later on, when she has calmed down, point out the things she did that you're proud of. Discourage your child from making excuses. When it's appropriate, ask, "What did you learn from this?"

■ **My son's baseball team lost the district championship on a bad call. What do you do then?**

Welcome him to the real world. Your son is going to learn sooner or later that life is unfair, and it sounds like in this case that it was sooner. You should have an attitude that views unfair results as character-building opportunities. For instance, there may come a time when your son doesn't get to start the game at shortstop even though he's the better player. Perhaps your son can look at setbacks as an incentive to work even harder on the ball field.

■ **The other night at family devotions, my son asked for prayer that his football team would win the big game against our cross town rivals. I told him that instead of praying to win the game, he should pray that he would do his best. Was I right?**

Of course. Besides, if families on the *other* team are praying for victory, what is God going to do? Instead, you should pray with your child that God's will will be done. Don't pray to win. Your prayers should include a gratefulness for the opportunity to perform. Praying to demonstrate a Christlike attitude before others will also give your son a broader purpose for his endeavors.

■ **We've heard what to say to a chilg when he loses. So what do you say when a child wins?**

Make sure your child understands the correlation between hard work and victory. Help him be humble. Constantly remind him of the Scripture, "For everyone who exalts himself will be humbled, and he who humbles himself will be exalted" (Luke 14:11).

In the end, though, you want your children to treat victory and defeat just the same. Tell them their performance has nothing to do with your estimation of them. A simple hug and a warm smile can set the stage for a more fruitful conversation later on about what went wrong. Remember to love your child unconditionally, as Christ loves us. In that context, the pressures of our success-oriented world will lessen as we encourage our children to strike a healthy balance in their pursuit of God's best.

This material is adapted from writings by Nancy Thies Marshall, a former U.S. Olympic gymnast now living in Salem, Oregon.

4

All About
School Issues

22

Preparing Your Child for School

. . . .

Editor's Note: Though we don't go to school with our children, our concerns do. While some children love school and breeze through, others have a more difficult time. For a small minority, school is one of the most exquisite forms of punishment the world has ever invented.

As parents, we are caught in the middle. We want more than anything in the world for our children to get something worthwhile from school. We also want to see them enjoy it.

We often get the idea, however, that we are somehow outside observers, trying to catch a glimpse into that mysterious monastery set on a hill that swallows up our children each morning and spits them back to us each afternoon. How can we make school profitable for our children?

In the course of a year, Dr. Cliff Schimmels, a Christian college professor of education, visits more than 200 classrooms in more than seventy-five schools. Thus, his opinions are based on personal observations. What follows are some of the most prominent questions Dr. Schimmels hears parents asking, and they are answered in his voice.

■ **How early should a child learn to read?**

Everybody has an opinion on this—which is all right—except no one agrees with anyone else. What's a parent to think? One expert says start at age two. Another says start at eight. Which one do you listen to?

I am not sure I have the right answer, but I do have an observation. Teach your child to read when he *wants* to read. If you watch your child, he will tell you when he is ready. In fact, a lot of children teach themselves to read before any adult even knows about it; then one day they surprise the world by revealing their accomplishment.

Most parents are usually embarrassed at this point. They celebrate the achievement, but they feel a bit guilty the child learned something on his own without having to be taught by the parent. Aren't children wonderful? If your child shows signs of wanting to read at three or four or five, don't be afraid to encourage him.

You can do several fun things to get him started. You can make name tags for items around the house, such as a stove or table, so he can easily pick up the written symbol for that item. (Remember that reading is the process of interpreting symbolic language.)

Help your child learn to recognize the sounds of language. Help him discover the sound in a specific word. Then you can introduce him to hand-drawn flash cards with those sounds on them. With that foundation, he learns that reading is the process of putting sounds to letters.

■ **Our son has been going to first grade for six weeks, and he hates it. He cries every morning. What could be his problem?**

I assume that this is his first all-day school experience. If he hasn't gone to an all-day kindergarten or an all-day preschool, he is making a tremendous adjustment.

No matter what the age, moving from the home to the school is a major transition in a youngster's life. Let's look at some of these adjustments.

► *Social adjustment.* School is about friendships. It is almost impossible to function in school without some friendships. You need a friend to line up with you in the bathroom line. You need a friend to share your eating spot at lunch. You need a friend to help you study. You need a friend to lend you a pencil when yours wears out.

Establishing all those friendships is an exhausting enterprise, even for gregarious children, because there is a risk involved. You send out your feelers, and if no one picks up on them, you stand there with your emotions all exposed.

Let's see if I can make this into a general principle: ANY

CHILD WHO DOESN'T HAVE A FRIEND IN THE CLASSROOM WILL HATE SCHOOL. Well, it may be a little harsh, but I'm willing to live with it.

► *Adjustment to the routine.* Learning to go to school is learning to live with having someone in control of your body, mind, and soul from 9 A.M. to 3 P.M. The teacher really expects you to sit still, read when she tells you to, walk straight to the bathroom rather than looking at all the neat stuff in the hall, get a drink when she tells you to, and keep from looking out the window even when a man is mowing the grass.

► *Adjustment to authority.* When a child is at home, the only people who boss him around are those who love him. When you go to school, everybody tells you what to do—the bus driver, the teacher, the lunchroom monitor, the school secretary, and the principal.

► *Adjustment to the ever-present threat of failure.* Failure is as rampant in school as success is. You can fail in many different ways. You can misspell a word everyone else knows. You can color outside the lines. You can read too slowly. You can drop your books during quiet time. You can go to the bathroom in your pants.

In other words, if you aren't careful, you can make a complete fool of yourself. You always have to be on your guard, and that not only wears you out, but it makes life miserable as well.

Help your son establish a friendship with someone in the class, even if you have to invite someone over every afternoon for a week. At this point, you need to be diligent and frequently express love for your son (or daughter). Pick him up and hold him. Hug him when he isn't expecting it.

■ **We've never had any trouble with school until this year. Our daughter is in fourth grade, and her teacher is terrible. The class is in constant chaos. How damaging could this year be for these children?**

It depends on the individual student. Some students are so sensitive that a year like this one could have repercussions for a long time, not only in what they lost in subject matter, but also in just being able to relate to a teacher.

On the other hand, some students just adapt, accept what is, and go on with their business.

How are *you* responding to this? If you are panicking and fretting, you will surely pass part of this on to your child. If you are cool and accepting, your child will have a better chance of learning to adapt to an unfortunate situation. In fact, if you are particularly skillful, you might even turn this into a learning experience.

Obviously, you will have to make sure this is a true report. Go to the school and get the evidence for yourself. If the teacher *is* doing a poor job, you need to consider a few things that could go wrong with a teacher.

1. The teacher has trouble handling her own authority. When this happens, one of two things occurs. Either she is so inconsistent and disorganized that the classroom is in a state of chaos, or she comes down so hard on students that she controls through sheer fear. Either way, the students don't get much work done.

2. The teacher is lazy, tired, and burned out. Some teachers simply spend so much energy that it finally catches up with them. They don't care anymore. They quit preparing lessons, or at least they don't prepare thoroughly enough. They don't read and grade students' papers. Students soon catch on to a teacher like this. They not only quit working, but they begin to play around in class.

How you are in a better position to help? Let's explore some steps you can take:

1. Help your daughter understand what is happening to her. Help with her lessons. Supplement, if you have to. And while you're doing that, help her understand that not all human beings she meets in life will be pleasant people.

2. Go see the teacher. If at all possible, see her under friendly terms. Try to find out what might be bothering her. You may find that she has some personal or family matter making her life miserable. Offer to help, and later explain the situation to your daughter.

3. See the principal. Again, go in a nonthreatening but straightforward way. If the class is in total chaos, the principal probably already agrees with you but may not be able to admit it. State your displeasure. Give specific examples if you can. If the principal has a course of action, give that new plan time to work. Offer your support, but at the same time make sure the principal knows the problem.

■ **Our sixth-grade son tells us he's going to take typing. Isn't that a bit early?**

With so many children beginning to use computers at early ages, some as early as kindergarten, when is the appropriate time to teach students how to use a keyboard?

Some experts tell us a child can properly finger a computer keyboard as soon as he's old enough to finger a piano. Others say youngsters can't be effective until high school.

I'm not sure with whom I agree, but I do have a couple of observations: (1) I've seen sixth graders master the fingering process, so they *can* do it; (2) every student must take typing sometime.

Let me restate that. Every student growing up in the last decade of the 20th century *must* learn to master the keyboard. It should be criminal to let students out of high school without this skill, but we are doing it.

■ **Our sophomore daughter is taking geometry this year. She started the school year working hard and doing well. She worked on homework almost every night. She studied hard for tests, and she had a B average. But just after Christmas, she missed three days of school with the flu. Since then, she hasn't even tried. Now she's failing the class. What happened? Could missing three days of class make all the difference?**

What an excellent question! Students and teachers everywhere will thank you for asking it. The answer is an emphatic *yes*. Yes, missing three days of a class like geometry could make all the difference in the world.

The reason is rather simple when you think about it. Geometry—and other classes—build concept upon concept. Every day the teacher sets out to present a new concept to the class. In fact, the good teacher will write one new concept on the board so the whole class will understand the objective for the day.

But the teacher often covers three other concepts before he gets to the main one. If a student misses any one of those preliminary concepts, he won't be able to get the main one. When a student is absent, a good teacher will be deliberate in showing the student the main concept, but even the best of teachers forget about all those other concepts en route.

How do we know which concept is missing? We don't get far asking a general question such as, "What don't you understand?" If your daughter knew what she didn't understand, she would probably find it somewhere and learn it on her own. At this point, however, she doesn't understand *any* of it. She needs to go through a series of specific questions until she and her teacher can identify the missing concept. I know this sounds like tedious work, but I don't know of a shortcut.

■ Is it possible for my child to get a value-free education in the public schools?

No. How's that for a short but frightening answer? Let's face it: There is no such thing as a value-free education; there never was and never will be. Education, by its very definition, is an enterprise in preparing people for a future. To do this, someone has to guess what the future holds and what is the best way to prepare for it. Those constitute values. We can't escape it.

Let's look at some of the ways human values are consciously or unconsciously incorporated into the school process. For starters, just the structure of the school day teaches certain values, such as the importance of being on time, the importance of following instructions, and the importance of the mind.

Students really don't have any options. If they go to school, they are going to learn that we Americans believe in being on time. That is the way the program operates. Teachers make hundreds of value judgments every day. They decide which piece of material gets three days of emphasis and which piece only gets one day. They decide what to explain and what they don't explain. They decide what is a good piece of work and deserves an A. Conversely, they decide what *isn't* a good piece of work and gets a D.

I don't want to frighten anybody, but a lot of what we adults value is what we learned from some teacher whose name we probably don't even remember. No, there simply is not something called a value-free education.

■ Aren't extracurricular activities just frills that weaken the educations of our young people?

No, I don't think so. Still, I do hear those cries for emphasis on the basics, and I agree. We must be diligent in teaching young people the skills of reading, writing, organizing, calculating, and using their minds. This is what school is all about.

Yet, at the same time, extracurricular activities can—and should—contribute to that mission, at least in a couple of ways. For one thing, the student who takes an active role in extracurricular activities is usually more excited about school and about learning. Because of this excitement, he is more highly motivated to apply himself to the sometimes difficult task of learning the basics.

One thing that we have learned from recent research is that the more students enjoy coming to school, the more they learn. That point is so obvious that we probably knew it long before the research proved it to us.

Besides, extracurricular activities carry some significant lessons. Notice how many corporate executives were active in a variety of extracurricular activities. Notice how many military leaders were high school athletes. These activities provide young people a practical arena in which to develop such skills as leadership, commitment to a group project, dedication, and personal discipline. I am prepared to argue that these lessons are just as important as the lessons of reading, writing, and calculating.

For these reasons, I think extracurricular activities are valuable. I would hope that we have enough variety—sports, music, speech, yearbook, etc.—that every student has an opportunity to participate. Providing a broad base of extracurricular programs within the school structure is one of the strengths of American education.

■ Do Christian students really have much influence in the public schools?

Yes, yes a thousand times yes! Christian students have an impact on other students, on teachers, and even on the community at large.

There may be a few laws restricting what Christians can say in a public place such as a school, but there is no law keeping a Christian from being a Christian; from thinking as a Christian; from looking at other people through the eyes of a Lord of love; and from keeping a lifestyle that is not comformed to this world, but is transformed by spiritual commitment to a righteous God.

Some Christian students witness by doing quality work. Frequently, teachers will comment that students from "church" families are easier to teach. What they are saying is the solid family unit that has God at the center makes a difference in the lives of young people.

Let me give another example. Brian and Susie were a perfect match in high school. Susie was a cheerleader, straight-A student, and homecoming queen. Brian was president of a couple of student organizations and captain of the football team. It seemed obvious to everyone that the two shouod be "seeing each other."

But there was one small hitch. Susie was a Christian and Brian wasn't. Finally, when Brian got the nerve to ask Susie out, she agreed on the condition that Brian would attend church with her each Sunday night. Since Susie was one of the prettier girls in school, Brain decided the price was not too high. He agreed. Shortly after they began seeing each other, Brian responded to the message of the Gospel and became a believer.

The two continued to be an "item" through high school, but when they went away to different colleges, the romance faded into just another high school memory.

Today, Brian is a successful minister, pastoring a large church in the Midwest—an effective servant of God who was first introduced to Christ because a high school girl was not afraid to stand on her convictions.

This material is adapted from Parents' Most-Asked Questions About Kids and Schools *(Victor) by Dr. Cliff Schimmels.*

23

Which School for Your Child?

One of the biggest decisions parents must make is what school they will send their children to or whether they will home school. In this chapter, we will discuss three options: private Christian schools, public schools, and homeschooling.

The Case for Christian Schools

■ At church the other Sunday, a seventeen-year-old senior, Amy, was asked to speak to the congregation about the local Christian high school she attended. Amy is a bright, articulate, nice-looking girl, and she did a fine job describing the benefits of Westminster Academy to the congregation. I was very impressed, but I guess I wasn't as impressed as another couple, who called their architect the next day and canceled a contract to build their "dream home."

"We've decided to take the money and put our kids in Westminster Academy next fall," the father told me. "If Amy is the type of person that school produces, that's what we want for our children." His actions have had a profound effect on me, and now I'm wondering if I should take my two children out of the public school and put them in Westminster Academy.

If you did, you wouldn't be alone. More and more Christian parents are choosing a Christian education for their children. Sure, it's a financial sacrifice, especially for young families. At Christian schools around the country, tuition can range from $1,500 to $5,000 a year. But school administrators say they've heard story after story of how God met the financial needs of parents once they chose Christian schooling.

■ **Why is tuition so high in some Christian schools?**

Often it's because the school has decided to pay its teachers on a par with the public school system. Some Christian schools cut corners with salaries and suffer rapid turnover. That does not build a strong school. You want to look for a school with veteran teachers.

The teachers' commitment is one reason why the education equals and often surpasses anything you'll find in public schools. Class size is usually small—about twenty students per classroom. Top Christian schools stress pure academics—language arts, reading, and mathematics. Many have computer labs, art, music, theater, and physical education.

■ **I've seen brochures from Christian schools that stress a "Christ-centered environment." What does that mean?**

Generally, this means that every class will have an awareness of Christ at its core. In a Christian school, every side of an issue—including the spiritual—can be explored and debated. That's forbidden in public schools. Such was not always the case, however. Before the Civil War, most schooling took place in a church-related environment. Even when towns and communities built common schools with public money, the curriculum was based upon traditional Christian values. That began to change rapidly after World War I.

The Supreme Court's decision in 1962 to ban school prayer signaled the beginning of the end. Today, the public school system doesn't allow God in the classroom. It's gotten so bad that many school districts are even afraid to call Christmas vacation "Christmas vacation." The two-week break is called "winter holiday," while Easter has become "spring break" in many parts of the country.

■ **Are there any biblical reasons why I should have my children in Christian school?**

Some Christian educators stress that God gives us a *biblical mandate* to provide Christian schooling for our children, no matter how good the public school is perceived to be. Proverbs 22:6 says, "Train a child in the way he *should* go. . . ." That doesn't give us permission to deliberately school our children in the way they *shouldn't* go!

Similarly, Deuteronomy 6 commands us to surround our children all day and all night with constant reminders of God's presence and involvement, while Psalm 1 says, "Blessed is the man who does not walk in the counsel of the ungodly. . . ." Only once in the history of the church have Christian parents deliberately placed their children in non-Christian schools in contradiction to the biblical mandate, and that has been in the 20th century.

■ **Some friends at church believe God has nothing to do with art, history, math, social studies, biology or basketball. Another told me that a child can be adequately equipped in a *secular* setting for a lifetime of *kingdom* work and service.**

Actually, children are cheated in a school system that excludes God. By law, public schools cannot teach the whole truth about life, and, by deliberate design, textbook companies and teacher unions have purged God from texts and lesson plans. This institutional bias leaves children with huge gaps in their learning that are rarely filled later.

Many parents don't believe this, however, and they believe that the Great Commission in Matthew 28 calls us to infiltrate the "real" world of public schools with our sons and daughters. Such thinking is nonsense.

■ **Why's that?**

First of all, the "real" world is where *God* is present and adored. Where He is ignored is the phony world of make-believe. Second, exposing our children to a curriculum handcuffed by a biased legal system and, in many cases, to the pagan influence of a non-Christian teacher who thinks and operates away from the authority of the Bible is like sending eleven- and twelve-year-olds into combat.

Our troops in the Gulf War were mature, hardened, well-trained servicemen and servicewomen equipped for battle. Our children in public schools are fodder for cannons. No, the Scriptures are clear. Public schools are mission fields for Christian teachers and administrators (and we should encourage and pray for each one), but they're not suitable schooling environments for children of Christian parents.

The Case for Public Schools

■ **Those arguments make sense, but let us tell you about our situation. My husband and I had sent our children to several different Christian schools, but we found something objectionable in each one. The first school tried to indoctrinate our children with the tenets of their denominational beliefs. They told our kids that unless they believed this about baptism and that about the Holy Spirit, they weren't saved. Our kids came home confused. We put them in another Christian school, but the kids picked on them. That school was very cliquish.**

We tried two more Christian schools: one didn't have many extracurricular activities for the kids, and at the last one, the headmaster was found guilty of sexually abusing one of the students. So we put our children in the local public school. They just love it. Both my husband and I are involved in the parents' organization, and we've met many other wonderful Christian parents.

Let's not give people the impression that Christian schools are known for abuse. Nor should we assume all public schools are problem-free. The bottom line is that it is not right to make broad, sweeping generalizations.

Actually, much depends on the school, the parents, and the children. All public schools aren't bad. All Christian schools aren't good. All homeschooling isn't done because parents are withdrawn from society. It's dangerous to the cause of Christ for Christians to engage in such quick judgments.

■ **I also resent it when people harshly judge the public school system. After all, a public school teacher led me to Jesus Christ as my personal Savior. But I'm the first to admit public schooos** have problems—lots of problems. I also believe, however, that many problems exist in the homes and the churches of America. I'm not about to give up on the family or the church, nor am I ready to give up on our public schools.

Keep sticking to your guns. For the most part, public schools offer more for the student, including competitive sports, extracurricular activities, and advanced curriculum— especially in the areas of math and science. The greater good can be served when Christian parents keep their children in the local school and work to make those schools even better.

■ **We've heard the biblical support for Christian schools. What spiritual case can be made for public schools?**

In Matthew 25:40, Jesus said: "Whatever you do to the least of these my brethren, you do unto me." What about the "least of these" who will never have any alternative other than to attend public schools? Don't we need to make public schools the best we can for them? If we love Jesus, we must look beyond our own children to those who have no one to care for them.

That's why you should get involved in your local school district. You will discover people who really care about kids. Mothers should consider joining—or starting—a "Moms In Touch" prayer group, because prayer works wonders in our schools.

In the public schools, you'll also find dedicated Christians serving Christ. True, they cannot openly "preach" to children, but nothing prevents them from living out their faith before the students. Numerous Christian parents are involved in their children's educations. They know what's going on in the classrooms, and they're working to change the curriculum where needed. By their commitment, they're not only part of an exciting mission field, but they're touching lives for eternity.

Chuck Colson once said, "Be a witness for Christ. If necessary, use words." The countless thousands of Christians who teach in the public schools are powerful witnesses for Jesus Christ. They realize that the best way to brighten the darkness is not to condemn it, but to shine a light in it.

The Case for Homeschooling

■ **I first heard about home schooling on a "Focus on the Family" broadcast in 1982. Dr. Dobson interviewed an education expert who listed symptoms of burnout in third-grade school children. He was describing Joel, our first-grader! In preschool and kindergarten, he had been well behaved, but now he was wandering around the classroom, unable to pay attention.**

Our child is already ruined, **I thought. But as I researched child development, I discovered it wasn't too late. As my husband, Larry, and I talked and prayed, we realized we were responsible for our children's education and that we could offer them more than traditional schools could. We also realized we weren't facing just an educational issue, but a spiritual one. Without hesitation, we took Joel out of school and started working with him at home. We've never regretted our decision. But along the way, we've found that many people have misconceptions about homeschooling.**

The biggest misconception people have about homeschooling is the schedule. Many think Mom and the kids slough off much of the day.

A regular schedule is adhered to in many homes. The school day usually begins at 9 o'clock with Bible study and prayer. Grammar and vocabulary exercises follow, along with assignments for Friday's history lesson. After lunch, they finish their work and read.

Wednesday afternoons are for group activities with other homeschoolers. Sometimes they have a park day or take a field trip. On Friday, the children from several families may meet at one home for history. The moms will divide the responsibilities: one leads devotions, one teaches the main lesson, and another takes the accompanying hands-on activity, such as supervising the making of salt-dough maps or costumes for a historical play the students write.

After lunch, Mom may lead the children through an assignment in writing, literature, or music. When studying ancient Rome, the children may read *Julius Caesar.* For a study of ancient India, the students may write a play and perform it for their fathers in the evening.

■ **Can homeschooling parents be confident that their children are getting a good education?**

Recently, the National Center for Home Education checked the academic progress of home-schooled students. They found that the average student scored above the 80th percentile on national achievement tests, such as the Stanford Achievement or Iowa Basic Skills. The average public school score, of course, is the 50th percentile.

■ **But what about socialization? Aren't homeschooled kids looked upon as weirdos?**

Yes, but many parents work hard to "socialize" their children. This is done through "class" field trips with other homeschoolers, band practice at the local public school, sports such as soccer, gymnastics, and Little League baseball, and being involved with the youth group at church.

■ **How can moms stand to have their children home all day? I think I would go nuts.**

Homeschooling moms don't see their day as a chore—but rather as a privilege. They believe God has given them the responsibility for their children, and when they stand before Him to give an account, He's going to ask how they handled it. They believe He has established families as the center of society. Strong families result in a strong society.

Homeschool parents say all parents need to ask themselves, "Why does a child need an education?" The world tells us one thing; Scripture tells us another. If you've thought through your biblical responsibility before the Lord and can fulfill it through a traditional school, that's fine. Homeschooling parents believe such schools have replaced the final authority of the parents. The best way we can educate our children is through one-on-one tutoring.

■ **Yes, but how does homeschooling prepare children for "real life"?**

The family *is* real life. It contains sickness and sorrow, as well as joy and laughter. All the emotions in the outside world are in the microcosm of the home.

■ **Other moms say they'd love to homeschool, but they can't because of younger children.**

Granted, younger children make it more difficult but not impossible. The six-year-old doesn't need to be on an all-day lesson schedule. Often he needs just an hour of "formal" education. You can teach the rest through informal projects such as baking cookies, cleaning, and gardening—things that are going on in the home anyway. You just need to look at the activity with an eye for turning it into a learning experience.

■ **Many mothers worry that if they homeschool, they won't have time to do all their housework.**

You can't do it all. You may decide that while the children are young, a spotless house and gourmet meals every night just aren't important. The children's education ranks higher than a waxed floor.

This material is adapted from writings by Ken Wackes, superintendent of Westminster Academy in Ft. Lauderdale, Florida, former "Teacher of the Year" Guy Doud of Baxter, Minnesota, aod home-schooling expert Susan Beatty of Anaheim, California.

24

Your Child Can Succeed in Public School!

. . . .

■ **We recently moved our family of five to Oklahoma City. The two older boys were adapting well, but Joel, our sixth-grader, was our greatest concern. His elementary years were academically tough, especially throughout fourth and fifth grades. Now his standardized test scores in math totaled only 15 out of 100, and 27 on language. How can a child facing these learning difficulties cope in a new public school?**

Prayer is always a good place to start, since God can lead you to a solution, such as volunteering in Joel's classroom. By being there each week, you will get to know his teachers, see what is expected of him, and learn how to make the most of the materials they are teaching. For instance, many classrooms have supplemental resources—sheets such as "Reteaching Long Division"—that will help Joel work on his math every day after school.

Start by doing half of the problems together, then let Joel do the rest himself. Check his work, and help Joel rework the problems until he understands what he is doing. You can also make spelling flash cards, read aloud the science and history textbook pages, and use a globe, atlas, and extra books to enliven the material.

■ **We have no Christian schools in our small town, and I'm not** the homeschooling-mom type. Thus, our children attend public school, but I feel guilty about it. Should I?

Not at all. We all want to see our children succeed in school, whether they go to Christian, private, or public schools. Although many Christian parents opt for religious schools and homeschooling, 90 percent of all children from American Christian homes are in public schools.

So, how can parents of children in public schools help them succeed? The answer is *parental involvement.* More than 50 research studies demonstrate that when parents get involved, those schools improve dramatically; their children are more motivated and better behaved in the classroom; their diverse needs are met more effectively; and scores on achievement tests are significantly higher.

A PARENT'S CHECKLIST

► Schedule a teacher conference within the first month of school, as well as after each major grading period or semester. Although special times are sometimes scheduled for parents employed outside the home, you may need to take off work to attend the conference. If an employer gives you trouble, suggest that an "ounce of prevention" now may mean less time off the job later on.

► Ask the teacher for "Grade Level Expectancies" and a list of the classes' monthly themes.

► Be sure you oversee your children's work and review any graded tests.

► Read the school newsletters.

► If you are a working parent, inform school personnel of your schedule and how to reach you by phone during the school day. Make
continued next page

■ So you're saying that when parents consider their child's education as their own personal responsibility—not the school's—their kids come out better.

Right. You need to see teachers and other school personnel as helpers in meeting educational goals for your children. Public school may be where their children obtain part of their education, but the parents provide additional academic enrichment opportunities for their children.

■ Can you give me a word picture?

Let's say you're in the construction business, and your company builds housing tracts.

Wise parents build relationships with teachers much as a general contractor does with his subcontractors (the framers, trim carpenters, plumbers, etc.). By meeting with the "subs" and going over the plans, you'll be letting them know your expectations for their craftsmanship. If there are problems, you will figure out the cause and come up with solutions.

In similar ways, parents are the general contractors of their children's education. They may have many teachers along the way, but the parents are their primary instructors and guides. Parents "sub out" parts of the educating task, but they must oversee, provide support, and take the initiative to keep in touch.

Remember that you are your child's most important teacher. It is you, not the principal and teachers, who are ultimately responsible for his education. It is you who will be held accountable to God.

■ **At conference time, the teacher asked me if anything had changed at home. My daughter, Cheryl, had always been a good student, but over the last six months her grades had fallen drastically. She seemed moody and distracted, and her enthusiasm for learning had disappeared.**

"Yes," I reluctantly reported, "her father and I have not been getting along well, so we are trying a trial separation. I guess the whole thing is taking a larger toll on her than we thought."

This is a common example of how family stress can present a barrier to a student's learning. A good student with no previous problems suddenly performs poorly in school. Some outside event

sure your child knows your work phone number.

► Express appreciation to the teacher several times during the school year.

► Help your child set a time and place for homework. Be sure to provide support, materials, and encouragement.

► Have regular read-aloud times at home, which are especially important for elementary-age children.

► Consider a volunteer opportunity, such as helping out in the classroom, assisting in a school fund-raiser, or joining the class on an outing.

► Remember this thought: If you let your children know that school is a very important place and what they learn extends far beyond the classroom, you'll pave the way for an excellent education.

was responsible, but in some cases, the negative influence isn't always easy to identify.

A balance exists between a student's emotions and his or her academic performance, and emotional difficulties can impede classroom learning. With that thought in mind, here are some ways you can help your child cope with stress:

THE AIR JORDAN BLUES

by Roberta Rand

"But Mom! ALL the kids at school are wearing these!"

My 11-year-old son is pointing to the advertisement for a $125 pair of sneakers. *Here we go again*, I sighed inwardly, steeling myself for a predictable onslaught of whining, pouting, pleading, and door slamming.

"I don't care what the other kids are wearing. We do not have $125 to spend on a pair of shoes that you are going to outgrow in a matter of months!"

All parents wrestle with their kids wanting to be like the other kids on the block. Feelings of guilt can easily cloud your good reason. Children, as precious as they are, can be clever manipulators—even mercenary—to get what they want.

So how do you head these pleas off at the pass without sounding like a bad caricature of your own mother ("When I was your age, we paid $5 for a pair of Keds and were happy just to have shoes on our feet!")

Contrary to what your son insists, not every kid on the playground is wearing $125 sneakers.

continued next page

1. *Be aware of what's happening with the child's emotions and within his or her environment.*

Problems tend to occur when stress accumulates little by little. Kids as well as adults can find themselves burned out without realizing they're overwhelmed.

The need here is to pay attention. If your daughter tells you she tossed and turned all night before a volleyball tryout, assure her that she's normal, perhaps by telling a story about the time something similar happened to you.

2. *Develop a positive perspective about stress points.*

Eighty percent of a child's coping power comes from his perception of the event. If he believes he can deal with a situation, it's likely to happen. But if he is pessimistic about his ability to overcome an obstacle, chances are high he will fail. It all boils down to a matter of perception.

3. *Practice healthy living habits.*

Make sure your child gets adequate sleep, stays physically

fit, and eats a healthy diet.

4. *Teach your child how to relax.*

Try the following: (a) have him realize what is bothering him; (b) get him to relax his forehead, eyes, nose, mouth and neck; and (c) have him take a long, deep breath and then exhale slowly, letting his jaw go limp. While he relaxes, think of biblical promises that will encourage him and provide hope.

5. *Reduce or eliminate possible stress points.*

Do everything you can to reduce the amount of change, competition, and other stressors in the child's life. If she has too many extracurricular activities, try to cut back. If competition is extracting too high a toll, move her to a less-competitive level.

Solomon declared, "There is nothing new under the sun" (Ecc. 1:9), and that includes stress. No matter how severe and frustrating a situation looks, God has been there before. We're not left to our own resources. God is for us (see Rom. 8:31), and this kind of hope can give your children the ability to cope with stress. They don't have to accomplish everything in their own power.

■ **I'm very much concerned about religious freedom. What "rights" do my children have on a public school campus?**

That's a very important question in this day and age. But first of all, your children have the right to meet with other reli-

Don't let your child's Oscar-caliber tantrums sway your good judgment. Besides, we are not doing our children a favor when we communicate the message that *things* will make them happy—or that *fitting in* is the most important goal in life. Giving in to a child's appeal for extravagant purchases reinforces a message that can only hurt later in life.

Stand firm. Keep impressing godly values into your children. Instill in them the precepts of integrity, generosity, and compassion. Remind them that it is not clothes that define their value as human beings, but God who cherishes them simply because they are His. You may still have to endure some world-class hissy-fits, but in the long run, they will learn what is truly important.

When it comes time to buy shoes, your kids will probably get along fine with the Air Jordan "knock-offs" at Payless. It's a pretty good bet that a respectable number of kids on the playground will be wearing the same sneakers. And isn't that what they wanted in the first place?

gious students. The Equal Access Act allows students the freedom to meet on campus for the purpose of discussing religious issues.

■ **What about talking about God on campus? I hear that you can't even mention Jesus Christ by name at some schools.**

Your child has the right to talk about his or her religious beliefs on campus. Freedom of speech is a fuodamental right mandated in the Constitution and does not exclude the schoolyard. In addition, your child has the right to distribute religious literature on campus. Distributing literature on campus may not be restricted simply because it is religious.

■ **Do students have the right to pray? When I went to high school, I can remember asking for God's help just before my big chemistry tests.**

Yes, by all means, today's students have the right to pray on campus. Students may pray alone or with others so long as it does not disrupt school activities or is not forced on others. In recent years, the "See You at the Pole" prayer event every September has been a huge success, with over a million students around the country gathering to pray around the flagpole before the start of class.

■ **Can students carry their Bible onto campus?**

Again, the answer is yes. Students have the right to carry or study their Bible on public school campuses. The U.S. Supreme Court has said that only *state-directed* Bible reading is unconstitutional, so if you hear about a teacher asking your child to keep his Bible out of sight, that is illegal.

■ **What about mentioning God in writing projects?**

Students have the right to do research papers, speeches, and creative projects with religious themes. The First Amendment does not forbid all mention of religion in public schools. On the flip side, students have the right to be exempt from activities and class content that contradicts their religious beliefs.

■ **How about the right to celebrate or study religious holidays?**

Music, art, literature, and drama that have religious themes are permitted as part of the curriculum for school activities if presented in an objective manner as a traditional part of the cultural and religious heritage of the particular holiday. This means Thanksgiving can be recognized as a day for thanking God, and Christ stiln remains the reason for the season during the Christmas holidays.

This material is adapted from Helping Your Child Succeed in Public School *by Cheri Fuller. Copyright © 1993, Cheri Fuller. Used by permission of Focus on the Family,* Help! My Child Isn't Learning *by Grant L. Martin, Ph.D. Copyright © 1995, Grant L. Martin. Used by permission of Focus on the Family, and* Students' Legal Rights on a Public School Campus *by J.W. Brinkley and Roever Communications. For more information, write Roever Communications, P.O. Box 136130, Ft. Worth, TX 76136, or call (816) 238-2000.*

25

Discovering Your Child's Learning Style

. . . .

■ **One night our fourth-grader, Alison, had thirty irregular verb forms to memorize in the present, past, and past perfect tenses—that's ninety words! She had been sick one day and missed the class explanation, so at first the task looked overwhelming.**

Nevertheless, I went over the list orally with her. I've learned that Alison needs to hear and verbalize information in order to understand and remember it. I helped her record on tape each verb and its forms, which she enjoyed thoroughly. We played the tape over several times, and she recited along with it. Then I gave her an oral practice test and circled the missed verbs. She studied the ones that gave her trouble, saying them aloud. The whole process took half an hour.

The next morning, Alison used her recording to practice the verbs during breakfast. At school, she received a 95 on her test—and a jolt of confidence.

That's a good example of finding a "learning style" that works for your child. Teachers will often look out at their students and think what a difference it would make in their learning if their parents actively helped. For most children, school could become a more positive, successful experience.

Whether your youngster is in a private, public, or home school, *you* are his most important teacher. Former U.S. Secretary of Education, William Bennett, once said, "Parents are their children's first and most influential teachers. What parents do to help their children learn is more important to academic success than how well-off the family is."

■ **Unfortunately, I am probably like many parents who don't know how to help their children learn. What can I do?**

A good way to start is by understanding and then utilizing your child's learning style.

■ **What is a learning style?**

Just as your child has a distinct temperament, personality, and spiritual motivation, he also has a particular way of learning. There are twenty-one different factors that make up a learning style. Perhaps your child learns best alone, or when studying with peers. Maybe he needs a structured setting with an adult. Some kids learn best in a quiet room, others with background noise; some learn in logical steps, while others see the whole picture.

The senses through which each child absorbs and retains new information are the *auditory, visual,* and *kinesthetic.* Some children, like Alison, are auditory learners. They learn best by learning and verbalizing new information. Others need to see and retain a mental picture; they are visual learners. Kinesthetic learners need to touch and use movement to process new concepts. They learn by doing.

■ **I have three children. Let's pretend they each have a distinctive style of learning. What are some ways to maximize their learning at home?**

Let's say your daughter, Meghan, is an auditory learner. Meghan talked early and constantly, with a wide and colorful vocabulary. Her clear speech sounded like a little adult as she related riddles and creative stories to her family. She is a bright, sociable child, but she often has difficulty with spelling and math.

Meghan spells everything phonetically, so her words are often written incorrectly. She also has trouble remembering multiplication tables, which slows her during arithmetic tests. And Meghan is easily distracted in class. She verbalizes everything and needs to hear information and then say it in order to learn it.

Meghan should use her mind's ear to "sub-vocalize" when she's reading, studying spelling words, or doing math problems. By saying to herself what she needs to learn, difficult information will be recalled.

A tape recorder is the auditory learner's best friend and will boost Meghan's comprehension. Tape-recorded addition, subtraction, and multiplication facts can help the auditory learner gain speed in doing math. She can use flash cards with the tape recorder, or summarize a chapter on tape and play it back for review. When studying spelling at home, the auditory learner should say the word aloud and write it several times.

Because auditory learners are distracted by background noise while studying, they need to study in a quiet room.

■ **I think my second-born son Brian is a visual learner. What should I do here?**

Brian relies more on seeing things and visualizing them. As a baby, Brian could be quieted by the sight of your face or by the movement of his crib mobile. As a toddler, Brian learned colors quickly. When traveling in a car, he looked attentively at passing billboards, often noticing some detail that his parents missed. Brian loves to draw, and has a great imagination. But he cannot listen for long periods without beginning to doodle, squirm, or daydream.

A strong phonics-based reading program at Brian's kindergarten has been difficult for him. He is already behind in reading. Since he learns best by seeing and retaining a mental picture, he

WHAT IS YOUR CHILD?

To determine a young child's learning style, imagine you are reading aloud from a book with a repeated refrain like "and the rabbit went hop, hop, hop" or "There once was a boy with a little toy drum; with a rat-a-tat-tat and a rum-y-tum-tum." Does your child:

► Come up close, perhaps insisting on being on your lap, to see the pictures? This is a sign of a visual learner.

► Mimic the words of the refrain or interrupt to talk about the story? This is a sign of an auditory learner.

► Move around and do what the refrain says—hop and jump? This is the sign of a kinesthetic learner.

can learn to make his own flash cards for vocabulary and spelling words (with the word in bright marker on one side and his illustration of it on the other side). This can be done for math, too.

The visual learner is easily hooked by television, so TV time should be limited, and parents should provide plenty of interesting and accessible books and magazines.

The visual student is also distracted by a disorderly study area, and he works best on an organized, neat table or desk. He will enjoy working alone and taking responsibility for assignments, but he should also do oral drills before tests.

Visual memory can be improved by organizing a simple memory game using a variety of interesting objects. Place the objects on a tray and cover them. Then take the cover away and let each person view the objects for thirty-to-forty-five seconds before covering them again. Whoever can list the most objects is the winner.

■ Finally, I think my other son Josh is a kinesthetic learner.

Josh was a wiggly baby. As a toddler, he was in perpetual motion. He explored things by pulling and taking them apart. He was also an athletic prodigy. At age four, Josh delighted your family with his ability to ride a bicycle without training wheels. Today, he excels in a local gymnastics class and is the star player on his soccer team.

Because of his constant squirming and short attention span, however, Josh has not been a teacher's favorite. Learning to read has been a frustrating experience, and all academic subjects are hard for Josh.

A kinesthetic child like Josh needs a multi-sensory phonics reading and math program using plastic or sandpaper letters and numbers to emphasize touch in learning. At home, one of his best tools will be a large chalkboard. When learning new spelling words, Josh can write them in large letters and then erase them. Or, he can practice writing spelling words on large sheets of colored construction paper, first with a marker, then a pencil, then a bright crayon.

The kinesthetic learner often lacks good listening skills. Using games and activities at home will improve his auditory memory. Listening to taped stories and books is valuable, and read-aloud books with plenty of action will hold his appeal.

■ **Are there any cautions I should be aware of?**

Being a visual, auditory, or kinesthetic learner does not mean your child cannot learn in any other mode. About 30 percent of children have no specific learning style.

Moreover, as a child grows, learning styles can shift, blend, or develop. Infants through kindergarten children are very kinesthetic; most children develop visual skills by grade two, and auditory skills strengthen by grade six.

Develop your own ideas for your children's homework and study time. As you understand how they learn, you can be more supportive when they need help. With these secrets to school success, both you and your children will find joy in learning, and you will help prepare them for the special purpose God has for each of their lives!

This material is adapted from writings by Cheri Fuller, an author and former schoolteacher from Oklahoma City, Oklahoma.

26

Dealing with
Report Card Panic

. . . .

■ **Last week, my fifth-grader stood silently before me while I reviewed his report card, which was littered with Cs, Ds, and an F. Grasping at anything to break the deafening silence, my son said, "Do you think these grades are the result of heredity, or could it just be my environment?" I didn't know whether to laugh or strangle the little guy.**

Who can blame you for not being amused, but the lad may have had a point. Parents *do* influence the classroom behavior of their children. A twenty-year study at Stanford University focusing on parents' reactions to poor grades and their impact on the future success published these unequivocal findings: First, most parents express negative emotions in responding to poor grades. Second, this is the worst reaction possible since it creates greater tension within the child.

■ **Yes, but I want to see my children do well in school. So can I avoid report card panic?**

The first thing you want to do is provide an emotional safety net at home. During the early days of building the Golden Gate Bridge, some twenty workers died or were seriously injured when they fell into San Francisco Bay. Finally, construction was stopped, and a giant safety net was installed under the work area. Over the next several years, only four men fell off the bridge. Not only did the net make work conditions safer—but it also made workers feel more confident and less likely to fall.

Parents can provide the same security net for their children by making the home a safe place, even when scores tumble. Positive support, rather than faultfinding, increases the likelihood of success in the future. Berating and criticizing a student for poor performance will not make the child work harder, but it will actually create more tension, which can result in even worse grades.

■ **But my child looks like he doesn't even care that he got lousy grades.**

Sometimes struggling students hide hurt behind masks of apathy. When this happens, a poor report card requires extra understanding by parents. When a parent replaces judgment with mercy, the child begins to trust Mom and Dad to help, not hurt.

■ **OK, I promise not to fly off the handle next time. How do I offer grace in this tense situation?**

First, separate *who* your child is from the grades he has received. It is no compromise to say, "I know you are disappointed with these marks, but they don't mean you're stupid, and they don't mean I don't love you."

Set up a nonthreatening discussion with your child. Go out for ice cream or hot chocolate to talk over his struggles. Look him in the eye and tell him that grades are serious and important. Then ask your child how you can help him set the course for better grades the next time around.

■ **My son may not have any ideas. Do you have any?**

If a child has a routine schedule and a place to do homework, studying will become second nature. The area needs to be quiet and uncluttered. A desk in a bedroom is ideal, but a kitchen table can work too (especially since you can keep an eye out for him that way).

A dictionary, atlas, and other elementary reference books should be easily accessible, as well as pens, pencils, and paper. The goal is to create the best study conditions for the student, not to force him into a setup he will resist.

■ **But what if my daughter is taking classes that are over her head?**

You can help ensure that your child is in the right classes by discussing this situation with your daughter's teachers. With a growing sense of achievement, your child will become more eager to master new material and new skills.

■ **Every afternoon my middle school children and I have a fight: They want to plop themselves in front of the TV; I want them to do their homework. Any suggestions?**

Television can be a roadblock to academic success, and we (the Yorkey family) know it. That's why we have a hard-and-fast rule: No TV during the school week, except for very special exceptions *after* dinner.

For those families unable or unwilling to keep the television off during the late afternoon, use it as a reward for completing homework. While it's true that "you can lead a horse to water but you can't make him drink," it's also possible to salt his hay. For some students, a simple reward such as watching a half-hour of TV or listening to music can be the "salt" that motivates them to get their studies done.

Finally, ask the school or teachers to send home progress reports to be signed by the parents. That way you have a good idea of how the kids are doing and where the child may need help while there is still time to turn things around.

■ **We hear a lot about "success" and "achievement" these days in school. How should I define those terms?**

We should all strive to have "success" and "achievement." The Apostle Paul wrote that he "pressed on" to reach the high calling and was constantly "laboring" in his ministry.

If you want to motivate your children toward greater achievement, let them know they are on the right track—and they have the *ability* to achieve. Your encouragement will empower your children. Success feeds success! One successful learning experience primes us for the next one because we expect to succeed the next time we try something new.

What's the most common ingredient of successful people?

A study was once done of 120 successful people, and they all had one important common denominator: parental involvement. The parents often sat with them while they did their homework or during practice. They cheered them when they won and comforted them when they lost. You must find things to cheer about in your kids!

What's the difference between praise and encouragement?

Praise and encouragement are not synonymous. Both have their place, both are good, but they are different. Praise focuses on performance. Encouragement focuses on effort or improvement. Praise takes place when achievement takes place. Encouragement is wrapped up in who the child *is* and *can be* rather than what he or she *does*.

What are some ways I can give my children an "edge" at school? Academic success is important to my family.

These three activities will give your children the tools for achievement: conversation, questions, and reading.

Ah, come on. It can't be that simple.

Why not? A study entitled, "The Disadvantaged Child and the Learning Process" by Martin Deutsch found that in homes where conversations, questions, and reading were *not* encour-

---

A PARENT'S REPORT CARD CHECKLIST

Have you . . .
► Avoided critical reactions?
► Expressed love to your child despite his grades?
► Set up a study zone in your home?
► Given help to your child when needed?
► Contacted your child's teacher if necessary?
► Affirmed your child's potential to succeed in the future?
► Controlled the use of the TV?
► Used incentives to motivate your child?
► Expressed your standards firmly but with affection?
► Sensitively listened to your child's needs and struggles?

aged, the child entered school significantly short of his peers. When compared to his higher-achieving classmates, he asked fewer questions, used shorter sentences, and had a smaller vocabulary and shorter attention span.

■ **What was usually the reason?**

Mom and Dad just didn't devote large quantities of time conversing with and reading to their children. Perhaps it was because conversations were actually monologues—the parents telling the child something. Certainly, this type of communication is important, but it needs to be balanced with conversation.

Questions are important for discovery and learning. Questions are like keys that unlock doors. The right question can bring the right answer to open up whole worlds of understanding. Children need to be curious and seek answers. It also helps if *you* ask the right question to your child.

■ **Give me an example.**

When your child comes home from school and you ask, "How was your day?" the response from your child may often be, "Fine." The question was too open-ended. It didn't require any thinking on the part of the child.

Next time, try asking, "What was the most interesting thing you did today?" Don't let your child get away with answering, "Nothing." Other specific questions could be: "What is one thing you learned in history today?" "What did you do today about which you felt good?" or "What was the funniest thing you heard today?"

■ **How do I find out how well my child reads?**

Casually test your child by having him read aloud to you. If he struggles, begin tutoring him. The time you spend with your child will be the best investment you can make for his future.

■ Reading to my children is a great idea, but what about silent reading?

Sustained silent reading should be started from the elementary school years and become a regular family routine. The U.S. Department of Education has observed that school children spend between seven and eight minutes reading at school. Most time is spent on reading drills rather than just reading.

This material is adapted from writings by Dr. Les Parrott, a professor at Seattle Pacific University in Seattle, Washington, and Charting Your Family's Course *(Victor) by Eric Buehrer.*

27

Facing a New School

. . . .

■ **When the school year is over, our family will be moving. Helping our children adjust to a new school following a family relocation is important stuff. How can I smooth over the transition?**

American families are on the move, and the odds are high that your child will have to change schools some time before graduating from high school. Each year nearly 20 percent of school-age children and their families move. Conventional wisdom tells us that any move will be disruptive. Such expectations can have a powerful effect on a child, and they could negatively influence his achievement and classroom behavior.

But moving has its good points as well. For some children, moving can improve academic performance. Oftentimes, youngsters are stimulated by the change in surroundings. New teachers and administrative staff may be better able to meet the child's needs. That's why children need to hear the message that they can adapt positively to a move.

■ **Our family has moved a half-dozen times in the last fifteen years. We've found that living in different parts of the country is a great way to get involved in activities unique to each area. In Minnesota, we learned to ski and canoe, and the kids tried ice**

fishing and wilderness camping. In Arizona, the kids loved swimming and horseback riding.

Moving has brought your family closer together. In a new place, you're all in the same boat, so you have to be each other's best friend for a while. One thing to keep in mind is that learning to meet the challenges of moving can prepare children for later changes in life. Moving can broaden their horizons and develop confidence. In addition, supportive parents and teachers smooth the child's adjustment, making it easier to continue enjoying learning and developing.

■ **How can I start helping my children adjust to a new school before the moving van arrives?**

In whatever ways you can (depending on the age of the children, of course), involve them in the preparation of moving. Have a family meeting to discuss why you're moving. Be sure to involve the children in the family's house-hunting plans and be prepared to answer any questions they might have.

Although you and your spouse may be sad about leaving family and friends behind, recognize that your attitude is important in helping your child make a good adjustment. Remember: children are always listening, even if you think a conversation with your spouse is out of earshot. Talking about a move in a positive way will help your youngster make the transition.

SOME THINGS YOU'LL NEED

When moving, it's imperative to collect your children's school information before you leave town. Realize that some schools may not release records until the day your child withdraws from school.

Don't accept the old school's promise to send along your children's records. Take the records with you. Otherwise, this can delay his placement in the right grade or classes. When you enroll your child in a new school, take along a manila envelope with the child's name clearly marked on it. Inside should be copies of:
► the birth certificate
► medical, dental, and orthodontic records
► immunization records
► a list of the textbooks he has used
► a description of the grading

continued next page

■ **We know it's important to buy or rent our new home in the right school district. But**

how can we fiod out about the quality of the schools in the new city?

You can get information about local schools—both public and private—from relatives or friends who live in the area, real estate agents, and owners of the homes you're looking through. You should also visit any prospective schools. Ask to sit in on a few classes and talk to their prospective teachers. If you can't visit, write ahead and compare different districts. Either way, keep these questions in mind:

- What are the facilities like?
- What is the extent of special programs, such as those for learning-impaired or physically-handicapped children?
- What are the teachers and administrators like?
- What is the average class size and teacher-pupil ratio?
- How does the school stack up when you compare standardized test scores?
- What provisions are made for textbooks, school bus service, hot lunch programs, and extracurricular activities?
- How good are the athletic programs?
- If it's a high school, what kind of college prep classes are offered? Are vocational programs offered?

■ **We are facing our first major move this year, and I know the experience will be traumatic for the kids. We know the kids will be mourning the loss of friends and familiar surroundings. And when school starts in late August, they'll be adjust-**

method used by his former teacher
- a statement from his teacher indicating the student's current level of achievement, interests, and any special programs in which he was involved.

For an older child, call ahead to the new school and ask what is needed for sports eligibility and when athletic tryouts are scheduled. Most schools require transfer students to present a letter from a doctor certifying that he's had a physical examination within the past twelve months. If your child has already had a physician's checkup for a summer camp, take a copy with you. This could save some much-needed time and get him on the practice field, where he'll have a better chance of making the team.

ing to new rules and trying to find new companions. How can we ease the pain for them?

Before leaving town, buy your children address books and let them collect the addresses and phone numbers of their friends. Allow them to exchange photos as well. They can make their own "change of address" cards—decorated with colorful stickers. It helps too if you let them invite a few friends over for a good-bye dinner.

As the Girl Scout song goes, "Make new friends, but keep the old; one is silver, and the other gold." You can foster continuity by helping your children keep in touch with a few friends back home. Provide stationery and encourage them to correspond regularly. Besides being a great boost to writing skills, corresponding with several "best" friends provides a sense of connection.

■ What can I do to ease the transition into a new school for my children?

WELCOMING NEW FAMILIES

When a new family arrives on the block, go right over. Introduce yourself and offer specific help—extra arms while unpacking a room or offering to read to a small child while Mom directs the movers. Bring a plate of sandwiches and a thermos of juice, or whip up a house specialty to welcome them. Anything is appreciated: banana bread, a casserole—even a plate of store-bought cookies!

Sharing information with the new family is a great way to help. You can provide a list of phone numbers and addresses of the nearest pharmacy, cleaners, florist, and doctors (someone in the family is bound to

continued next page

Ask if the school has an orientation program. Some schools place pictures of newly arrived students in the school's entry hall. Other schools assign a "buddy" to show the new student around and help him find the cafeteria, library, and classrooms during the first few difficult and confusing days.

One family found pen pals for their children before the move (they wrote the new school and asked for names of students of similar ages and interests). After corresponding for a few months, the children's budding friendships provided a great support when they arrived at their new school.

Keep in close touch with the

new school counselor or reading specialist who handles the testing and placement of transfer students. Know what's being taught and what the new teacher expects. Find out what books will be read and how much homework is usually assigned. You can also share information that can help your child's teacher understand him quickly. Finally, be aware of "tracking" procedures in the new school (assignments to low, average, or honors classes).

If your child already has a strong interest in a particular sport or activity—such as gymnastics, tennis or art—encourage him to be involved. This interest will help smooth the moving process as he meets other youngsters with common interests, rather than being isolated in a strange new environment. A talent or sports skill boosts self-esteem and provides a way to become known in the new setting.

■ **My child has special academic needs. How do I make sure she gets into the right classes?**

Don't leave it to time or chance for the teacher to discover them. Meet with the school principal to go over the child's records and discuss how the new school can best help your child make the adjustment.

■ **Does the impact of a move vary with the children's ages?**

If your children are less than four years old, they haven't developed binding social ties outside the family. Youngsters in the early elementary years are starting to develop friendships, so it sometimes takes longer for them to let go of loyalty to past friends and make new ones. Teens have the toughest time, often facing loneliness and shaken identity.

get sick with all the work associated with a move). Include *your* name and phone number. Also, a list of baby-sitters may cause the new family to nominate you for sainthood.

Ask the new family if they're looking for a new church home. If they respond positively, let them know where your church—and others—are located. If they visit your congregation, invite them to an upcoming social.

Moving during a holiday time can be especially hard on newcomers because they often leave family and friends behind. Invite them to a Labor Day picnic, Christmas Eve services, or a Fourth of July parade.

Even the simplest gesture of caring helps a new family. As one moving mom said, "There's nothing you can do that won't be appreciated!"

Adjustment occurs at different speeds, but the following are representative of the usual stages in the child's transition process:

- ▶ *Denial:* "I'm not going. I'll stay with friends and go to school here!"
- ▶ *Anger:* "Why me? Why did Dad have to take that promotion and move me to this boring little town?"
- ▶ *Acceptance and adjustment:* "Here I am. Maybe I can do better here than I did back home. I guess I'll go out for basketball and join the Spanish Club."

When Sandra moved her four children from Idaho to Maine, she was determined to understand what they were going through. "It's OK for them to mourn their past life and loss of friends," she says. "We should allow them to say what they miss about the old school and what they don't like about the new situation. By accepting their feelings—rather than trying to gloss over negative reactions—we provide a needed balance."

If our children stay angry or depressed for an extended time, which can drain their motivation to perform in school, they need extra support. By listening, staying positive, and getting additional assistance from the school counselor or a trusted pastor, we can help our children make a positive adjustment.

Finally, be sure to pray for your children. Young people feel a sense of support when their parents pray for them before leaving for school or at bedtime. Praying together brings a family together—and that's a good idea whether you're moving or not!

This material is adapted from writings by former schoolteacher Cheri Fuller of Oklahoma City, Oklahoma.

28

Help with Homework Hassles

■ **The beginning of the school year always brings mixed feelings for us. While we are glad our children are returning to school, we are also concerned about adding the role of study hall monitor to our already hectic lives. Busy schedules, schooo apathy, and the pressure to achieve educational excellence also increases stress and the number of disagreements we seem to have. Is it possiboe to increase our child's success and decrease the homework hassles?**

Let's discuss the purpose of homework first. Children's reasons for completing homework influence their attitudes and abilities. Some children do their homework because they have to, while others do it to acquire knowoedge. Of course, some do it to please teachers or to get you—the parents—off their backs. (We were never like that, were we?) When you stress learning, and not just finishing and grades, you help to build right attitudes.

■ **Building the right attitudes about homework? That sounds like a tough task around our household. What do you mean?**

Instead of asking, "Are you finished?" you can ask, "What's one thing you learned?" And when looking at graded papers with your children or talking about their day, you can discuss the topic being studied at least as much as the grade earned. When children know learning is important to you, they may view homework as a more positive part of life. Grades, responsibility, and attitudes often improve when the focus is on learning.

Remember that your child's belief in himself influences his attitudes toward school and homework. The identity component of his self-esteem is a key. Those children who see themselves as learners and believe they are smart will more likely complete homework assignments responsibly.

■ **I have a son who feels stupid, so he doesn't want to do his homework. He tells me that studying just makes him feel dumber. What's your answer to this?**

Many believe they were born dumb, so they can't control the amount they learn and base their grades upon. You can help by pointing out your child's academic growth and complimenting your son for the positive qualities you see.

One month from now, your son may still believe he is slow at completing his math homework. What he may not realize is that although it is taking him just as long as it did at the beginning of the year, he has been assigned more math problems, and they have increased in difficulty. So actually, he is improving. Being able to point out that improvement is one reason to save old assignments.

Perhaps last year you constantly battled with your son about the messiness of his assignments. This year, try concentrating more on what he communicates rather than the way he communicates it. He will be encouraged when you tell him how creative, well-thought-through, detailed, or organized his answers are. This may then result in iocreased pride in his work, whicj may show up in increased neatness.

Also mention the papers that are neatly completed, what is important, and how you believe he was able to be neat. This way he will come to believe he can be neat in the future.

■ **Sometimes, homework assignments are taking too long, and my child is often confused. That drives me nuts. What should I do?**

Let the teacher know. It is difficult for teachers to know how long it takes to complete homework, whether their directions have been clear, if children have the necessary supplies at home to do the work, or if parents have time to assist, etc. Don't suffer in silence. Teachers may be able to adjust assignments and, if nothing else, they will at least be aware of your problems.

■ Does homework work?

According to a recent U.S. Department of Education report, student achievement rises significantly when teachers regularly assign homework and students do it. With a little organization and diligence, you and your kids can work together to take the hassles (well, most of them) out of this nightly chore.

A Homework Checklist

- ▶ *Allow your child some time to unwind after school.* A break and a healthful snack will help with concentration.
- ▶ *Agree on the rules.* When and where will homework be done? What will happen if the assignments aren't finished?
- ▶ *Set a minimum amount of time each day for studying.* For example, multiply the child's grade by ten minutes—a fourth-grader should study forty minutes a night.
- ▶ *Set up a quiet, well-lighted work area.* Be sure to equip it with the necessary supplies and resources.
- ▶ *Help your child keep a homework log of assignments and a calendar of deadlines.* Note longer projects on the calendar to avoid hasty last-minute discoveries of a project due the next day.
- ▶ *Don't focus unduly on performance.* The outcome counts but so does the process of learning.
- ▶ *Encourage independence.* Don't do your child's homework for him or her, but be available for consultation.
- ▶ *As mentioned before, limit—or ban—TV viewing on school nights.* Decide at the beginning of the school year how much TV is acceptable—and stick to it! You may discover that there's no time for TV.

This material is adapted by writings from Kathy Koch, Ph.D., from Ft. Worth, Texas, and Sharon Sheppard of St. Cloud, Minnesota.

29

Is College Too Expensive for Our Kids?

■ When I filed past my husband's casket, I viewed him for the last time. Only days before, Bob had suffered a heart attack while riding his bicycle through our hometown. With no warning, my five children were left without a father.

As I watched my son Roy say good-bye to his dad, I wondered if he was also saying farewell to his dream of becoming a doctor. My heart ached. I pictured the day he told his father he wanted to pursue a career in medicine. Even then, he had wondered if med school was possible with our large family, but we encouraged him to pursue his dream. Now, as we stood over his father's grave, we both knew it would be nearly impossible.

With each day, I watched my carefree, exuberant son lose his zest for life. Though he was already two years into his undergraduate program, he wanted to give up. Even though Roy worked part time, we could barely make ends meet.

How can I help him reach his goal? Is it still possible even though my husband's gone?

Those nagging questions are similar to those being asked by millions of parents these days, including two-parent households. Unless you've been able to save a considerable chunk of money, the answer is in pursuing financial aid beyond the scholarships your child could be receiving.

That may mean spending countless hours in libraries, poring over financial aid manuals, scholarship applications, and books on federal aid. There are hundreds of resources available—resources that can help your children move one step closer to getting a college degree.

■ Where's a good place to start?

Federal and state aid is the logical place. The federal government finances about 75 percent of all financial aid through six major programs. Unless otherwise noted, the programs are based on financial need, which is calculated by financial aid administrators on college campuses.

► Federal Pell Grants, which do not have to be repaid, offer more than 3 million students a maximum of $2,300 each per year for college expenses. As with most federal programs, you must reapply each year.

► Federal Supplemental Educational Opportunity Grants provide up to $4,000 a year to undergraduates. The grants are based on students' needs beyond what Pell grants can cover. The money does not have to be repaid.

► Federal Work-Study Program provides money to colleges and universities to pay the salaries of students who need to work to attend college. The money your student receives from his or her part-time job cannot exceed the amount of your financial need as calculated by the financial aid administrator at your college.

WHERE'S THE MONEY?

Every year, more than $24 billion in financial aid is available for students who want to go to college. But chances are you won't see one cent of that money if you don't get moving! Start with these sources, which can usually be found in your local library:

► *How to Put Your Children Through College without Going Broke* (New York: The Research Institute of America, Inc.)

► *The Scholarship Book.* Daniel Cassidy and Michael J. Alves (Englewood Cliffs, N.J.: Prentice Hall Publishers)

► *Directory of Financial Aid for Minorities* and *Directory of*
continued next page

- Federal Perkins Loans allow undergraduates to borrow a maximum of $3,000 annually for up to five years at 5 percent interest. The money must be repaid in at least ten years, and repayment must begin nine months after the student graduates, leaves school, or drops below half-time status.
- Federal Stafford Subsidized Loans, which are more widely available, allow students to borrow up to $2,625 at a variable interest rate of 7 percent. The Stafford Unsubsidized Loan is also available, and any family is eligible regardless of income.
- Federal PLUS Loans are available to parents of dependent students regardless of need. There is a variable interest rate starting at 9 percent, and repayment begins sixty days after the money is advanced.

Any student can apply for federal student aid by filling out the Free Application for Federal Student Aid (FAFSA) and the Financial Aid Form (FAF). You can find these forms in the financial aid office of your local high school or college. The information you give—which is based on your tax return—is used to determine your family's contribution and the student's eligibility for aid. Check with the college you've chosen to see if it requires both. For more information or for a copy of *The Student Guide*, call the federal student-aid information line toll-free at (800) 433-3243.

Financial Aid for Women. Gail Ann Schlachter, editor. (Redwood City, Calif.: Reference Service Press)
- *Paying Less for College*. (Princeton, N.J.: Peterson's Guides)
- *Winning Money for College*. Alan Deutschman. (Princeton, N.J.: Peterson's Guides)
- *Need a Lift?* (Indianapolis, Ind.: The American Legion)
- For information on the federal aid programs, call the Student Aid Information Center at toll-free (800) 433-3243.
- For information on cooperative education, write to: The National Commission for Cooperative Education, 360 Huntington Ave., Boston, MA 02115.

■ What about state programs?

In addition to federal aid, each state has at least one financial aid program. Florida, for example, offers eligible students $1,150 to $2,000 a year through its tuition voucher program. Some states require you to fill out an aid application, such as the Student

Aid Application for California (SAAC) or the Pennsylvania Higher Education Assistance Agency form (PHEAA). For more information on what financial aid each state offers, read Peterson's *Paying Less for College* (see sidebar).

■ **My husband and I discovered that loans from the federal government are best used as a last resort, since free money is often available from the school. Are we right?**

Though the federal government offers the largest amount of financial aid that does not have to be repaid, colleges and universities rank a close second. Here are some awards they make:

▶ *Merit-Based Scholarships.* Schools throughout the country give scholarships based on a student's academic achievement, special abilities, academic interests, or characteristics.

Some of the qualifying characteristics: minority children, twins, children of educators, handicapped students, children of current students, first-generation college students, children with deceased or disabled parents, and students who have excelled in music,

---

PREPARING YOUR CHILD FOR THOSE COLLEGE YEARS

If your son or daughter is college bound, you've probably spent hours filling out forms, discussing loans, and deciding which college to attend. Here are a few more things to consider:

▶ **Teach your child the basic skills to survive dorm life.** Does he know how to operate a washer and dryer, stick to a budget, handle a checkbook, live with strangers, and use time responsibly?

▶ **Prepare your teen for the negative aspects of campus life.** Too often adults present a rosy portrait of college ("the best years of your life!"), and students who have less-than-wonderful experiences feel like failures.

Remind your child that homesickness is to be expected and that he can call anytime—collect—to chat. A warm letter from home can often be the best tonic for a homesick teen.

▶ **Help your teen prepare for moral temptations.** Campus life has changed dramatically in the past few decades; coed dorms are common, and boys and girls mingle freely at all hours. Being a Christian is certainly not "politically correct" in the '90s.

Tell your child that his faith will be put to the test as never before.

continued on next page

sports, or forensics.

▶ *Special Programs.* A student willing to fulfill a service obligation after graduating from college can receive free tuition, textbooks, and living expenses from the Army, Navy, and Air Force ROTC programs. Check with the college of your choice or the military recruiting center to see whether it has a military program.

Enrolling in cooperative education can also ease the strain on your family's pocketbook. In such a program, classroom study is combined with supervised off-campus work, enabling the student to earn wages while gaining experience related to his or her field of study. For more information, write to The Natiooal Commission for Cooperative Education, 360 Huntington Ave., Boston, MA 02115.

■ **I read that thousands of students abandon their dreams of finishing college each year because they don't have the money to finish. But this article also said that millions of dollars in scholarships from**

Stress the importance of hooking up with other Christian students, joining a Bible study, and regularly attending church.

▶ **Send an occasional treat.** Since collegians are on a tight budget, an unexpected "goodie" package will make your child feel cherished. Easy-to-mail packages include candy, popcorn, cans of pudding or soup, peanut butter, jelly, and cocoa mix. If the dorm has a microwave (and most do), enlarge the menu. Consider the nonedibles, too. Fill a padded mailer with socks, a current magazine, and a tube of toothpaste or shampoo—just the thing to balance an overstretched budget.

▶ **Be enthusiastic when your collegian comes home.** Let's face it—even though you miss your teen, it's nice to regain custody of the bathroom, refrigerator, and telephone. But if you make your child feel like an intruder, he may decide to go to someone else's home for future vacations.

If you can, make room for an occasional friend too. "I learn more about Jim's adventures from his roommate than from Jim," one mother said.

Going away to college is a milestone for everyone, a time of preparation for the final letting go. With prayer and planning, it can also be a time for growth and happiness.

corporations, fraternities, church groups, and other community organizations go unclaimed because students in need are unaware that the money is available. Is this true?

Yes it is. Let's look at a breakdown of this private aid.

▶ *Foundations, companies, and industries.* Companies like Allied Signal and U.S. West Communications offer scholarships to members of employees' families. The American Legion publishes a booklet, *Need a Lift?* which outlines information on educational opportunities, careers, loans, scholarships, and employment.

Your life insurance company may sponsor contests for public relations reasons and give scholarships to the winners. Companies often select winners based on their talent in writing, speaking, and music. Alan Deutschman's book, *Winning Money for College* (see sidebar) is an excellent source for learning more about contests around the United States.

▶ *Denominations.* Some mainstream religious denominations provide scholarships for their communicants. The Presbyterian Church U.S.A. for instance, offers a renewable National Presbyterian Scholarship to academically qualified high school seniors who are communicant members of this Presbyterian denomination and who plan to attend a college connected with the Presbyterian Church U.S.A. Check with your denominational headquarters to see if they offer financial help to its members.

▶ *Community organizations.* Though the bulk of private aid comes from major companies, don't discount local service organizations such as the Lion's Club, Alpha Kappa Alpha fraternity, the YMCA, and the Kiwanis Club. Students competing for these scholarships often have a greater chance of receiving aid because the pool of candidates is smaller.

Small towns often agree to pay a student's tuition with an understanding that he or she will serve that community for a period of time after graduation. Sometimes rural areas are willing to finance a medical student's education if the student will serve the community as a doctor.

■ What are some ways to creatively save for college or make it cheaper?

There is more than one way to save for college. Consider these options:

► *U.S. Savings Bonds.* Beginning with bonds purchased in 1993, the interest earned on Series EE Savings Bonds can be excluded from federal income tax if you pay tuition and fees at a college, university, or qualified technical school during the same year the bonds are cashed. For information on how savings bonds can help you pay for your child's education, write to: Office of Public Affairs, U.S. Savings Bonds Division, Washington, DC 20226.

► *Advanced Placement.* If your child is still in high school, he or she may be able to earn some college credit before graduating. By passing advanced placement tests in subjects like English, Spanish, history, and physics, students can complete college in less than four years.

► *Junior College.* Enrolling in a two-year community college may put your child one step closer to his or her educational goal. Besides saving on room and board, you will find tuition at junior colleges much cheaper than at state universities.

► *Housing Costs.* Consider alternatives to dormitory living, which drives up the cost of going to college. Though many schools require students to live on campus the first year, you may appeal on grounds of financial need.

   If the college you've chosen is close to home, the student can commute back and forth. If not, can a relative or friend living near the college provide a room? Elderly people often exchange housing for help with household chores, and sometimes single people with large homes rent rooms. At the very least, your student can team up with several friends attending the same school and rent a house, condo, or apartment.

► *Peace Corps.* The federal government will forgive a portion of school debt if your child agrees to serve in the Peace Corps for two years following graduation. In 1993 the White House administration initiated the AmeriCorp program, which also provides repayment of college loans or substantial payment toward tuition in return for community service. For information, call (800) 942-2677.

► *Waiting.* If your child doesn't have a specific goal in mind for college or if he can't secure needed financial aid, consider postponing school. A year of work could provide career focus, and the money saved could be used to reduce college costs later.

► *Trusting.* No matter how many hours you spend at the library or how many financial aid applications you send, God can open doors that no man can close. Stay on your knees, ask Him to provide, and trust that He'll do what is best.

This material is adapted from writings by Corinne Bergstrom of Longmont, Colorado, and Joan Wester Anderson of Prospect Heights, Illinois.

5

All About
Family Issues

30

How to Talk to Your Kids About Sex

. . . .

■ **I'll admit it. I have sweaty palms and a flushed face when it comes to talking about sex with my children. Like millions of parents, I dread this subject. So how can I speak to our kids about sex without getting all uptight?**

In a word, simply. Talk is only one part of it, though. The bigger part is giving our children the *desire* to be chaste, and then giving them the practical help they need to follow it up.

Sex education begins in the parent's mind, long before the baby is born. It begins with the mother's and father's attitudes: Do we respect the human body as part of God's creation? Do we believe that God called His creation "good"? Are we comfortable with being a woman? A man?

If we are comfortable with our own sexual nature, we can be comfortable with our children's—and with our job as our children's primary sex educator. But skimping on the details—and failing to impart Christian values—is more likely to produce promiscuous offspring.

■ **Imagine the scene. We were at Aunt Priscilla's tea table, and Junior chirped up in wonderfully clear diction: "Why doesn't Susie have a pee-pee like I do?" I turned purple and Aunt Priscilla looked like she just swallowed her crumpet. "Jason!" I screamed. "We don't talk about things like that!" Since then, I've noticed that**

my son is reluctant to talk about his anatomy.

When you silenced Jason in front of proper Aunt Priscilla, you probably silenced him for good. He has just learned that bodies are not to be talked about with adults, not even with *Mommy*. That's precisely the wrong lesson.

To Jason, his question was no different than, "Why is it raining?" Bodies and weather are all part of the world he is discovering, and he's interested in both. Of course, he popped that question at an embarrassing time, but how was he to know that Aunt Priscilla's living room table was not the place?

Far better if you had begun sooner, in the bathtub, with telling Jason all the parts of the body. You should use correct, clinical terms, not silly, baby words that will embarrass him later in front of his friends. In such an environment, Jason's questions could come out spontaneously and be easily answered.

Jason can be taught too that we only talk about our bodies when we're in private, or in our own home with Mom or Dad. At the same time, he can be taught where other people are *not* allowed to touch him.

■ **I'm aware that my children are hearing messages about sex all the time. Is this something I should be overly concerned about?**

Attitudes are formed early, early on. We mustn't forget that *we* want to be the adults who guide and form our children's attitudes. If it isn't us, then who should it be? The TV? Teachers? Classmates? Friends in the neighborhood?

These influences may not be bad, but we can do a lot more to keep our children wholesome and *reinforce* proper attitudes about sex.

■ **Recently I was walking in the park with my three-year-old son. Two teens were doing some serious necking on the park bench. I hurried us past and hoped my youngster wouldn't notice. Did I handle this right?**

That's a judgment call, but if your child *does* notice, he may think necking on park benches is an OK thing to do. So what do you say? Something like: "I sure hope those two are married. People shouldn't kiss and cuddle like that unless they're married. And even then, they should do it at home." Yes, you may start a conversation, and so much the better. That's when you can build on that foundation of instilling correct behavior.

■ **What type of expectations should we have regarding behavior around the house?**

Expectations of modesty can be conveyed: a gentle correction to a pint-sized streaker running through the house naked; an observation to a preteen that a pair of shorts are too tight to be worn any more; and a quiet explanation to a high-school-age child why you don't want him to see a "teen sexploitation" film.

■ **When should our child know the differences between males and females and the facts of reproduction?**

Generally speaking, if your child hasn't learned the "birds and the bees" by the time he is ten years old, you have no time to lose. Why? Because he will soon hear it from somebody else. And if he hasn't heard your values, he will probably accept somebody else's attitudes about sex.

■ **What's the first thing I should do?**

Read some adult-level books that fill any gaps in knowledge you may have. Read up on the subject to more than your heart's content. The idea is to know the topic to the point that it isn't strange or mysterious to you.

■ **But what should I do if I don't know the answer to one of my child's questions?**

Tell her you'll find the answer. Then, at an appropriate moment, bring up the subject again. "Oh, Kimberly, remember last week we were wondering how twins are made? I found out the answer for you."

When parents say, "I don't know," children usually assume that's the end of the subject. If *you* bring up the topic again, they'll be really impressed. They'll know your "I don't know" was genuine. This will indicate your sincere desire to answer their questions and to have open lines of communication. That's why it's important to follow up and deliver an answer later on.

■ **I'm embarrassed by sex. I just know my discomfort will show when I try to talk to Ryan. I'm not very good at pretending. How can I get over my embarrassment?**

The younger your child is, the easier it will be, because he won't read anything into your embarrassment. Just tell him straight out: "I want to talk to you about something very special and very holy. I've never talked about it before with anybody, so if I seem a little nervous, that's why. Grandma and Grandpa never had a conversation like this with me, so this is the first time I've talked about it with anybody."

Plunge right into it and get the focus of attention off you and onto the subject by asking, "Do you know how babies are made?"

If your child is close to puberty, she's going to be embarrassed about the subject. She's probably agonizing in private over the physical and emotional changes she's noted in herself. Wherever she is right now, she may be wondering, *Where were you when I needed you?*

You might start out by saying, "Sally, I can tell your body is well on the way to womanhood by now. I probably should have talked to you sooner, but do you know the saying, 'Better late than never'? Well, before you grow up anymore, I want to make sure you understand why God made your body the way He did." Then proceed candidly.

Again, focus on the information you are imparting; in this case, emphasize God's plan for sexuality. Even if Sally is a senior in high school and you can rea-

THE TOP TEN REASONS NOT TO GIVE YOUR CHILDREN A FORMAL SEX TALK

10. You're not too sure what the right answers are yourself.

9. They would sense your anxiety about the subject, and it would probably give them some deep-seated hang-ups.

8. They probably know more about the subject than you do.

7. Your spouse already took care of it.

6. They've already heard the TV sitcom dads give "The Talk" a few dozen times, and you can't think of anything else to add.

5. Perhaps they haven't thought about s-e-x yet, and as they say down on the farm, "If it ain't broke, don't fix it."

4. It would only encourage them.

3. They might ask if you and your spouse still do that.

2. The story about the stork still works for you.

1. They will never be old enough.

sonably expect that she studied human reproduction in tenth grade, she'll be interested in hearing the biological information again. She may not show it, though.

In fact, Sally may frown and say, "Mom, I've known all that for years." Your reply should be, "Well, good. I wanted to make sure you knew. I want to be certain you have accurate information. Your future happiness will depend in part on how you use that information, you know. And I truly want you to be happy. Your Dad and I have lived through twenty years of marriage, and we've learned a few things. If any of our knowledge can help you, we want you to ask."

■ **My children are six and seven. They seem too innocent. I don't think they need to be burdened with all this yet.**

What is "all this"? Is knowing that God made every part of their body for a special purpose a burden? It shouldn't be. Is knowing someday they will probably get married a burden? It shouldn't be, and they should be absorbing some basic principles.

For example, they can know that marriage is forever, that one of its major purposes is to take care of the children God causes to be born, and that a lot of self-sacrifice is involved in marriage. Children need to learn these truths from the very first time they start thinking about marriage and the differences between mothers and fathers. They start noticing those differences by age four, whether they tell you about it or not.

You are not "bothering" them when you tell them they are temples of the Holy Spirit, created by God for a special purpose. In fact, if they get to fifteen and sixteen and don't know that yet, they will have a real burden in trying to understand why they are the way they are.

■ **I know my child is hearing things on the streets, but he hasn't approached me. I don't know how to bring up the subject, but I want to. Any suggestions?**

Create a situation involving both you and the child, such as watching a wildlife program on TV that includes reproduction. You could also rent a video. Or take the child with you as you pay a social call on a new mother. Driving there and back alone with your child, start a conversation about where babies come from. Discussions like this can be helpful in telling you what your child already knows.

If you know somebody whose cat just had kittens, ask if you can come see them. All children think kittens are adorable, and the sight of nursing kittens can give them a reassurance about the subject of reproduction.

■ **My mother was visiting us and heard me answering my four-year-old's questions in the bathtub about the different parts of the body and what they do. I was giving simple but frank answers. Later, my mom hit the roof. She says I never knew anything until I was a teenager, so why should I do anything different with my daughter? What should I have said to my mother in that situation?**

The first thing you should have said is, "Mom, I love the way you raised me," or something positive about your upbringing. Continue this way: "But Mom, the world I grew up in was so much simpler. My husband and I have talked about how dangerous it is today, and we've decided to answer all of our child's questions. We think this is the best way to protect her against getting wrong ideas."

If the subject isn't laid to rest easily, point out that children whose parents talk to them are *less* preoccupied with sexuality than children whose parents stay mum on the subject.

■ **I'm divorced, and my ex-husband has liberal visitation rights. If he talks to our ten-year-old son about sex, I'm afraid he won't be on the same page as me. What should I do?**

If your ex has worldly ideas, you might try gently introducing a book to your boy, such as Jamie Buckingham's *Let's Talk About Life*. When your son reads it, tell him you're willing to discuss the subject further. Use a light touch, but be straightforward. Explain that because you love him, you want him to have the facts, both about his body and the moral consequences of premarital sex.

■ **My daughter is thirteen, and I think some of the girls in her crowd are pretty fast. Every time I try to talk to her about Christian values, she pooh-poohs me. She says the "new morality" gives women what men have always had—equality in sex-**

ual behavior—and that she's not going to be bound by some medieval standard of morality. How do I respond?

With prayer to begin with—incessant prayer that the Holy Spirit will touch her heart. But you also need some practical tips.

Such a girl seems to be a victim of feminism and the Planned Parenthood agenda—that the individual can decide his or her own values. Somebody needs to tell her that the sexual revolution is the worst joke ever played on women by men. Even some prominent feminists agree.

Go to the public library and thumb through some back issues of *Ms.* or *Cosmopolitan* magazine. Find an article making the same statement. Bring home a photocopy, but don't present it to her with a flourish and say, "I told you so." Wait for the right moment, then present the article in love, without being pushy. She'll probably want to talk to you right away.

Is there anyone in her circle of acquaintances whom she respects? Maybe one of them can talk to her. Does she associate with the youth group at church? If so, talk privately with the youth pastor and clue him into the situation. He might arrange to stage a conversation on sexuality with you present.

One point he might mention is that it's far easier for a man to repent and change a promiscuous lifestyle than it is for a woman. Why? Because women become much more emotionally involved in sex than men, and once she has tarnished her reputation, her self-esteem takes a nosedive. When a young girl has a certain "reputation," she practically has to move to another state to change it. It's extremely difficult to live down gossip in the peer grapevine.

■ **I just found out the school nurse gave my daughter's fifth-grade class a lecture on "safe sex" last week. My daughter is wondering why I never told her about family planning.**

"Family planning" for children is a euphemism for giving a false sense of security to fornication. Sex education advocates imagine (or pretend to imagine) that by giving out contraceptives and encouraging young people to use them, they are protecting children against the consequences of their actions.

Nothing could be further from the truth. Armed with a false sense of protection, young people plunge into promiscuity, and we end up with the highest teen pregnancy rate in the world.

Did you know this lecture on "safe sex" was coming to the fifth grade? If you didn't, you might want to talk to the school principal and your school board to protest this invasion of parental rights.

■ **I think it's unrealistic to expect our kids to wait until marriage before having sex. Fact is, I wasn't a virgin at my own marriage. Why should I expect my son or daughter to wait until marriage?**

Because you love them and you want them to have a better, happier, more virtuous life than you. Children can become self-fulfilling prophecies—they will act as they believe you acted. Listen to what one mother said:

"When I was about fifteen years old, I was having a conversation with my mother. She told me no one was a virgin when they got married and I wouldn't be either. Up until that time, I thought my mom, who was a Christian, expected me to be a virgin until I was married.

"To me, her comment was like a license to go ahead and lose my virginity—and I did, a short time later. I'm not putting the entire blame on my mother. The main thing I want to convey is that parents must be careful what they say to their kids."

One thing is important: our children need to know that we, their parents, care passionately about their character and lifestyle. We care through our instruction, our love, and our actions. They may rebel, but deep down, kids have a way of expecting of themselves what parents expect of them.

Some may reject our teaching and depart from the path of righteousness. But sooner or later, they will find themselves unhappy. And then, in a dark moment, the Spirit of the Lord will be able to bring to their minds our words, our example, and our love.

They will know where they need to turn. And in that moment, though it may be years later, the rebelliousness will be forgotten, and the teaching and the caring will bear their fruit.

This material is adapted from writings by author and speaker Connie Marshner of Front Royal, Virginia. The "Top Ten" List is from Faithful Parents, Faithful Kids *(Tyndale) by Greg Johnson and Mike Yorkey.*

31

We Really Love You, But . . .

. . . .

■ We lived on the corner of 4th and Sycamore for the first fifteen years of marriage in a little pre-World War II bungalow. Then about the time the kids hit junior high, we built our dream house up on the rim on the city's south side.

The kids are grown now, and the house is often quiet, except for the times the grand kids come over. Our daughter, Shana, is twenty-eight and expecting her third child. She, her husband, and their girls live in a little bungalow down on—you guessed it—4th street.

But the two-bedroom place is quickly getting cramped, and they aren't sure where to put the new baby. They definitely need a larger place. They could probably sell the bungalow, but they have only enough equity to buy a slightly larger tract house in a tough neighborhood.

For months Shana has been anxious over what to do. Finally she came upon a marvelous solution. "Since you like to travel more and more and don't want to spend all your time taking care of such a big place, why don't you guys move into the bungalow, and we'll move up here? This would be such a great place to raise the kids!"

Normally, this would be an easy no, but Shana is *our* daughter, and Baby #3 is *our* grandchild. What should we do? Should we trade houses?

We all have times when we—the adult parents—have to say no. In the case of trading houses, the answer is clearly no, but in many others ("Dad, can you help Larry get a job at your office?" or "Mom, can I borrow $1,000 to buy a motorcycle?"), the decisions are not so simple.

On those occasions, you need to *listen*. Make sure you've heard the whole story. The initial request might sound like this: "Mom? It's me. Listen, I know it's noon Friday, but something's come up, and I really need you to keep the kids for the weekend."

To which you might stammer and reply, "Oh, Honey, this is Daddy's weekend to rebuild the deck. He'll have boards and nails and stain all over the place. Why don't we make it next weekend instead? Is it really that special?"

"Mom, Wayne and I wanted to go to the boat races in Seattle because. . . ."

"Boat races?" you interrupt. (You think, *They decide two hours before they leave that they're going to the races and don't want to take the kids? She could have called me weeks ago!*)

"Oh, it's OK, Mom," she sighs. "I'll talk to you later. Bye."

But that wasn't the whole story. Before sounding discouraging (or even encouraging), what if you pressed your daughter into a little more explanation?

"Well . . . it's not just the races. Brad and Carrie Robinson will be there—you know, Wayne's best friend in college. Brad's about the only Christian guy Wayne's really close to, and, well, to tell you the truth, we've been going through some tough times in our marriage. I mean, it's nothing we can't fix.

"But Brad and Carrie have been putting on marriage seminars; they know how to talk to people. Wayne just got a call from Brad this morning, inviting

---

A TIME TO LEAVE THE NEST

If you have children in high school, you should be mentally preparing yourself for the day when they are no longer in the home. Keep in mind that you want to "finish strong," and as parents, we are always working ourselves out of a job. We want to instill within our children a sense of responsibility so that they will be able to stand on their own by the time they are late adolescents. We are working toward healthy relinquishment of our children, hoping that when they leave home, they won't need us anymore.

Some of the best psychology is practiced by eagles. The mother

continued next page

us to come along. It would be all right to take the kids, but if we want to do any serious talking, we better go by ourselves.

"Anyway, I don't want you and Daddy to worry. This is just something we need to work out, and I thought maybe Brad and Carrie were the ones to help us."

Suddenly the request takes on a different importance. Maybe rebuilding the deck can wait another week . . . or month . . . or year.

■ **Let's say our married daughter, Martee, calls and says, "Mom, the contractors won't have the house finished until the middle of January, and the people buying this place want to move in by the first of November. Do you think that Devin, the kids, and I could camp out with you and Dad until they finish the house? We could rent a storage place for the furniture." What do I say then?**

The question to ask is, "How much time do I have to think about this before you need an answer?" Up to some obvious limits, the more time spent considering a situation, the better the decision will be.

Otherwise, you have three options:

1. You could instantly say, "Yes!"

2. You could blurt out, "What? You must be kidding!"

3. You could reply, "Wow, that does put you guys in a bind. Listen, let me talk to your father. When do you need to know?"

The third option is almost always the wisest. It gives you some time to discuss it with your mate and to consider all the ramifications. For instance, this might be the year your son, Kory, and his family will be flying in from Maine and spending two weeks

and father eagle spend a lot of time with their young, but the time comes when the parents literally shove their half-grown young ones over the edge of a cliff.

The eagles don't do that when the young offspring are helpless babies. They wait until they have developed enough strength in their wing muscles to fly, even though the young ones don't realize their powers. Halfway down the cliff, those young eagles begin to flap their wings in automatic response. Suddenly, they discover they can fly. If young eagles were never challenged, they would never learn to fly.

during Christmas with you. Try as you may, you just could not put three families in your home.

On the other hand, maybe this is the year you and your spouse are flying to Maine for a couple weeks to be with Kory and his family. In that case, the home would be vacant anyway.

Maybe you've been telling the kids for six months that the house will never be done in time, and that they will have to make plans for intermediate housing, and yet they waited until the last moment and then popped this on you. Or maybe every time Martee and you spend extensive time together you end up arguing about how to care for the children. Or maybe you've been wanting a way to get to know your son-in-law better.

Think about it. Take all the time allowed. You'll have a better shot at making a good choice.

■ **My husband, Miles, has always been a pushover for our daughter, Shandi. When she was six and wanted a five-foot, $100 stuffed bear, he worked overtime for a week to afford it. When she was seventeen and insisted on a $650 designer original prom dress, Miles sold his golf clubs and bought her the dress. When Shandi got married, she wanted a deluxe affair, and so Miles mortgaged the house for another $10,000 and gave her an incredible wedding.**

Now, Shandi feels cramped in her marriage. She told her dad she needs some breathing room to sort things out. She asked him if he would rent her a condo at Malibu for six months while she "gets my head on straight."

This request sent me

HOW TO SAY NO NICELY

▶ **Be reasonable.** You answer should be supported by good reason and open to reasonable questions.

▶ **Be gentle.** Fill your answer with tenderness.

▶ **Be distinct.** Let your statements be clearly yes or no.

▶ **Be edifying.** Choose words that help another's moral, intellectual, or spiritual improvement.

▶ **Be peaceful and strengthening.** Show the confident assurance that God is still in control even in the midst of a tough situation.

▶ **Be concerned about long-term goals.** How will this decision stand up a month, a year, five years from now?

through the roof. "You've spoiled that girl for almost 30 years! It's time you forced her to grow up!" I screamed. Now I need to know what to do.

Talk over the situation carefully with your mate. Absolutely no decision should be made until you and Miles come to an agreement about parenting Shandi.

When your adult children have asked you to make a major decision, make sure you're talking to them too. What exactly are you being asked to do? At what cost? For how long? Talking out everyone's expectations saves future headaches.

Finally, don't forget to pray about these big decisions. There is divine wisdom. There is a response that will work for the eternal good of all involved parties. But you'll never find it unless you take time to talk to God. Confess your own limitations in knowing what to do. Ask Him for the wisdom needed to make the right decision.

When your heart tells you one thing, and your mind tells you something else, let your spirit cast the deciding vote. Your decision, whether yes or no, should be one that you feel at ease with in the presence of God. If you find yourself justifying your answer before Him, then you are not listening to your spirit. But I am convinced of this: As we ask, He will help us parent even our adult children.

This material is adapted from Just Because They've Left Doesn't Mean They're Gone *by Stephen Bly. Copyright © 1993, Stephen Bly. Used by permission of Focus on the Family, and* Parents and Teenagers *(Victor) by Norm Wright.*

32

Reaching Out to Single Parents

. . . .

■ We have some neighbors going through a tough stretch. Linda is newly single and the mother of two young boys. They are a Christian family, but their marriage failed.

Recently, I ran into Linda at the supermarket, and we made small talk for a few minutes. After a lull, I said, "We'll have to get together sometime. Maybe while our boys are at soccer practice."

Linda smiled. "I'd like that. But if you want that to happen, you'll have to make the call. I'm on the phone so much, calling my lawyer, talking to the Friend of the Court, that I just don't have the energy to make any more calls. I'd love to get together, but could you take the lead?"

I was taken aback, but I quickly recovered and promised to call before the boys' next soccer game. Since then, we've become closer friends, and I can sense that we're gradually building a friendship. But if Linda hadn't said something, I'm sure she never would have called, right?

Absolutely. Reaching out to others is difficult. Sandra P. Aldrich, a former senior editor at Focus on the Family and frequent radio guest with Dr. Dobson, has been on both sides of the reception room.

Once, she was a beloved wife who attended every social event with her husband, but her spouse's death from cancer thrust her into a single-parent role before the two kids were out of elementary school. Now she wonders—perhaps like you—how often she unintentionally ignored the single parents in her church. After all, developing a relationship with a single parent requires the same elements needed for any relationship—time and understanding of one another's schedules and limitations.

Single parents don't want two-parent families to treat them with an annual good deed. They really desire friendship. But some of them, like Linda, are so exhausted or have been so wounded that they can't take the first step toward getting together.

■ Where should I start?

Here are some ideas:

▶ *Talk to single parents.* When you see single parents in church, offer a sincere greeting. If their children are young, then the single parents are especially hungry for adult conversation. They often feel awkward in church, and your smile and greeting on Sunday morning will make a big difference.

▶ *Talk to their children.* When Sandra Aldrich and her family attended a small church in New York, one of the couples invited her son, Jay, over for a Saturday lunch and an afternoon of working on the car. Jay was delighted to be doing "guy" things with a young husband, and even a two-minute conversation with the men on Sunday morning made him look forward to church. Don't discount the importance of just a few sentences. You can have a wonderful influence on a child too.

▶ *Pray for them.* Single-parent families may appear strong, but the load is heavy. If they're new to this role, they're struggling with unfamiliar territory and need all the encouragement they can get.

If they're already friends, they would welcome you to pray with them for a few minutes each week—perhaps before Sunday School. They love praying with their children, but they miss hearing an adult voice take their concerns to God. But if they haven't developed that closeness yet, please pray for them—and their children—in your own quiet time. If the Lord gives you specific direction, please listen. He knows their needs, whether it's help with grocery money or for someone to take their sons to a church event.

Sandra remembers the first father/son banquet after her husband died. Several sports figures were going to be in attendance, so Jay casually mentioned he wanted to go. She couldn't ask one of her friends to include him, because she knew they'd want to enjoy the special evening with their own sons.

Since Sandra wasn't into Rent-a-Boyfriend, she had no choice but to take Jay herself. Being the only woman at an all-male event didn't bother her until they walked into the hall and she realized they didn't have assigned seats. Sandra would have to approach a table full of men and their sons and ask if they could join them.

With shaking knees, she put on her brightest smile, approached an available table, and asked, "Are you gentlemen secure enough to allow a woman to sit at your table?" (She cringes now to think of that statement, but it was produced by fear rather than arrogance.) They laughed and welcomed mom and son, but in that moment she made up her mind to have a weekend trip planned when the next banquet was scheduled.

■ But wasn't that a rude question?

Yes, but sometimes those who are hurting the most can't take one more rejection, so they put up emotional walls. It takes a strong person to help them ease them down. One way to help is by making single parents feel emotionally safe whenever they're in your presence by not judging them; they're doing the best they can. They didn't want their lives to turn out this way. They didn't plan on being single again, and they weren't trained for this role.

■ It sounds like single parents can be defensive at times.

That's right. They will also confess that they're a little afraid of you, especially that you'll blame their children's normal misbehavior on their growing up in a single-parent household. They read the newspaper reports that present the statistics about kids from single-parent households having more discipline problems than others. More trouble with the law. More time in jail. Rather than condemning them, please remind them that the statistics are just that—statistics. They're often frightened by them. Please help them not to be.

■ **And how do I do that?**

By being a sounding board. One of the greatest things they need is someone to bounce ideas off of—whether they're wondering about normal behavior for their children, buying a used car, or maintaining their home. If they're struggling with what is usual behavior for an eleven year old, it helps if you'll share a similar experience in your own family. And if they're facing home repairs, they may need someone to interpret the jargon.

When Allison, a single mom, needed to repair her roof, she gathered the usual price quotes but realized that each contractor was suggesting different ways to correct the problem. She called her brother in another state to get the interpretation of such phrases as "four-inch pitch" and "floor joists." But not all of us have helpful relatives, which means they may have to turn to you.

Another thing you can do is offer occasional encouragement. If you see single parents doing something right, please let them know. Some days are so bad that they can't see anything but their mistakes, and your words make a difference.

Clare is the mother of rambunctious eight-year-old twins who love to poke and tease each other as they jostle their way to the parking lot. Clare's weariness often grows under the raised eyebrows of parents with "perfect" children.

One drizzly morning, another mother approached Clare and said, "I wish you could have seen how helpful your boys were at church last Sunday. The boys were leaving the Sunday School building with Mrs. Reynolds. You know how she is still a bit unsure of her footing since she fell last winter? Well, as she hesitated on the steps, the boys let Mrs. Reynolds put her hands on their shoulders as she walked

> **QUICK FACTS**
>
> The U.S. Census Bureau states that in 1992, single-parent households under eighteen rose to 10.5 million, a 40 percent increase since 1980. Those 10.5 million homes have 17 million children, which means that 30 percent of our nation's children—your children's classmates—are from single-parent households.

to the car. You really are doing a wonderful job with those boys." That simple comment encouraged Clare for months.

■ **I see what you mean. What are some things that churches can do to reach out?**

More and more churches are having an auto day, in which single moms can bring their cars for tune-ups, oil changes, or winterizing. Other churches keep a file of handyman teams who are available to trim bushes or caulk around the windows. But sometimes their needs are a bit more bizarre.

When Jay Aldrich was in the fourth grade, he had to wear a tie for his spring concert. Sandra struggled with it for a while, trying to remember the way her husband had tossed the long, wide part of the tie around the short, narrow part.

After several frustrating attempts, she had to admit she didn't have the foggiest notion how to tie a tie. Her neighbor Cathy rescued her. With the expertise of a veteran mother of two boys, she explained the procedure as she tied the fabric in a perfect four-in-hand.

As Sandra thanked her, she said, "That's what friends are for."

Another young mother was having trouble potty training her two-year-old son. She didn't have any male relatives close by to give the little guy an example of how to tackle this milestone. One evening, as she purchased toddler diapers from the grocery stores, she ran into her neighbor Liz. With some embarrassment, she stammered her frustration that her son just wasn't catching on. Liz, bless her, didn't shrug and flippantly say that the child would figure it out before he got to college. She had a practical suggestion: Bring him to her house each evening after dinner so her husband could give the little fellow a lesson. It worked!

Besides, yours may be the only "normal" family a single-parent's children see. What a wonderful impact you can have by letting them join you for a family night. Invite them into your home just as you would any other family. And please accept when they invite your family to their home.

So go ahead and make someone feel welcome. It's as easy as saying, "Hi, my name is Frank, and this is my wife, Susan."

This material is adapted from Sandra Aldrich's book, From One Single Parent to Another *(Regal).*

33

Raising Color-Blind Kids

. . . .

■ **I know racism still exists, but I have high hopes for raising "color blind" children. I'm eager to see them accept other ethnic groups. What are some steps I should take?**

Jan Johnson asked the same question when she lived in Inglewood, California, a predominantly black suburb of Los Angeles. As a white woman who had a lot of day-to-day contact with other races, she was particularly sensitive to black-white relationships.

One time, she was sitting in a restaurant with her six-year-old daughter, Janae, and a black friend.

"Mommy, why are those ladies over there staring at you?" asked Janae.

"Because I'm sitting with Rose," answered Jan. "Some people don't think blacks and whites can be friends."

Janae looked up and wrinkled her nose. At six years old, she didn't see skin color an issue yet. *So far, so good,* thought Jan. She wants her children to understand that most people are basically alike, regardless of their skin color. They want happiness and security for themselves and their families. At times her children grasped this better than Jan did.

■ **How so?**

For example, one Father's Day, Jan's kids picked out a card that surprised their mother. The dad on the front of the card was not white like their father.

When Jan pointed this out, Janae said, "But he's smiling like Dad."

Jan started to explain, but nothing made sense. Many of Janae's friends' dads are black. Some are Hispanic and others are Asian. The color of a dad's face didn't make much difference to her.

■ I understand that we shouldn't let racial differences divide us. How can I get started along the road toward reconciliation and understanding?

First of all, you should enjoy the cultural differences, which can make life more interesting and expand our perspectives. When a Hispanic family moved across the street from Jan Johnson, she had ulterior motives for being extra neighborly. They had two teenage daughters with all kinds of mothering attitudes.

"Crackerjack baby-sitters!" she told her husband. And they were. But Jan learned a lesson one time when she popped over to pick up one of the daughters to baby-sit. Angela, the mom, motioned for Jan to wait. Then she blushed and sputtered in broken English, "I'm glad you're my neighbor. I hope you're comfortable in our house."

Jan left in amazement. No other neighbor—black, brown, or white—had ever said anything like that before.

■ What should I *not* say around ethnic families?

If you stop and think about it, it's obvious: racist language. The "N-word" is particularly offensive in the black community, but so is referring to sections of town by their ethnic make-up.

■ How can I learn more about the different cultures around me so I can better understand my ethnic neighbors?

Ethnic celebrations take place during the year. For instance, Black History Month is every February. You might look for a local "expo" during one of the weekends that month, or watch specials on public television. Be sure to tell your children what you remember about race relations when you were growing up.

Cinco de Mayo is celebrated on the fifth of May to commemorate a Mexican victory over French forces, and it can be a holiday around your house as well. On the Chinese New Year, prepare an elaborate Chinese meal and bake almond cookies for dessert. It makes sense to observe holidays that have become part of the American melting pot.

■ What happens if I encounter someone who still harbors racist feelings?

Ethnic acceptance is a condition of the heart and not easily changed. The sad fact is that you probably won't be able to influence many people you come in contact with, but you can certainly work with your children. You do that by inviting friends of all races to your home. People may know each other at work, school, or church, but crossing each other's thresholds is a key.

Jan Johnson remembers the first time a black couple ate dinner with them. Her son, Jeffrey, caught her peeking during grace. They were staring at the same thing. Their clutched hands created an "ebony and ivory" effect—black and white and black and white.

Jan thought it was pretty neat. She admits she's a little radical when it comes to racial interaction. She's eager to see her children accept other ethnic groups. To her, racial acceptance is also a spiritual issue. Being "color blind" is one more way she can teach her children to shed selfishness and pride.

Once, Jan read Philippians 2:4, which says, "Each of you should look not only to your own interests, but also the interests of others." Being "color blind" forces her family to be *others*-centered, which is one of her primary goals as a Christian parent.

This material is adapted from writings by Jan Johnson of Simi, California.

6

All About Teen Issues

34

Teenage Ups and Downs

. . . .

■ **I have two teens, and let me tell you, parenting has become a challenge. Why do I feel like I'm in the wildest ride of my life?**

Perhaps you feel like you're on a roller coaster, and you're going higher and higher until you see only blue sky. Then the cars hurtle toward the earth, pushing you hard into your seats with your breath caught in your throat. Joyful screams muffle other sounds as the cars jerk quickly to the right, sharply left, up again, then down and around.

Roller coasters pack sixty seconds of thrills into every minute. It's great once or twice or even three times. But what if you were subjected to days and weeks of continuous ups, downs, and stomach flip-flops?

Welcome to what many parents are feeling every day.

■ **Our thirteen-year-old daughter Trish slinks down the stairs five minutes after having been called to dinner. Sullen and downcast/ she sneers at me when questioned about her tardiness. During the rest of the meal, she exhibits sadness about a relationship, excitement about a boy, happiness about her plans for the weekend, anger at her brother's comment, and laughter at a silly joke. Is Trish psychotic? On drugs? Suffering from lack of sleep?**

Trish is experiencing a roller-coaster ride of emotions. But the ride is not solo—the whole family is with her, and that's why you are exhausted and exasperated by the whole thing. Besides, Trish is a typical early adolescent, junior high teen.

As children approach the teenage years, parents probably feel more helpless and unsure of themselves than at any other time. How do we know when our sweet little son or daughter is about to embark upon this difficult adventure? There are several warning signs:

One symptom of adolescence involves the radio. These kids often start listening to rock stations, talking about their favorite artists, and buying albums. Along with this push into pop culture comes another phenomenon: the desire to see previously prohibited movies and TV shows.

Then there's the telephone. When Stuart McDowell's daughter Kara was in junior high, she and her best friend did almost everything together. Once he drove her and the friend home after a full day of classes and basketball practice, only to hear Kara's parting line—"I'll call you." Neither sex holds a monopoly on the telephone phenomenon; boys and girls alike can tie up the phone for hours.

■ **I've noticed my daughter is getting cauliflower ear too.**

WAYS TO TELL YOUR TEENS YOU LOVE THEM

Teenagers may not be the most lovable creatures in the world, but they probably need more love during those turbulent years than at any other time in their lives.

If you're a parent who finds it difficult to say "I love you" to your teen, take heart! You can tell your teen you love him without actually saying it. Here are some ways:

► **Give plenty of hugs.** It's been said that human beings need twelve hugs a day. Sounds like a good idea. If you haven't hugged your teen lately, don't be embarrassed. Just do it!

► **Show respect.** The way you speak says as much as your words. Even if you're correcting your teen, do it in a respectful way.

► **Share time and energy.** You know that parenting requires massive doses of time and energy. Regardless of what you may think, teens do notice the little things you do, such as ironing clotkes, paying part of their car insurance, and asking what they would like for lunch.

► **Set reasonable limits.** Even when teens try to talk their parents out of curfews, they feel secure knowing someone cares. Scott, a high school junior, says

continued next page

Explain this "junior high" thing in greater detail for me.

Besides relationship stresses and adolescent irritations, other serious problems arise. Junior highers can argue about everything. Privacy is a big deal. They lock the bedroom door, write journals or notes, and talk in whispers on the phone. They don't want anyone listening, especially their parents. Violation of their space triggers arguments, as do discussions of friendships, curfews, studying, or church and other extracurricular activities.

Another problem is the crisis in self-confidence. Early adolescents want to be good at something. So they take lessons, try out for teams, run for school offices, and audition for plays. When they don't make the team or get elected or win the part, they often feel like failures.

In junior high, more definite social groups emerge. Some are negative, including gangs. Close friends part ways, and new best friends are found. In elementary school, a child plays with children in the neighborhood. But that changes in junior high, where relationships are forged through common interests, activities, and values. The former close friend may now be in another social group. Friendship stresses and changes can be painful for kids this age.

that when his parents tell him no, they are trying to keep him from getting hurt. That understanding might not have come if his parents hadn't first explained to him why they'd said no to a later curfew.

► **Forgive and forget.** Suzanne, now a grown woman, was eighteen when she lost her virginity. The news crushed her parents. "When I saw their faces," she remembers, "I wanted to die. If only I coulg have undone it." Suzanne was prepared for anything—except forgiveness.

"We all cried together," she says, "but I'll never forget what happened after I went to bed that night. My dad crept into my room, bent down, and kissed me on the forehead. He actually kissed me! It was the most incredible feeling." Her parents' forgiveness was a turning point in her life. "If they could forgive me, I knew their love—and their religion—was real."

► **Keep praying.** Perhaps the most loving thing a parent can do is pray for them. Be bold and ask to pray with your teen before he goes to bed. You can even slip in after he's sleeping and pray by his bedside.

Jeff remembers waking up in the night and finding his dad praying over him. "I knew that spelled 'love,' " he says.

■ **Has anyone figured out the causes of this behavior?**

The underlying cause of all these symptoms and problems can be summarized in one word—*change*. Early adolescents experience change in every area of life: social, mental, spiritual and physical.

> ▶ *Social.* In addition to leaving behind old friends and finding new ones, junior highers are experimenting with new social skills. They become conscious of the opposite sex, trying to determine who's going out with whom. Also, groups of friends become important as these kids try to find a place to belong. Listen to junior high conversations. The topic will probably involve relationships: gossip, conflicts, and opposite-sex intrigues.
>
> ▶ *Mental.* Children think in black-and-white, concrete terms. Most adults can think conceptually. The change in thinking from the concrete to the conceptual usually occurs during the adolescent years. Kids who haven't made this change may struggle in many areas of study and feel left out of most classroom discussions.
>
> ▶ *Spiritual.* In junior high, religion isn't cool. That fact is learned quickly by junior highers who are sensitive to what their peers think.
>
> Junior high kids speak in extremes like "Church is stupid!" or "Youth group is dumb!" Because these kids don't yet think conceptually, they may find they don't understand the sermons or the Sunday School lessons. Most church youth groups draw from several different schools, and many kids would rather be with their friends from school than with the kids at church.
>
> To complicate things, many churches offer little involvement for this age group. The kids are too old for traditional children's programs and too young for youth group. Many junior highers fail to see the relevance of Bible stories and church identity. They just don't relate to the changes in their bodies, their emotional ups and downs, or their temptations to drink, smoke, and have sex. Consequently, junior high kids often become disenchanted with the church scene.
>
> ▶ *Physical.* Perhaps the most obvious changes during this time occur in the physical area. Girls grow earlier and can feel like

giants. Boys who grow late feel like shrimps and may never achieve the coveted roster spot on the basketball team. And kids this age can be cruel to one another—mocking fellow students for being short, overweight, or physically limited.

Sex can also become an obsession as raging hormones twist and turn adolescent emotions. The sexual organs develop, and girls begin to menstruate. With all their new sexual awareness, kids often begin telling dirty jokes, acting tough, and swearing. Some kids even begin to experiment with sex.

■ I'm feeling depressed already. What's a parent to do?

Although we have painted a dreary picture of the junior high/middle-school years, there's a brighter side. These kids are a rewarding group to work with. If parents don't get psyched out but work hard to relate, there will be many opportunities to teach and develop their children's godly character. Here's what you can do.

- ▶ *Understand.* If you grasp what early adolescents are going through, you will be more forgiving and able to deal with their needs and problems. Remind yourself every day of the problems occurring during this time of adolescence.
- ▶ *Communicate.* One woman named Julie took a proactive approach to communicating with her son. "In my first conflicts with Ben during junior high," she said, "I explained that I had never been the parent of a teenager before, and we needed to learn together. We had to work at forgiving and being forgiven—and at keeping the lines of communication open."
- ▶ *Have a good attitude.* Too many adults make fun of junior highers, belittling their styles, physical characteristics, musical tastes, and friends. That leads to confrontation and alienation. Instead, hold your tongue whenever you are tempted to snap back with caustic, cutting or sarcastic comments. Remember the teaching of Ephesians 6:4: "Fathers, do not exasperate your children; instead, bring them up in the training and instruction of the Lord."

  A positive attitude also means carefully choosing your battles. Every day you will find issues to argue about, but most of those concerns aren't that important. Is Jason's room a mess?

Instead of nagging him to clean it, shut the door. Does Danielle slouch in the family room and try to study with her music on? Let it go as long as her grades don't suffer. Some parents use up all their ammunition in the skirmishes. Then when something serious happens, they have no reserves for the battles.

► *Listen.* Communication involves listening with your eyes as well as your ears. Look for clues in your son's or daughter's body language. Your son may be brooding because he is depressed about his height or anxious about basketball try-outs or angry at someone who's been picking on him at school.

When junior highers talk, you need to listen. Don't just look at them, waiting for your chance to speak. Real listening means taking seriously what your teen says.

One important aspect of listening is choosing the right time to talk. When Melissa was in seventh grade, she sometimes made outrageous statements at the dinner table about a friend who got into trouble at school, or about an R-rated video or about how much she hated a certain teacher. Her parents' natural reaction was to respond immediately with their opinions.

Each time they did that, disaster followed. Melissa became defensive and angry with them. The parents learned to listen quietly and let Melissa talk it out. Later in the evening, when her father was helping her with homework, he would often broach the controversial subject with her. Usually she would be much less defensive and more open to talking.

► *Talk their language.* Effective communication also means using words that your child understands.

A few years ago Bob Welch was coaching a sixth- and seventh-grade girls' basketball team. During one practice, his fellow coaches and him were teaching the girls how to play zone defense. One of the coaches said, "If the girl leaves your zone, you don't have to worry about her. The onus is on the player over here."

Bob almost laughed out loud as he looked at the puzzled expressions on the girls' faces. *Onus? What's an onus?* they thought as they checked their clothes to see if they had any onuses on them.

If you want to get through to your junior high kids, you should keep the vocabulary simple and concrete. Ask for feedback to see if they understand what you are saying.

■ **Sometimes I need to apply rules and discipline to my middle-school son, but then I need to repeat them and explain the consequences of violating them** *again*. **How can I get him to understand what the rules of the house are?**

Some parents put the rules in writing to avoid misunderstanding in areas like schoolwork, church, curfew, chores, and respect for others.

Take time to talk things through. Don't just dismiss your child's views and exert your authority. According to a number of adults surveyed by Greg Johnson and Mike Yorkey in *Faithful Parents, Faithful Kids* (Tyndale House, 1993), some off the least effective ways to resolve conflicts include these statements made by parents:

"I'm the parent."

"Because I told you so."

"I don't have energy for this."

"Don't sass me."

"Go to your room."

The survey also showed that children hate being yelled at. Some hear ultimatums every hour, and eventually the threats lose their impact.

■ **What are some other things I want to keep in mind with my teenagers.**

Keep looking for those teachable moments. Great opportunities for positive communication occur almost daily with junior highers. But you need to be sensitive to the teachable moments and take advantage of them when they occur.

Because early adolescents are focused on competence, this is a great time to teach them skills. Good coaches spend hours teaching their players the basic skills of the game—kicking, pitching, throwing.

Junior highers also need to learn skills to help them win in the game of life—studying, getting along with the opposite sex, and handling money. Spiritual life skills should also be taught—praying, studying the Bible, and witnessing to others. Although they may look and sound uninterested, children look to their parents to teach them practical skills for living as an adult.

■ How can I show love to my junior highers? It gets hard sometimes, especially when I want to strangle them.

By choosing to act in love toward them, even when they aren't lovable. Some parents assume that adolescents are becoming independent and consequently don't want them around. These parents withdraw emotionally and physically from their kids. But studies show that early adolescents want a close family, and they still enjoy having their parents involved in their lives.

Many parents take literally the emotional comments and quick reactions of their early adolescent children. For example, Scott might say, "I don't want to go to youth group. It's stupid and boring." Not wanting to push Scott, his parents might find it easy to give in and allow him to stay home. Instead, they should take him to church and trust competent youth group workers to minister to him.

This principle also holds true for parental involvement. My junior high ministry team is composed almost entirely of parents of kids in the group, and the involvement of those parents has improved the relationships with their kids. Don't be intimidated by what you think your junior high child might feel about your being there. Look for ways to get involved.

Loving also means arranging time and emotional energy to spend with your child. If you are too busy at work, in the community or at church, you won't have time or energy to teach your child. Learn to say no to unnecessary commitments and reserve that time for your child.

It is easy for junior highers to feel as though they can't do anything right. They hear a continual barrage of criticism and correction from parents, bus drivers, teachers, coaches, neighbors, and friends. It is up to you to give positive feedback. This means catching your children doing something right, then praising them for it.

If you have taught your son how to make cookies or lasagna, praise your young chef for what he did right. Don't point out the imperfections in the final product. If you watch your daughter's volleyball game, look for actions and incidents to affirm—her enthusiasm on the bench, her quick footwork, or her encouragement of other team members.

No matter how much young teens push against the rules, they need and want limits. Without rules, guidelines, punishments, and rewards, early adolescents feel insecure.

■ **A few years ago, I was driving my daughter and a friend to a basketball game. They chattered nonstop in the backseat and then began talking about a certain teacher. Megan's friend said: "He's not a good teacher. He lets us get away with anything." What was my daughter's friend really saying?**

She was expressing what most adolescents feel—they want someone to set limits. Some parents are afraid to exercise discipline with their children at this age. Fearful of alienating them or intimidated by the child's aggressive arguments, these parents just give in.

Instead, explain and then enforce the rules. In Proverbs 15:1 we read, "A gentle answer turns away wrath, but a harsh word stirs up anger." Firm enforcement of the rules does not mean you must be loud and angry. Gentleness is more effective.

Discipline is more than punishment; it is a positive action to direct behavior. Our goal as parents should be to teach our children to become self-disciplined so they will do what is right when they have moved beyond our surveillance and rule enforcement. It's never too early to begin teaching children that their actions have consequences.

■ **Any final advice then?**

Parenting an adolescent can be a difficult time—a roller-coaster ride that never seems to end. But it does. And there are things you can do to handle this challenge successfully. By understanding, communicating with, and loving your teen, you will make a big difference for both you and your child. So buckle up and enjoy the ride!

This material is adapted from Parenting Passages *(Tyndale House) by David Veerman and from writings by Dayle Shockley of Spring, Texas.*

35

When You Don't Like Your Teen's Friends

· ·

■ **My older son, Bob, a high school junior, has befriended a class-mate who dresses in combat fatigues and sports a mohawk hair-style. When my son's friend is around, he rarely speaks to me. I've also noticed that Bob is more quiet. Should I limit my son's contact with this boy?**

When your children were smaller, their choice of friends was usu-ally based on chance; they played with kids in the neighborhood or from the soccer teams. But as youngsters mature and begin attend-ing larger schools, friendships often develop by *choice*. Young teens usu-ally gravitate toward companions who share common interests, and they will often look to them to supply the support and comfort they need during the pains of adolescence.

■ **Yes, but Bob has chosen a friend we don't approve of. What practical guidelines can I follow?**

First of all, keep quiet as you take stock of the situation. You may be upset because Bob's new pal has a weird haircut and wears com-bat fatigues, but that doesn't mean he's done anything wrong.

Remember that kids "try on" a variety of images, and many of them are short-lived—provided parents don't have a cow!

■ **But last week Bob missed curfew by a half hour—the first time that's ever happened.**

If your teen has broken your rules—anything from missing curfew to cheating on a test—it's time to step in. You may decide to limit your child's contact with his "friend" to occasions when they both can be supervised. You might tell your son, "Tim is perfectly welcome here, but with his poor driving record, I cannot let you go anywhere with him." This is a logical reaction. It also leaves some room for change, should Tim decide to clean up his act.

■ **What about extreme cases, such as alcohol abuse or drug abuse?**

No way around it: You'll have to forbid your son or daughter to associate with his or her friend. Prepare for a great deal of sound and fury, but stand firm. Remind your child that you would rather be an object of contempt than grieve over a death from an alcohol-related car crash or drug overdose.

Agree with your teen that life isn't fair, and suggest that he or she pray for the friend. The friendships our adolescents make today often have long-reaching results. While we cannot control their choices, we can influence them, and that's worth a try.

This material is adapted from writings by Joan Wester Anderson of Prospect Heights, Illinois, and Faithful Parents, Faithful Kids *(Tyndale House) by Greg Johnson and Mike Yorkey.*

THE TOP TEN WORST WAYS TO SPEND TIME WITH YOUR TEENAGERS

10. Checking out the Fox TV network's fall lineup.

9. Staying awake in front of the TV set.

8. Sleeping in front of the TV set.

7. Trying to convince them that *your* music was much better than theirs.

6. Playing video games—and losing to them every time.

5. Letting them drag you to a movie that requires your presence in order for them to get in.

4. Bailing them out of jail.

3. Trying to influence their taste in fashion or hairstyles.

2. Driving them around town and getting only one-syllable responses to your comments and questions.

1. Nodding off while they tell you about their day.

36

How Not to Lose Your Teen

■ **My worst dreams are coming true. Oh, God, it hurts . . . I'm losing my teens and I don't know what to do. How in the world did it happen? Things seemed to have started right, and when my two children were born I thought I'd never have problems.**

As the years rolled by, they could be angels; other times I wondered if they were possessed by the devil! But I kept working at it. Then came the teen years. Why do I feel like disaster has befallen me?

During the teen years, many parents feel that they have lost the children they once felt close to. They can become strangers living in the same house. Problems include drug and alcohol abuse, depression, and one-way communication. Tragically, in extreme cases, teens can end up as runaways or suicide victims.

Below are five ways to *lose* the your teens, but if you can turn the negatives into positives, you'll keep them.

1. *You'll lose them if you don't know their world.*

In a popular television commercial for a major name-brand cereal, a man is concerned about his wife. He's talking to his daughter about the situation.

The mother has had a great burst of energy. She's competing in sports, as well as wearing clothes only teenagers would wear. Her husband can't understand how this could be. Then the daughter picks up a box of cereal. Could it be that Mom has eaten this cereal and reverted to being a *teenager?*

YOUR CHILDREN'S FRIENDS

Ever take a close look at your children's pals? You need to recognize the wrong kind of friends as a potential danger signal.

If the way their friends dress and act concern you, you may have a problem. It's easy for us to blame others for being a bad influence. Too often we think our own offspring can do no wrong. But they tend to gravitate toward like individuals.

What do you do if your children run with the wrong pack? Here are some suggestions to get them under the right influences:

▶ **Make sure they go to a Christian camp every summer.** This usually works because it changes behavior patterns. When young people go to camp, they're surrounded by Christian kids. If a good speaker is on board, everybody wants to follow his suggestions. Peer pressure is enormous, but this time the crowd is a Christian crowd acting in a Christian way.

At camp, young people get saved, filled with God's Holy Spirit, and learn to identify with the good kids—because being good is the "in" thing at camp.

Ask your pastor about the great church camps your denomination
continued next page

■ **So you're saying that if I don't wear short skirts, know the latest dance, or use the newest slang I'll lose them?**

Of course not, but you *do* have to understand where they're coming from. Life is different today. Tomorrow it will be even more so, and who knows what a year may bring? Do everything you can to understand the world your teens live in *today.*

Music changes. Styles change. As we both know, teens often seem to do the most ridiculous things imaginable, but it's their world. Try to understand it.

The Apostle Paul may not have raised teens, but he was right when he said in 1 Corinthians 9:22, "To the weak I became weak that I might win the weak. I have become all things to all men that I might by all means save some."

■ **What's the second point?**

Your teens are going through enormous physical and emotional changes. They've been thrust into a new world they don't understand. And they are frustrated. That frustration can boil over to disputes and little communication between teens and parents. That's why:

2. *You'll lose them if you lose patience with them.*

God knows about this problem. Hebrews 10:36 says, "For ye have need of patience." In fact, it is a fruit of the Spirit that He wants to develop in us (Gal. 5:22).

■ **I have a Japanese friend who gave me a wonderful definition of patience: "Peace under pressure." Is that what you mean?**

By all means. One way to develop that characteristic is to get your teen to read the Book of Proverbs. Since the thirty-one chapters neatly fit into a month, many parents encourage their teens to read the chapter corresponding to the day's date.

A word of caution. Before you encourage them to read the Scriptures, you'd better start yourself. Your advice probably won't take if you aren't reading God's Word either. But keep in mind that your youngsters won't always be teens. Later on, you'll laugh about some of the things you went through together.

One father recalls taking the family on a long driving vacation, and sometimes he'd lose patience with the kids' squabbling in the back seat. "Cut it out back there!" he'd command.

Now that his children are married and have their own fam-

provides. Some independent organizations, such as Camp Kanakuk-Kanakomo in Branson, Missouri, have camps with exciting sports programs, excellent music, and enthusiastic speakers. In this atmosphere, children are exposed to the Gospel, and God gets a chance to work in their lives.

Of course, going to camp isn't cheap. But don't let those costs stand in your way. Maybe you'll have to do without something else so your children can go. Maybe it will be something as simple as saving a little money each week during the year. But camp is a worthwhile investment.

Some churches have scholarships for those who can't afford camp. If the money is absolutely beyond your means, don't be embarrassed to ask your church leaders about available help.

► **Plan activities to counteract the "Saturday Night Syndrome."** Saturday night is still the big evening for young people. At school, they talk all week about "getting blasted" on Saturday night. It's party night.

Young people's activities at the church can counteract this. Or you can invite a group of young people to your home that evening. Or take them to a professional or collegiate sports activity.

continued next page

ilies, they recently told him they would make motions with their fingers, like scissors cutting, in response to his order to "cut it out."

Of course, he couldn't see that while he was driving, but he'd heard the kids giggling. They can laugh about it now, but back then it was serious business. You too will have times of laughing about things that bother you now.

■ **What's point number three?**

3. *You'll lose them if you're not cool.*

Don't try to be perfect. Sure, you feel it's important to show your best side as a parent. Still, you need to let your young people know the mistakes you've made.

And don't ever give them the line, "When I was a kid. . . . " We try to impress our kids by telling them about our own childhood. Things aren't that way anymore, and they can't identify with walking several miles to school or working sixteen hours a day when you were sixteen, or whatever.

They want to see the real you. Don't hide it.

■ **So you mean that if I'm encountering difficulties or experiencing failure, I should tell them what's going on?**

Yes, and have your teens pray for you at the same time. But it also refers to times when you

Another great idea is to open your home as a gathering place after a school sports activity, whether or not it's on Saturday night. Some young people have the idea that the thing to do is to go out and drink. Take the initiative by inviting them over to your house for a party. There, you'll have control over what happens.

One forward-looking church has a party for its youth after every major school sports event. It works just fine.

▶ **Be firm about those your children go with.**

Sometimes, it's necessary to sit down with your children and explain what kind of people they should select as friends. If they've selected someone you don't approve of, tell them why you don't approve.

Of course, you'll have to use discretion—and have valid reasons. In the process, be positive and suggest possible friends. Then offer to take them and those friends to an activity.

Breaking so-called friendships is difficult both for children and parents. Yet some will have to be broken. Ask God to give you wisdom to deal with this problem.

lose your temper and cut someone off on the road, or the time you said something unkind about the pastor. In those occasions, ask your teens' forgiveness. James said it right in James 5:16: "Confess your faults one to another." Do that, and you'll be cool in your teens' eyes.

■ **Sometimes, I feel so inadequate with my teens. All the time I'm saying to myself, They must think I'm the biggest fool. I once read that I should be a hero to my kids, but how can I do that?**

Keep this thought in mind: Hero worship is still in. What greater hero than you?

Holiness is a word teens care little about if they can't see it in your lives. Somehow, you've got to show them. What's your standard of holiness?

Unfortunately, even some Christians haven't answered this question in their own lives, so their teens have no idea what standard to maintain.

Perhaps when you grew up, women couldn't wear makeup, cut their hair short, or even wear slacks. You thought that was holiness. But it wasn't.

You should be talking about what happens on the inside. You may even ask your teens, "What's your idea of a *real* Christian?" You may be surprised at their answers. Rather than thinking a Christian is someone up on a pedestal, they probably would think of someone who is a "forgiven person," or someone who cares for others and thinks about what Jesus would do. Which brings us to point four:

4. *You'll lose them if you're not living the Christian life.*

■ **The encouraging of wickedness in our society can be overwhelming. How do we counteract it?**

Begin to share with your teens what the Bible teaches about holiness. Psalm 146:8 says, "The Lord loves the righteous." First Peter 3:12 states, "The eyes of the Lord are on the righteous." Matthew 5:6 says, "They that hunger and thirst after righteousness will be filled." Our life can be full if we have that desire.

Discuss with your teens what it is to live a righteous life. Ask them what they think. It may be a revelation to you.

■ **You mentioned five points about not losing your teens. What's the last one?**

Here it is:

5. *You'll lose them if you don't instill hope for the future.*

You've probably heard the illustration of a glass containing water. Some people look at it and say it's half full; others say it's half empty. That's what the future is to us.

Some well-meaning people are forecasting disaster. Earthquakes, famines, war—you name it. It's coming. Others recognize that these things *could* happen. But no matter what, Christ is going to be with us.

That second attitude is the one you must promote. Young people today are bombarded with the evidence of a difficult future. Their peers are killing themselves. Materialism is rampant. Drugs are everywhere. The AIDS epidemic is here. What next?

Instead of getting depressed about the future, get together with your teens and pray with them. They *do* have hope, so start emphasizing the positive aspects of life and minimizing the negatives. Be sure to remind them that they have much to live for.

If you think you've lost your teens—or are afraid you will—do yourself a favor. Have them read this chapter and ask them, "What do you think?" You may be surprised to find that things aren't as bad as you thought.

The material is adapted from writings by John Benton, president of the Walter Hoving Homes in Garrison, New York, and Pasadena, California.

37

Teens and Sexual Pressure

. . . .

■ **My teenage daughter has started dating a young man whom I don't trust. Should I say something to her?**

Yes, you should, but you also may want to say something to *him*. It's a good idea to pointedly, yet politely, interrogate your daughter's date.

This practice is both acceptable and advisable, especially with the phenomenon of date rape. One dad who took this approach would tell his daughter's date, "My daughter is a Christian and belongs to Jesus Christ who lives within her. To honor Him, she has decided to remain a virgin until marriage. She will not have sex before marriage. Do you have any problem with that?" Wouldn't you just love to have a videotape of a teenage boy hearing those words?

■ **What telltale signs can parents look for when their adolescent or teen is struggling with sexual desires?**

When a young person reaches puberty, it's safe to assume the struggle has begun. You can make a number of observations to try to determine the intensity of your child's struggle.

How does your son look at girls? Have you found pornographic magazines in your teen's possession? How does your daughter talk about boys? Does she emphasize only their looks and not their personalities? When with a member of the opposite sex, does your teen constantly need to be touching?

Answering these and comparable questions should help you gauge your teen's battle with sexual desires.

■ My teenage son says I have no right to go through his dresser drawers. I disagree.

Why not go through his mind rather than through his dresser? Ask him what he's doing, and spend enough time with him to see it first hand. Get close enough in the relationship so that you really do know what's going on. Then discuss some of the dangers that exist in our sex-saturated society.

■ What are some ways I can tell if my child is sexually active?

Sexual activity *does* affect a young person's behavior. The physical act unleashes a myriad of emotions and spiritual struggles. A young person who becomes sexually active will probably demonstrate guilt symptoms, which include an aversion to spiritual things and the desire to pull away from Mom and Dad. If your child won't look you in the eyes or turns her head whenever you address spiritual matters, you have to begin to suspect that something is wrong. Anything or anyone who reminds her that she is wrong will instigate a guilt response that often is seen in the form of anger.

Also keep in mind that sexual desires, when they are fed, tend to dominate a young person's mind. If a teen manipulates a parent to get alone with a boyfriend or a girlfriend, you should suspect sexual involvement.

■ I think I see some of those signs that my child is sexually involved. What should I do? We have not been close for some time.

Since you probably do not have an open and honest relationship with effective communication, anything you do at this point probably will not work and may even make matters worse. Where should you begin? By investing time with your child in a positive atmosphere. That way, you can "defrost" the frozen communication lines with relaxed and informal interaction. Do something fun together that he or she enjoys. Then begin to look for gestures that indicate your child's heart is opened to you.

Is there eye contact and spontaneous conversation and spiritual closeness and touching? Once these begin to surface, pray for the opportunity to ask about your child's sexual behavior.

You may discover in the course of rebuilding your relationship with your child that you have been negligent in communicating spiritual truth. Consider asking your child for forgiveness and expressing your desire to help him or her understand what God says about sex. Admit that there are a number of things you wish you had discussed years ago. But remind him or her that it's better late than never.

■ **While putting away my son's clean socks, I found a condom in his dresser. What can I do? He's only fourteen years old.**

Here are several steps you should take.

1. *Pray for wisdom and protection for yourself and for your son.* He is terribly young to be worrying about "safe sex."

2. *In a comfortable setting, when he would least expect it, ask him very directly, "Are you having sex with someone?"*

Observe his response to determine the truthfulness of his answer. If he is uncomfortable, no matter what he says, you had better assume the worst.

3. *If he is sexually involved, tell him that for his benefit you will take several steps to make sure that he stops.*

Have several steps in mind when you confront him:

▶ You may have to inform the girl's parents.
▶ You will probably have to restrict his social activity.
▶ You may have to consider a better school environment.
▶ You should get your youth pastor involved.
▶ You will have to increase the time you spend together in order to build up the relationship.
▶ You will have to teach him what God says about sex.

4. *If he is not sexually active, ask him why he needs a condom.* What does he have in mind anyway? Then proceed to discuss with him the fact that there is no "safe sex" and that there are incredible spiritual and physical dangers in premature intimacy.

■ **My young son is exhibiting some effeminate behavior, and I am getting more and more concerned as he gets older. What should I do?**

God designed men and women to function and act differently. He expects parents to cultivate a boy's maleness and a girl's femaleness. If by effeminate behavior you are referring to casual gestures and mannerisms, you can probably correct the behavior by constantly praising him for appropriate male gestures.

Accentuate his maleness, and if possible, ignore feminine mannerisms. If this doesn't work in a couple of months, you might want to seek professional counsel. The effeminate behavior you referred to may be far more serious. If your son only wants to play with girls, wear girls' clothes, and says he wishes he were a girl, then seek professional counsel immediately.

A BIBLICAL BLUEPRINT

A good summation of God's advice on sex can be found in 1 Thessalonians 4:1-8. Perhaps you should go through this passage of Scripture with your teen:

▶ Living a pure life pleases God (v. 1).
▶ God's will is that we avoid sexual immorality (v. 3).
▶ God wants us to learn how to control our bodies (v. 4).
▶ Our methods of controlling our desires must be holy and honorable (v. 4).
▶ How we control our bodies will differ from the methods of unbelievers (v. 5).
▶ Gratifying our sexual desires outside of marriage offends and detracts from the other person (v. 6).
▶ We should not take advantage of another person in order to satisfy our sexual desires (v. 6).
▶ These instructions come from God, not from man (v. 8).
▶ If we disobey these instructions, we reject God (v. 8).

■ **If we overprotect our children, won't they be overwhelmed when they finally go out into the world? I have heard of some children from Christian homes who go absolutely wild.**

Yes—if we protect our children from the negative moral influences of our world and fail to prepare them to enter this world, they may well go morally crazy.

Yes—if we protect our children and they grow up in a hostile home where they never have fun, some will go berserk when they leave.

Remember, the strategy is twofold: protection and preparation. Preparation includes explaining and exposing children to the world *under our direction*. Like the father in Proverbs 5, we describe the allurements of the world and the consequences of being trapped by them.

Granted, some young people will give themselves over to the world no matter what we do. It's their choice, and in some cases how they were raised won't matter.

■ What should I say to my daughter about bathing suits? What is modest these days?

Go to any beach or lakeshore in mid-July, and you would agree that modesty has been abandoned in our day. As for your daughter, finding an attractive and relatively modest suit won't be easy.

There are several important concepts to communicate to your daughter about a standard of modesty.

- ► Don't dishonor your body by flagrant exposure and inappropriate display. Make sure to read 1 Timothy 2:9-10 with her, which says, "I also want women to dress modestly, with decency and propriety, not with braided hair or gold or pearls or expensive clothes, but with good deeds, appropriate for women who profess to worship God."
- ► Pursue inner beauty over outward adornment (1 Peter 3:3-4).
- ► Don't wrong others by tempting them with your actions or dress (1 Thes. 4:6).

A great way to impress these principles on your daughter is to point out girls who are obviously selling their sexuality. Your daughter should be able to sense that a girl who flaunts her body also cheapens herself.

■ My husband and I didn't become Christians until our children were entering their teens. How can we begin to undo mistakes we made in the past?

If your children see Jesus Christ revolutionize your lives, it will be a catalyst to change their lives no matter what they have previously learned. Let them see supernatural change in you, your marriage, and the way you relate to them.

Then, explain to your children you would love to go back and raise them according to your newfound faith, but you can't. So the best thing you can do is start now and teach them about Jesus Christ and God's Word.

Don't apologize or continue to express your regrets over the past. Just let your enthusiasm make up for lost time.

■ **My husband is not a Christian and refuses to talk to our teens about sex. In fact, his attitude toward sex is so lousy I'm afraid of what he might tell them. What should I do?**

Why not use some of the ideas in this book to talk to your husband about sex? It may be a great way to get his attention and might show him the practicality and relevancy of the Bible. You might also read to him the Song of Songs and explain that it's an account of marital love. Some of the more explicit portions of the Song of Songs may motivate him to read the entire Bible. While attempting to cultivate your husband's understanding, take the initiative to talk with your children. Try not to discredit Dad. Make sure that if your children sense a disagreement, they see that it is between Dad and God, not Dad and Mom.

■ **The Bible forbids fornication, but it doesn't seem to forbid any sexual relations up to a point (necking, petting, etc.). What is the biblical basis for saying no to *all* sexual activity before marriage?**

Let's simply list several biblical principles and directives:

1. We are to flee—not fight—the "evil desires of youth" (2 Tim. 2:22).
2. We are to "flee from sexual immorality" (1 Cor. 6:18).
3. Lust is sin (Matt. 5:28).
4. Necking and petting are not "holy and honorable" ways to control your own body (1 Thes. 4:4).

There are practical benefits to obeying these scriptural admonitions. Tell your teen if he refrains from arousing himself by necking and petting, he will be a lot less frustrated and will consequently find it easier to control his sexual desires. Why pour gasoline on a fire that he doesn't want to burn out of control?

This material is adapted from What You Need to Tell Your Children About Sex *(Thomas Nelson) by John Nieder.*

38

Dating, No . . . Courtship, Yes

■ **We have two children in their early teens, and they are wondering if they will be allowed to date when they turn sixteen. My wife and I know all too well the pitfalls of teen dating, which range from broken hearts all the way to premarital sex. Some friends at church said they're trying a concept called "courtship." I've never heard of it. Is courtship some old Victorian thing where the young couple sits on a porch swing and talk to each other—within earshot of the parents? What is courtship all about?**

Courtship can mean different things in different circles, but for many families, it means that if a young man wants to date one of our daughters, he must contact the father first and ask to take the daughter out. (Of course, the mother can take this role in families where the father is not available.)

At this very first meeting or phone call, the father explains that the family believes in courtship, which means that the young man must be spiritually and financially prepared to marry her if they fall in love. Otherwise, don't even bother starting a relationship. There are no casual "tryouts" in courtship. (As for our sons, they know they must meet the same guidelines before they can begin courting a young woman.)

Since courtship is reserved only for young couples spiritually and financially ready for marriage, this effectively means no courtship or dating during the high school years, and perhaps not until after college graduation.

■ **Wow, that's pretty heavy. The advice we've received from Christian friends is to allow our children to date once they reached their sixteenth birthday. Can courtship work in the 1990s?**

Before you dismiss the idea as impractical, outmoded, or just plain weird, take some time to weigh the benefits of courtship against the drawbacks of dating.

Parents who believe in courtship say it has physical, emotional, and spiritual safeguards over dating. For starters, dating can be a setup for divorce. The current thinking goes like this: *If I like this guy (or girl), I'll go out with him a few times. If it doesn't work out, we can always break up.* It simply does not make sense to train for a *long-term* marriage by pursuing a series of *short-term* relationships.

Even in a lasting marriage, the baggage left over from previous dating relationships can be frustrating and painful. As Christian parents, we talk a lot about sexual abstinence, but what we forget is the need for *emotional* abstinence.

■ **So you're saying that dating, by its very nature, opens the door to heartache and disappointment.**

Yes, it does. Courtship, on the other hand, is a process by which young people can get to know and enjoy one another while maintaining their physical and emotional integrity.

■ **What are some of the practical benefits to courtship?**

For one thing, bringing Dad into the picture takes the responsibility for saying yes or no to a relatiooship off a daughter's shoulders. If one of your daughters is now interested in a young man, you (the father) can break the news gently without damaging their friendship or the young man's walk with Christ.

Perhaps the biggest benefit of courtship is that it also allows the family to better understand the person interested in one of your children. Dating waves good-bye at the door and says, "Be home by midnight," whereas courtship includes time spent with the entire family. In your home, a young man interested in one of your daughters might find himself playing basketball with your sons, or helping out in the kitchen after dinner.

■ How does courtship work?

While the benefits of courtship are intriguing, folks may balk at changing the way they've looked at relationship building between the sexes. Dating, as it has evolved in the twentieth century, is readily accepted and understood. It seems "normal," but is it?

Courtship, on the other hand, introduces a different set of guidelines and behavior patterns. If a young man is interested in a young woman, he starts by praying about the relationship. With a go-ahead from his parents and the Lord, he then approaches the girl's parents. The parents pray and, if the young woman has a reciprocal interest in the young man, her father talks through courtship and its expectations with the fellow.

Before a young man and woman actually begin courting, the girl's father and the interested fellow spend time getting to know one another, as discussed in the previous question. This relationship may be built through shared activities or—in cases where the two do not live near one another—through letters and telephone calls.

■ What's the next step for the young couple?

Courtship activities may include a family missions trip, prison ministry, or similar service-oriented endeavors. The idea is to give the young couple an opportunity to spiritually mature as they fulfill God's call on their lives. Other activities—from family games to neighborhood walks—can shape and reveal a person's character, responsibility, and resourcefulness. By allowing for this practical and productive time together, courtship enables a young couple to look beyond physical attraction to focusing on things that are truly important.

■ How "together" should the young adults be before entering into courtship?

Each person should demonstrate spiritual depth, a strong biblical character, financial responsibility, sexual and emotional purity, and the ability to lead a simple, practical lives.

■ **What about families who have tried courtship. What experiences have they had?**

Jim and Anne Ryun (he's the former Olympic runner and world record holder in the mile) have four children in their early twenties, and their decision to try courtship grew partly out of personal experience; as teenagers, they had encountered some of the drawbacks and dangers of dating. When Anne dated, her heart became emotionally tied to her steady, which created wounds of rejection that lasted for years. She and her husband wanted something better for their children.

At just about the same time, their twin sons, Ned and Drew, had turned sixteen, and they began closely observing the dating scene at their school. When they saw the broken hearts and hurt feelings following the latest school breakup, they believed there had to be a better way to protect their emotions while learning to be friends with the opposite sex.

The boys prayed long and hard about the situation. Finally, with Ned leading the way, he decided he would not date until he met the girl he thought he would marry—and then only when he was prepared to support her.

That incident happened nearly six years ago. Since then, the Ryuns have continued to practice courtship and they have seen some very encouraging results, including their children's desire to be available to the Lord.

WANT TO LEARN MORE ABOUT COURTSHIP?

The Courtship Connection has books, videos, and cassettes about courtship. Contact:

The Courtship Connection
3731 Cecelia
Toledo, OH 43608
(419) 729-4594

■ **Have the Ryuns experienced any challenges?**

Yes, they have, like the time one of their children became seriously interested in a person who, they later realized, was not the right choice in God's eyes.

Another time, their daughter Heather, who was a college student at the time, was asked to go out by a fellow student. Heather hesitated. Although she knew the young man standing before her in the college student union, she wouldn't accept his offer—at least not yet. Instead, his inquiry needed to be directed to her father. Would the young man be offended or think she was some kind of weirdo?

Heather mustered her resolve. "Well," she said, "I would really prefer that you talked with my dad first."

Then, without giving the fellow a chance to respond, Heather made a beeline for her dormitory. *I'm never going to hear from this guy again,* she thought. *In fact, I'm going to be the laughingstock of the campus.*

The young man did call Jim Ryun, and after he heard Jim's explanation of courtship, he decided not to pursue the relationship. But that was all right.

■ **Are any of the Ryun children married?**

So far, none of the children (ages twenty through twenty-five) are married, but they aren't worried, since they know God has a plan for their lives. The Ryuns also know plenty of families where courtship has been successful.

But like so many things that they've tried or experienced as a family, courtship has brought them together in laughter and in tears, and it's encouraged them to pray. The Ryuns pray for their family as a whole, for each individual family member, and for each of their children's prospective spouses, as God prepares them for marriage.

This material is adapted from It's a Lifestyle *by Jim and Anne Ryun. If you'd like to contact the Ryuns with any questions about courtship, write them at Rt. 3, Box 62B, Lawrence, KS 66044.*

7

All About
Mothers

39

A Pitch for Mothers

····································

■ **For more than two decades, mothering has been devalued in America. It has even become a status symbol for the modern woman to take as little time as possible away from work for full-time mothering. I know a first-time mother down the street who spoke with pride about delivering her baby on Tuesday and being back in the office the following Friday. Others are taking a few months off before returning to their careers. How can any mother create a sense of home for her baby in a few short weeks or months?**

Not very well, which is why a huge number of mothers are staying home by choice, providing their children with continuous presence and love. These mothers are home because they know that they, and not a child-care provider, can best nurture their children and give them a sense of home. They know children thrive in their mother's presence and suffer from her prolonged, daily absences.

The pendulum is beginning to swing again. As we move toward the next century, the ranks of mothers at home are swelling. Not only are countless women quietly at home nurturing their children, developing their gifts, and forging their intimate connections, but others who have spent years in the work force are listening to the logic of the heart.

Is mother at home today?

Yes, increasingly.

It *is* possible (as millions of families prove each and every day) for a mother to stay home to care for her family—even at a great financial sacrifice. With a voice that's beginning to be heard, men and women across this land are reaffirming the value of home and their ultimate human connections.

The home, recently viewed by some as a prison, is now being seen as a refuge for family members, as well as a necessary school for life. Increasingly, child development experts are saying what many mothers and fathers have known all along—that to be fully human a child needs to be intensely loved and cared for by someone who won't "pack up and leave at 5 o'clock." That someone is the child's mother.

MOTHERING MAKES A DIFFERENCE IN THE WORLD
by Elisa Morgan and Carol Kuykendall

At MOPS (or Moms of Preschoolers, an organization started in 1973), we're fond of the motto that mothering matters . . . because "today makes a difference tomorrow." We would be wise to transfer this truth to our mothering. Child expert and author Jeanne Hendricks warned in a speech at a MOPS convention that moms are more concerned about making a better world for their children than they are about making better children for their world.

Mothering matters not only to the child and to the mother, but also to the world in which they live. In fact, Leo Tolstoy in *The Lion and the Honeycomb* writes, "Yes, women, mothers, in your hands more than in those of anyone else lies the salvation of the world."

■ **Over the years, it seems some of our common sense for mothering has been lost. Why is that?**

Maybe it's because so many young mothers no longer enjoy the proximity of extended family, where skills and insight are passed from older moms to younger ones. Maybe it's because before we have kids, we think that knowing how to be a good mother and having the right answers just come naturally. But we soon learn better.

A *lot* is expected of moms today. Well-adjusted kids don't just happen. Developing their hearts and spirits must be the main thing, the central focus of our efforts. As the German proverb says, "The main thing is to make the main thing always remain the main thing."

Well-adjusted kids come from

families in which mothering is seen as a complex, beautiful challenge worthy of everything Mom can give to it. Mothering shapes lives and attitudes, one way or another.

■ **As a mother of a four-month-old daughter, my parental leave is about to end. I'm torn with what to do. I don't want my daughter to be in day care, but I don't want to lose my career, either. I still have college loans to pay.**

The truth is, motherhood can't be discounted. That's why it's disconcerting to see more moms fitting work outside the home into their schedules and having to deal with the issue of child care.

We're stepping into dangerous territory by talking about child care. Whenever Focus on the Family airs a broadcast or publishes an article about working mothers, regardless of what they say, they get critical letters from both sides of the issue.

Moms who work outside the home write, "Why are you trying to make us feel more guilty?" Stay-at-home moms write, "Why are you downplaying the importance of what we do?" It seems to be a real Catch-22 subject.

Nonetheless, because you love your children deeply and want to be the best mom you can possibly be, and because we want to help you toward that goal, we're going to venture boldly into this arena and say what we believe with all our heart.

We know there are many moms who have children still at home and who truly have no choice but to work outside the home. For them, it isn't just a matter of wanting to maintain a certain lifestyle. Even in those cases, however, as in all others, a mother's care is the preferred choice. We don't say that to make anyone feel guilty; it's just a fact.

If you must put your children in day care, do everything in your power to make sure that the situation is the best you can find for each child.

■ **My name is Kendall, and I'm a young woman who has worked at a day-care center for the past three years. This job has given me a stark view of where families, especially women, are headed. Motherhood is no longer valued, and it is seen more as a mark of prestige than as the precious gift it truly is. The little girls in our** day care are growing up playing office, banker, and travel agent while they take their baby dolls to a day-care center or sitter. Not all mothers who bring their children to day care are bad mothers. But I see a lot of tired women who don't have any patience at the end of the day. I see too many of them whisk their kids off to another babysitter for the evening while they take care of themselves.

We've heard other day-care workers echo your story. They say that little girls don't play house, that they never cook a meal; they microwave everything. The little girls never nurture their dolls. They just put them in a crib and have their friends take care of them. These little girls all want to be like boys. They're very competitive, but they're not at all nurturing.

■ **Kendall's story makes me shudder. But what does the scientific research say?**

You'll shudder more when you read what researchers are discovering as they study children placed in child care at early ages. This research doesn't point fingers at the abilities or intentions of child-care providers. Instead, it points fingers at the effects of parental absence. No matter how great the caregiver, the parent is needed most.

Brenda Hunter, writing in *Home by Choice*, said, "Babies need their mothers. They need them during their earliest years, more

WHAT IN THE WORLD DOES A MOM DO ALL DAY?

Being a mom is a job with a capital J. We work our fingers to the bone, push our nerves to the edge, and use every skill possible to accomplish the demands of the day.

Just what does a mother do all day? Today's college student can't imagine. Numbers of women are baffled by what they'd do with "all that time" if they had to be home. Sometimes Mom herself can't remember.

Well, what am I? I'm the following:

► baby feeder, changer, bather, rocker, burper, hugger, and listener to crying and fussing and thousands of questions
► picker-upper of food and debris cast on the floor
► problem solver, determiner of action, and the one who gives those talks to whomever needs them
► phone messenger
► comforter, encourager, counselor
► hygienist
► linguistic expert for two-year-old dialects
► trainer of baby-sitters
► listener—for the husband as well

continued next page

than they need baby-sitters, toys, or the material comforts a second income will buy. The evidence since 1980 indicates that when a baby is placed in substitute care, even good quality care such as with a nanny, for twenty or more hours a week during his first year of life, he is at risk psychologically. If a mother returns to work during her baby's first year, there's a significant chance the child will be insecurely attached to its mother and/or father."

Freud describes the relationship of a young child to his mother as "unique, without parallel, established unalterably for a whole lifetime as the first and strongest love object and as the prototype of all later love relationships for both sexes."

If that relationship is interrupted by child care substituted for the mother, the impact is immense. British psychiatrist John Bowlby states, "The young child's hunger for his mother's love and presence is as great as his hunger for food. Her absence inevitably generates a powerful sense of loss and anger." Young children desperately need the emotional accessibility of a parent. That stability forms the foundation for all relationships to come.

■ **Has any expert changed his or her mind after studying some of this research?**

Yes. The psychologist sounding the alarm today about maternal employment and infant day care is Jay Belsky, professor of human development at Penn

as the children—about their day, their needs, their concerns, their aspirations
► teacher of everything from how to chew food to how to drive a car
► assistant on school projects
► questioner, prober to promote thinking
► censor of TV, movies, and books
► reader of thousands of children's books
► planner and hostess of children's birthday parties
► planner and hostess of adult dinner parties
► short-order cook for meals budding athletes depend on
► central control for getting the appliance fixed or the carpet shampooed
► executioner of ants, roaches, wasps, and other pests
► resident historian in charge of photo albums, baby books, and school record books
► resident encyclopedia source for all those hard questions
► defroster of the freezer
► food preservation expert
► family secretary, confirming dinner reservations, travel, and accommodations
► keeper and locator of birth certificates and other valuable documents

continued next page

State University. But this was not always the case. Belsky said in 1977 that he found little evidence of any negative effects of infant day care. In fact, when Belsky and his colleague reviewed the material again in 1980, he concluded that "infant day care need not disrupt the child's emotional development."

Belsky has since changed his mind. Based on research since 1980, Belsky has said that placing a baby in day care during his first year may erode his sense of trust and order in the world. This may also lead to later personality maladjustment.

Belsky wrote in *Zero to Three*, "Children who initiated care in the first year . . . seemed at risk not only for insecurity but for heightened aggression, noncompliance, and possibly social withdrawal in the preschool and early school years."

Also on this side of the debate is John Bowlby, the psychiatrist mentioned earlier, who has twice received the American Psychiatric Association's highest award. One time, a young female physician, holding a sleeping infant in her arms, asked Bowlby when she could safely go back to work.

Bowlby did not equivocate in his answer: "I don't recommend at all that a mother return to work during the baby's first year. What's important is what's optimal for the child, not what the mother can get away with."

■ **I've heard child-care advo-**

- ▶ ironer of wrinkles
- ▶ appointment desk for the family's visits to the doctor, the dentist, the orthodontist, the barber, and the mechanic
- ▶ one who prays
- ▶ cleaner of the oven, the drawers, the closets, the garage, the curtains, the bedding, the windows, and even the walls
- ▶ refinisher of furniture
- ▶ emergency medical technician and "ambulance" driver
- ▶ hubby's romantic, attentive spouse
- ▶ enjoyer of those moments when nothing is happening, no one is calling, nothing demands attention

And what are some things I do? Well, among many others, the following:

- ▶ clip ten fingernails and ten toenails for each young child regularly
- ▶ return library books
- ▶ get film developed
- ▶ choose gifts, purchase gifts, wrap gifts for birthdays, Christmas, Father's Day, Mother's Day, wedding showers, baby showers, and anniversaries
- ▶ mail packages, buy stamps
- ▶ drop off the dry cleaning; pick up the dry cleaning

continued next page

cates say that a child naturally establishes strong bonds with a caregiver. What about that?

That isn't something necessarily good for the child. Author Richard Strauss wrote, "A child's mind is like a videotape recorder, carefully transcribing every word, right down to the tone of voice and facial expressions. And all of it contributes to the person he will become. Some psychologists say his emotional pattern is set by the time he is two years old."

Whom will your child pattern himself after? Whom will he see when he wakes? When he experiences the rushes of good feelings from being fed, changed, or bathed, who will be indelibly etched in his mind, you or a caregiver?

You're going to have to figure that others just don't have the deep concern for your children that you do. No one else is ready to make the sacrifices, to take the time to nurture and encourage as you are. So who could better care for your child, especially during his first years when he is so impressionable and easily molded?

Many people can carefully attend to your young child. Many people can provide quality food and supervision. But that doesn't ensure the emotional health, stability, or well-being of your little one. Mom, your child's identity will be indelibly stamped with the identity of the significant caregiver. His security and self-

- ► have pictures framed
- ► haul everything that needs repair
- ► attend recitals
- ► attend every school sporting event imaginable
- ► chauffeur everyone everywhere
- ► cover for my sick son on his 4 A.M. paper route
- ► comb a little girl's hairdo
- ► help in the classroom
- ► attend school PTA meetings and conferences
- ► act as a room mother, making things and organizing parties
- ► chaperone field trips and special events
- ► coordinate car pools (it makes men shudder)
- ► lead Scouts, Blue Birds, and a Sunday School class
- ► purchase most everything for the family and the home
- ► deliver forgotten lunches, forgotten homework, and forgotten athletic gear
- ► make bank deposits and withdrawals
- ► attend church, Bible studies, committee meetings, showers, weddings, choir practices, board meetings, potlucks, and neighborhood meetings just to "stay active and informed."

esteem will be permanently affected by his setting, especially if he has to establish himself in a crowd of other little folks all clamoring for attention, recognition, and regard.

You must look deeper than good food and supervision when you determine for yourself, "What is quality child care?"

■ **OK, I see your point on child care, but I *have* to work part time to help the family pay its bills. What are some practical guidelines you can give me?**

The bottom line is this: If you *have* to use child care, use it as a supplement to your nurturing, not a substitute. Treat your search for care with as much thoroughness as you would use in searching for the best heart surgeon. Use the following three guidelines in conducting your search.

First, **look for a home atmosphere,** with only one or two other children present, rather than a large-group setting such as a franchised day-care center. There's just no way kids can get the individualized attention they need in the large-group situation. The ideal situation might be to find someone who can come to your home and give your children the most secure environment of all.

Second, **do a thorough exam-**

TEN THINGS TODDLERS WISH THEY COULD TELL YOU

1. Walk in my small shoes.
A sad sight at shopping centers and grocery stores is a hurried mother carrying a baby and half-dragging a toddler whose chubby little legs must run to keep up. If you're shopping with toddlers in tow, slow down. You should also take a stroller that will permit your toddler to ride when little legs tire.

2. My attention span is limited.
Sure, it's fun to meet and greet neighbors in supermarket aisles, but your toddlers aren't interested in catching up on all the latest news. They'd rather wander, explore, touch. Instead of spending fifteen minutes chatting next to the Oreos and Ding-Dongs, promise to call your friend when you get home.

3. I'm afraid of strangers.
Few children appreciate being passed from lap to lap. Most prefer getting to know new people a little at a time—and on their terms. Be wary of forcing your toddler to accept strangers and new baby-sitters immediately.

4. I'm not a pet or a trained seal.
"Come on, Honey, say `Aunt Kathie.'"

continued next page

ination of all potential caregivers. Interview them closely, ask for references, and question all the references as well. It's not a bad idea to ask local churches for recommendations, but that's not foolproof, either. Examine those people as carefully as any others. And only consider people with a proven record of positive experiences.

Finally, look for caregiving situations that will allow you to **maximize your own involvement with your children.** Perhaps you can trade baby-sitting with a friend. Or you might find a job-sharing arrangement or a part-time position that meets your financial needs but doesn't require you to leave your children with someone else a full eight hours a day. Also explore the possibility of a home-based business if you have skills that can be used that way, such as word processing or craft making.

Mom, you have a unique place in your child's life, and you will make a unique impact—one way or the other. Make it the best that's within your power to give.

■ **My sister-in-law, Pam, just gave birth last week to a child. When Pam was asked if she planned to return to work, she replied, "Oh, yes," with enthusiasm, as she cradled her ten-day-old son in her arms. "I can't leave my job for long. My**

"Show Mrs. Dennis how you play pat-a-cake, Josh."
"Sing that little song you learned at church for Grandma."

These and other performance-on-demand statements place your toddler in a tough spot. Some small children delight in showing off. Others shrink away, risking a reprimand. If your child falls in the latter group, don't push it.

5. Don't be embarrassed if or when I don't respond the way you hope I will.

There is no need to apologize for your baby or small children if they:
► cry when someone new picks them up
► hide behind you during introductions
► refuse to sit on Grandpa's lap when he hasn't visited in a long time.

They aren't terrible kids. They're shy, frightened, and unsure of themselves in new situations. Too many parents feel an unresponsive toddler reflects unfavorably on them, and they react accordingly.

6. Please don't compare me with others.

Every baby and child is unique. Some learn to walk and say a few words before they are one. Others take longer. So what? Toddler development isn't a race, although to hear some parents, it appears to be.

continued next page

boss wouldn't like it. Anyway, I've only been with this firm for six months, so I can't take much time off. Besides, I've decided to put Eric in day care when he's three weeks old. I want him to be adequately socialized, so I'm planning to expose him to other children as soon as possible." Can you explain what's going on?

Pam believes her baby needs to be socialized through contacts with other adults and children. What she does not know is that during his first year, her son needs a close, continuous, and intimate relationship with his mother far more than the company of others.

For instance, child development experts who study mother-infant interaction know about the importance of the "dance," a metaphor for the dialogue that ensues between babies and their mothers.

According to child psychologist and author Evelyn Thomas, the baby's "dance"—which is actually communication at its most basic—comprises rhythmic arm movements, eye shifts, head tilts, coos, cries, fusses, gazes, and dozens of other behaviors. As a mother and baby engage in the "dance," the baby is establishing his first vital human connections. Over the first year of life, but particular-

7. I can't like everything you think I should.

Forcing toddlers to eat foods they actively dislike, or to force their interests in a specific way, can develop into bigger problems later. If your toddler doesn't care for a certain vegetable, choose another.

8. Handle me with care.

Toddlers may look sturdy, but they are still fragile. Overdone roughhousing, tossing babies in the air, and jerking little arms and legs can damage young, growing bodies.

9. Let me be my own age.

Some toddlers behave so well on occasion that parents forget they aren't little women and little men. Remember, toddlers are just past babyhood, and they must not be expected to respond like miniature adults. Enjoy them fully at ages two, three, and four. Soon you'll wave your kindergartner off in the mornings, and only memories of their toddler days will remain.

10. Be sure to tell me about Jesus.

Small children are wide open to learning about Jesus in the preschool years, and the Lord recognized this in Luke 10:15: "I tell you the truth, anyone who will not receive the kingdom of God like a little child will never enter it."

Create a godly home where you talk often about the Lord, and all who dwell within will be blessed.

ly between six and twelve months of age, every baby attempts to forge intimate bonds or attachment relationships with his mother first, then with his father. Bringing other children into the picture is counter-productive at that age.

■ **Why is that?**

Child development experts indicate that children do not engage in peer play until they are about two years old. Babies need their mothers.

■ **I once heard a famous child psychologist say with absolutely no conviction that babies need to be cared for by their mothers, but it was evident that he was pained to go that far. When asked why, the expert stammered, "Well, mothers who work feel so guilty."**

A lot of the experts want to shun controversy, although you will find folks who are outspoken proponents of day care, such as psychologist Sandra Scarr, the author of *Mother Care/Other Care*.

Dr. Scarr, herself an employed mother, believes children do not necessarily need to be cared for by their mothers at home. She writes that "day care can actually be good for children." She believes that "today's child," while sensitive to his environment, is nonetheless "resilient." Dr. Scarr suggests that bad experiences can readily be overcome by good experiences: "Today's child is not a china doll who breaks under the first environmental blow. Rather, our child is a tougher plastic doll; she resists breaking and recovers her shape, but she can be dented by later blows."

Although Dr. Scarr is an advocate for children's resiliency, she did write about an unsettling experience involving her third child, Rebecca. Dr. Scarr, who employed baby-sitters because of her irregular hours and extensive travel as a university professor, returned home one day to find her eighteen-month-old crying. Her daughter simply said, "Kathy hit me! Kathy hit me!"

Dr. Scarr found large, red welts on her daughter's body. "The sitter had beaten her badly," she said.

After she called the police and registered her complaint, Dr. Scarr learned this same baby-sitter had physically abused other children whose parents had filed complaints. But because no adult witnessed the abuse and could testify, the police told her they were unable to prosecute. Dr. Scarr writes with obvious frustration, "No one was there to prevent the abuse or to testify about it." The irony in her comment should not go unnoticed.

It is to prevent just this situation that many full-time mothers stay home with their very young children. They feel it is not always possible to effectively screen every sitter, and they don't want to pick up the pieces once abuse occurs.

■ **I'm staying home with my newborn. Can you give me any more encouragement that will keep me going through these sleep-deprived days?**

We are only home for a season. Since our time at home is short, let us make the most of the summer. Then with positive memories we can embrace more fully the world beyond our doorstep. We can dance into a winter of rich reward, rather than shuffle into a season of regret.

As parents, we invariably give our children a legacy of memories: A *sense of home or a deep, abiding feeling of homelessness.* It is only as we consider our children's well-being a high priority—and are willing to make the essential sacrifices—that we will give them a rich legacy of memories to treasure throughout their lives. In the process, we will not only strengthen society, but we will affect future generations as well.

■ **For the first nine years of my life, Mom stayed home. Those days felt so good, I knew Mom would be there when I needed her. But when I was ten, she went to work full time. Because I wanted to be her helper, I took on the role of being the mom myself. I cleaned the house, made dinner, and told my brother and sister what to do. When Mom came home tired, I tried to make things pleasant for her. Her praise was my reward.**

I think it's good for kids to help, but if Mom hadn't worked, maybe I would have played more with friends my age, doing what kids do. And maybe I would have learned that my significance should be based on who I am, not what I do.

Your mom started well. She just turned from nurturing to working outside the home too soon and forgot about giving attention to her children's special needs. Doing so has had lasting effects. Working wasn't the problem; her becoming sidetracked without realizing it was. And sometimes when we veer off course, it derails others as well. But we may not see the result until we look in the rearview mirror of time after it's too late.

Here's an example. Let's say you grew up near an apple orchard in central Washington, and learned that nurturing is a process. You don't plant an orchard and then say, "Mission accomplished, time to relax." And you don't raise confident kids that way, either.

It's hard to wait for results. But that's the way apple-growing and child-rearing works. It takes patience and diligence. If the formula doesn't have both time and attention, properly balanced nurturing doesn't happen.

To all the moms reading this: No investment you make in life will yield the returns you'll get from nurturing your children. So enjoy your role of protecting, feeding, encouraging, strengthening, and establishing these little ones. You'll never regret it!

40

Moms Getting Organized

■ **I've never been an orderly, follow-through type person. Growing up, I used to procrastinate when Mom asked me to straighten up around the house. I could never keep appointments because I could never get organized to know what I was doing. As a young mother, I need help!**

Recognizing that you have a problem getting organized is a great start. Resolving to manage your time better is difficult for busy moms, but if you can get a handle on it, you'll be the wife and mother you've always wanted to be.

The place to start is with a calendar planner. Diane Synder, a Wichita, Kansas mother, looked around for a calendar planner that would work for moms. Some were too complicated for her, she says. She needed a planner that would keep her on track but not overwhelm her.

After two years of experimenting with various ways to best organize her days, she designed a calendar called "The Fruit of Her Hands." If you're looking to get a handle on your time, here are some of Diane's suggestions:

> ► *Focus and prioritize.* This is most important in efficient
> time management—and effective Christian living. Spend

some time alone with God, prayerfully asking Him to show you talents He's given you, areas He's called you to serve Him. Jot down what He reveals. These subjects will be your highest priorities.

▶ *Plan ahead.* Remember, "Those who fail to plan, plan to fail." With your priorities in mind, schedule your days as far ahead as possible. But do leave room for the unexpected.

▶ *Learn to delegate.* Could someone else do this task as well, or as reasonably close, as you do?

▶ *Make choices.* You can't fit everything in. Making wise choices with our time means eliminating the unnecessary and choosing the best.

▶ *A guaranteed time-saver: Just say no!* This technique, along with prioritizing and focusing one's life, can solve 75 percent of our time problems. In our society, demands and requests bombard us from all sides.

■ **Boy, isn't that the truth. It always seems like I'm being asked to help out at school or do something for the Junior League.**

Those are noble things, but when you're volunteering *too much* time, you're costing your family. Refusing to take on those things that do not fit your goals or benefit your family is an art to be learned. These lessons are not easy because we don't like displeasing others.

Certainly, people don't enjoy

WHAT SHOULD A GOOD CALENDAR PLANNER HAVE?

The "Fruit of Her Hands" calendar planner has the following items:

▶ Scripture verses to encourage and uplift

▶ A self-check system to rate your effort that day and help develop good habits

▶ A place for planning special events, birthdays, anniversaries, and holidays

▶ A reminder section for doing household chores

▶ Listing of addresses and phone numbers

▶ Pages to write down gift ideas when they come to mind (important if you do your Christmas shopping months in advance in order to save money)

▶ A place to write personal notes, such as menu ideas, special thoughts, or spiritual insights being turned down, but with your new organizational spirit, you'll have time to fit them into your schedule, right?

This material is adaped from "Fruit of Her Hands" by Diane Synder of Wichita, Kansas.

41

When Mom Is a Perfectionist

. . . .

■ **Our home is a showcase. The furnishings, the decor—even the *Architectural Digest* magazines fanned out on the coffee table—are perfect. The drapes are hung without the slightest sag. Each picture is placed at the same height, to the exact millimeter. Even our pantry is alphabetized.**

Nothing is irregular in our house—except perhaps my wife's perfectionism. She constantly drives herself and our children to maintain an immaculate home. But I've noticed that the kids have difficulty relaxing and enjoying our beautiful surroundings. Rarely do they bring friends over a second time. I'm beginning to wonder if something is not right.

It's obvious that your wife pays meticulous attention to details; she is precise in everything she does. But is it ever enough? Does she always feel her home and her children continually fall short of the mark? What happens when you or guests shower her with compliments? Does she smile and think, *Yes, that's nice, but could it be better?*

Unfortunately, the amount of time your wife spends maintaining a showcase home is far out of proportion to the result. As a perfectionist, her standards are too high—impossibly high. And it's likely her parents' standards were just as lofty, programming her to accept nothing less than perfection. Now she is passing this malady on to *your* children as well.

■ **That's why I'm deeply concerned. Why is my wife hung up on having everything perfect?**

Perfectionism is a thief. It promises rewards but steals joy and satisfaction. In your wife's mind, an old and worn tape plays the same refrain over and over: *You're not good enough. Try harder. Don't make a mistake.* She is on a treadmill that will never stop.

When we demand perfection of ourselves, we assign our life to a set of rules. These often come in the form of "I must," "I should," and "I ought." Do any of these sound familiar? From the minute we are born, we are surrounded by advice, warnings, cautions, and directives.

But some of the urgent *shoulds* we hear in our childhood later grow into an unreasonable drive for perfection. The need to be perfect brings with it a strange companion—a high sensitivity to failure. The fear of failure—or even doing less than our best—is much more acute for the perfectionist because of the height of personal standards. The greater the distance between performance and standards, the higher the degree of pain.

In order to prove that they are good enough, many mothers strive to do the impossible. They set pie-in-the-sky goals for themselves and their children, and they see no reason why they shouldn't achieve them. But they are soon overwhelmed by the arduous task. Their standards are so high that *no one* could consistently attain them.

Besides, perfectionism is not all it's supposed to be. If you're "perfect," you have no opportunity to grow and very few people you can turn to. Raising healthy children includes letting them know you are human. If you believe you must be the perfect parent, you'll end up with doubt and loneliness. It's likely you'll be alienated from your children and frustrated that no one—not even yourself—will ever live up to your expectations.

■ **What are some of the unspoken rules that create tremendous stress for perfectionists?**

Here are some of the most common:

- ► *I must never make a mistake.*
- ► *I must never fail.*
- ► *I must play it safe so I always succeed.*
- ► *My children must be perfect, too, or I'll look bad.*

These rules come from deeply held beliefs. If change is to take place, they must be repeatedly challenged.

■ **But I've always been told that I "must always do my best." Are you saying that's an unhealthy attitude?**

A healthy revision would be "I prefer to do my best, but I don't *have* to be perfect. I feel better when I do my best, but I can learn to get along when I don't."

Another rule to challenge is this: "I must never make a mistake that others would see." That revision could be, "I would prefer not to make mistakes in front of others, but it's not the end of the world. I can stand it. Other people are not as judgmental as I think they are."

■ **What are the spiritual consequences regarding perfectionistic thinking?**

In his book *Living with a Perfectionist* (Oliver-Nelson), clinical psychologist Dr. David Stoop notes that perfectionism almost invariably leads to a distortion in our perception of God. He says perfectionists have an image of God as a "spiritual terrorist" who is really more like a demanding and critical parent.

So, attempting to live perfect lives means we are still living under the law and haven't learned to live by grace. It also means we probably react to our children in the same demanding way.

Perfectionism can interfere with our parenting skills as well. In 1 Thessalonians 5:11, Paul urges us "to encourage one another and build each other up." As parents, we are called to encourage our children, believing in them to help them believe in themselves. We are asked to accept their frailties and guide them to do the same. What we say is an important part of that process.

■ **What are some affirming comments a perfectionist should say?**

Here are a few:

► "You treat your friends nicely."
► "You have a wonderful ability with tools."
► "Thanks for doing such a good job on your chores today."

- ► "Your schoolwork has really improved."
- ► "I'm so glad you're my child."
- ► "You make my life more complete just by being you."
- ► "I'm glad I have you. You teach me so much about life."

■ **Those are nice, but my children aren't perfect. What happens if they make wrong choices or misbehave?**

Of course, they need to be corrected. But since we are concerned with nurturing them at all times, corrective messages must be delivered in a positive, affirmative way. We don't correct our children to make them feel bad but to help them discover a better way to do something.

Do you find it difficult to accept that your children are less than perfect? Have they, when upset, told you they can't be "perfect like you" and that they're tired of trying? Many children feel this way but never express it directly. They show it by giving up and tuning out.

Here are a few ways to offer correction in a nurturing way:

- ► "You can't do that any longer, but you can do this instead."
- ► "Here's a way you can do it that you might like better."
- ► "It sounds as though it's difficult for you to accept a compliment. Perhaps you need more practice accepting them, and I need more practice giving them."
- ► "I'm not sure you heard what I said. Tell me what you heard, and then let me repeat what I said."

■ **Growing up, my mother always said since Jesus was perfect, we have to be perfect too. I'm still dealing with that.**

Jesus does want us to reflect His presence in our lives, but the call to be perfect is a call to continually grow and mature, not to rid ourselves of mistakes or errors. Each of us can confidently express ourselves out of a sense of adequacy instead of a drive for perfection. God has declared us to be adequate because of what He has done for us through Jesus Christ.

We may as well accept it: We will never be perfect. The perfect world God created was marred by the fall of man, and we can never regain through our own efforts what was lost.

If you are a perfectionistic parent, part of your struggle is the cry of desperation that rises within you: *What if I fail? What if I'm not a perfect mother? What if my child isn't perfect?* Relax! Just know:

► You have failed in the past.
► You are failing now in some way.
► You will fail in the future.
► You weren't perfect in the past.
► You won't be perfect in the future.
► Your children will not be perfect either.

Failure will always be with us in this life. It's part of being human. When you fail, allow yourself to feel disappointment, but not disapproval. When you release your grip on perfectionism, the fear of failure will release its grip on you. You can fail and not be a failure!

You see, despite not being perfect, you and I are loved and—because of Jesus—accepted by God. You won't find a better offer anywhere.

This material is adapted from writings by author Norm Wright of Christian Marriage Enrichment in Tustin, California.

42

Beauty and the Best

■ Even though I was raised in a Christian home, I was nonetheless taught that appearance was of paramount importance. The clothes I wore, the accessories I picked, and the way my hair looked were all expected to be just so.

I don't know exactly where or when this emphasis began. I know it wasn't with my grandmother. She was a woman who spent little time on her appearance. In Grandma's time, women worked hard, married young, didn't drive, and wouldn't think of traveling alone. I don't remember Grandma wearing much makeup, if any, and her clothes were typically plain for women of that era. Her beauty advice mostly consisted of telling me to sit up straight and not to eat too many potatoes.

As if to defy this domestic dullness, my mother took up beauty's cause with a vengeance by modeling clothes at a local dress shop. She subtly conveyed the message to my sisters and me that how you look is an important part of *who* you are. Are we obsessed or what?

These days, in an age of obsession with appearance, things haven't gotten any better. What began as a trickle of beauty ideals and expectations in your mother's day became a veritable torrent in the '60s and '70s. It continues to sweep over us like a gigantic tidal wave. Few can resist its grip entirely.

As your grandma's generation passes away, the ones following display an ever-increasing preoccupation with beauty. Kids today take it for granted that they need to look a certain way, wear the right clothes, and have their hair permed—all before they're twelve years old.

Somehow, somewhere, between our grandmothers' generation and our own, we exchanged simplicity for sophistication. For most of us, it's only the size of our wallets that keeps us from investing even more money in looking better.

■ **Now that I'm older—and hopefully wiser—I'm wondering what God's Word says about beauty. Is there anything in the Bible about this topic?**

The Bible—not our culture, families, peer groups, or even churches—gives us the truth we need to fight the temptation to concentrate on outward appearances. Only Jesus can set us free from worrying about the way we look and make us who He would have us be through the work of the Holy Spirit. God's love—not our husband's, father's, mother's, sister's, brother's, or friends'—helps us accept ourselves the way He's made us: "Being confident of this, that He who began a good work in you will carry it on to completion until the day of Jesus Christ" (Phil. 1:16).

While beauty is evident everywhere in God's glorious creation, the Bible warns against beauty as a snare. Be aware of the paradox here. Scripture clearly dismisses physical beauty as fleeting while offering the rapturous celebration of married love in the Song of Songs: "How beautiful you are, my darling! Oh, how beautiful!" (1:15)

■ **What else does the Bible have to say about beauty?**

As with other unique qualities God gives, beauty is shown in the Bible to be a physical attribute He occasionally uses to further His purposes—as in the case of Esther, for example. But beauty definitely is not something to ask for, strive for, or believe in. That's an idea our culture has picked up from other sources.

In Scripture, physical beauty is never used as a metaphor for goodness or counted as any kind of moral virtue. In spite of the fairy tales that abound in our culture, beauty has no magical power to make bad people good.

Most fairy tales depict a "good witch" solution, not Christian salvation, as the cure for curses. Yet, according to the Bible, it took the horror of our Lord's crucifixion to turn bad people into good ones—not a blessed beauty's benevolence. As Christians, we know from Scripture that Jesus alone is truly good. Spiritual power is not ours to wield as we wish.

Over and over again, physical beauty is shown in Scripture to be a skin-deep quality distinctly separate from the condition of one's heart. In contrast to *physical* beauty and *adorned* beauty, the Bible shows us a *beauty of holiness* that belongs to the Lord. Words used in the Bible to demonstrate the beauty of God's holiness are "radiance," "glory," and "splendor." One day, when we see Jesus face to face, we'll see for ourselves the beauty of His holiness.

For now, we must settle for tiny glimpses of this delightful beauty in Christians. The Apostle Paul wrote, "And we, who with unveiled faces all reflect the Lord's glory, are being transformed into His likeness with ever-increasing glory, which comes from the Lord, who is the Spirit" (2 Cor. 3:18). Believers carry this spark of God's great beauty, no matter what they may "look" like.

■ **The thing that gets me about the Bible is one striking fact that stands out in the Scriptures: The majority of biblical women aren't described as "beautiful." We aren't told, for example, what Ruth looked like, though many of us picture her as being pretty. Nor are we told how Jesus' mother, Mary, appeared. In fact, the New Testament contains no reference to women's physical attractiveness at all. Why is that?**

The omission of beauty as a measure of a woman's worth in the New Testament is not an oversight. By telling us about the women's inner qualities, personal relationships, and love for the Lord rather than stressing her appearance, we have a uniquely Christian perspective upon which to build our identity as women—one that doesn't measure our worth by the beauty of our faces, the shape of our bodies, the style of our hair, the brand of our cosmetics, or the fit of our clothing.

If we believe what the Bible says, physical beauty is a nonissue for Christians. So why do we pay homage to it? How many people who claim that "it's what's inside that counts" truly believe it? Here, in the New Testament's only discourse on beauty, we are reminded of the truth:

"Your beauty should not come from outward adornment, such as braided hair and the wearing of gold jewelry and fine clothes. Instead, it should be that of your inner self, the unfading beauty of a gentle and quiet spirit, which is of great worth in God's sight" (1 Peter 3:3-4).

This is it! A kind of beauty that lasts forever, one that won't fade with the passing of seasons but grows ever brighter with the passage of time. A kind of beauty that can't be physically put on, made up, covered over, or taken off, but is 100 percent *real*. A kind of beauty the Bible declares "of great worth in God's sight."

■ **What would happen if we lived as though we took this truth seriously and based our ideals and expectations on God's opinion of beauty instead of on our culture's?**

It's a fact: No matter how hard we try, we can never make ourselves beautiful where it counts the most. Only Jesus can. Often the things we use for outward "beauty" actually pull us away from what Christ's beauty is all about: the fruit of His Spirit in our spirits, reaching the world for the glory of God's kingdom—and changing every aspect of our hearts and minds and lives.

43

When You're a Messie

. . . .

■ Growing up, my life seemed orderly. My mother folded and put away laundry, kept bills in one place, and got rid of what she didn't use. I held myself together in college—I had only half a room—but when I got married, life fell apart. What a shock it was to learn that home management took work! It seemed easier to leave the groceries in bags rather than put them away. It seemed easier to leave the clean laundry in the basket, but we were always hunting what we needed! Our apartment was not the happy, cozy nest I had envisioned, but rather a stressful, chaotic mess.

When the doorbell rang, we'd go through our usual panic as Jim and I scurried around hurling shoes from the living room floor into our bedroom, scooping unfolded laundry from the couch and dumping it onto the bed, and hauling piles of mail and magazines to stack against the bedroom wall.

One day after our visitors left, Jim complained, "This place is a shambles!"

"You could pitch in too, you know!" I snapped.

"It's your responsibility. You're the woman of the house!"

Disorder was our main source of conflict. I would fall behind, feel discouraged, fall further behind, feel more discouraged. It was a vicious, demoralizing cycle; it was my secret shame. I felt I would never gain control of my home, time, or life. I didn't keep house—it kept me.

Yes, your house sure did keep you. You are a Messie, a term invented by Sandra Felton, author of *The Messies Manual*. It's not that Messies don't have any system for keeping their house clean, but they change the way they do things around the house every day. One day bills go on the desk, the next day, the lamp table.

Confusion rules! As pack rats, they'll always have a reason for saving everything. Why do Messies save expired sale flyers? Because when the next sale flyer comes, they can tell if it's going to be a better sale.

The Messie's motto is "Be prepared for anything," but it's a double-edged sword. They usually *have* the item, but they can't find it.

■ **That sounds like me. Each year I think, I'm gonna send out Christmas cards with a personal note inside each one. But I never find the cards I had purchased before Thanksgiving, so I never write the notes.**

When one of the kids scrape a knee, I have Band-Aids, but I can't find them. One time I saved newspapers for months, storing them in two piles— each two feet high—under the sink. Then one day I noticed water oozing from under the stove. We had a leak that had gone undetected long because the newspapers had soaked up the water. By now, there

---

WANT TO GET STARTED?

► **Pray for vision,** help, energy, patience, and wisdom.

► **Adjust your attitude.** Becoming organized is a marathon, not a sprint! Don't expect overnight success.

► **Take action.** Write your goals out and break them down into small bites, like decluttering a desk. Save the big stuff (like cleaning the kitchen) for later.

► **Start at the front door,** and following the Mount Vernon Method, move around the inside periphery of your home, dejunking as you go. Have three boxes with you—one for throwaway, one for giveaway, and another to store.

► **Pace yourself.** An hour of decision making is all a person can take. It might take you three months to go through your entire house.

► **Don't deep clean;** just declutter.

► **When sorting mail,** throw away what you don't need. I have three stacking trays labeled "to file," "to do" and "to read."

► **Reward yourself when you're done.**

was so much damage to the wooden floorboards under the sink that we had to remodel the kitchen.

I'm angry! How can I change?

If you begin your quest at the library, chances are you'll find only books on "tidy tips" or "household hints" on how to starch shirts or stencil a border. What you need is help in basic organization, something called the "Mount Vernon" style of cleaning.

■ Mount Vernon? What are you talking about?

If you would take a tour of George and Martha Washington's estate, you would be mightily impressed with its cleanliness. How do they keep the old mansion that clean? Each day, the workers start at the front door, clean methodically around that room until quitting time, and the next day pick up where they had left off—until the whole house is clean.

That approach works for dusting and waxing. For instance, start inside your front door at a lamp table with one small drawer. Throw out old school calendars, classified ads, and other junk. Don't you feel like Superwoman?

Then go to the next piece of furniture, the one with six drawers. You might be intimidated at first, but you should be energized by your little victory. Throw out all the junk, and then go on to the next piece of furniture.

Realize that your family may resist your efforts. After years of "anything goes," they may say, "You're going overboard," "You've become a fanatic," and then really lay the guilt: "We liked you better before!"

But you'll like yourself better now. You're well on the road to becoming a "Cleanie."

This material is adapted by writings by Sandra Felton (A Messies Manual) *and B.J. Conner of Ann Arbor, Michigan.*

44

Dad Is Away

. . . .

■ **My husband is traveling more and more on business these days. We have a young son, and I've been trying to compensate for Dad's absences with fun outings, late bedtimes, special treats, and a whirlwind of activities. After a week of this, I'm exhausted and resentful, and my son is tired and cranky. Any suggestions?**

Seven days of nonstop nurturing, encouraging, disciplining, listening, diaper changing, and answering, "When is Daddy coming home?" 600 times can push many moms over the top.

The first thing you want to do is prepare the children ahead of time. Avoid having your husband "sneak off" when he leaves for the airport. That only undermines a child's sense of security. If the travel schedule involves a departure early in the morning, inform the child beforehand that Daddy will not be home when he or she wakes up. Some parents also leave notes for the child to open each day of the trip.

■ **Some well-meaning friends shower us with dinner invitations when my husband is traveling. At first I eagerly accepted every one. But I found it difficult to settle the children at bedtime. What's the best balance?**

Although parents and children alike enjoy some spontaneity, children need predictability too. Knowing that daily events such as meals and bedtime occur at the same time each day gives them a sense of security. If your husband is gone for a week, accept only one or two invitations, and on the other nights stay home and play games and read stories to your children.

■ **I'm all for routine, but when my husband is gone, one of my regular routines that gets dropped is my daily devotional time. How do I find time?**

That's understandable because you're so busy. But no matter how little time you have to yourself, it is important to spend at least a few minutes in God's Word and in prayer.

Whether you read several verses from Proverbs and say a quick prayer, or work through a Bible study geared specifically for mothers, focus on the Lord's will for you and your children. Obviously, the day that starts smoother will run smoother.

■ **My two-year-old son doesn't do well when Dad leaves. What should I do?**

Encourage your child to express his feelings. Young children often interpret Daddy's leaving as rejection or punishment for wrongdoing. Assure him of Dad's love and his planned return.

You can help do that by letting your son make a calendar to hang on the refrigerator. Letting him mark off the day each evening will give him a sense of when Dad will be returning.

In addition, Dad should talk each day on the phone with your son (and you too, of course!). This will do a lot to bridge the gulf between father and son.

■ **Those are some good ideas, but what about me—the tired and harassed mom?**

As the ad jingle says, "Give yourself a break today." Start by arranging some time for yourself. Get a new hairstyle you've been putting off. Read that new book. Some youngsters are reluctant to be left with a baby-sitter during their father's absence since they fear the loss of both parents. Do the next best thing: Trade baby-sitting with another mother and have your son play at a friend's house in the afternoon. If finances and distance permit, you might arrange for the children to visit relatives for the day.

■ **I live in New York City, and it's not safe to go out at night. What precautions should I take when my husband is away?**

If you are uneasy about being alone at night, arrange for a neighbor or friend to call you at predetermined times. You might consider purchasing an alarm system, but a cheaper alternative—and very effective—is getting a dog. And don't underestimate the power of prayer!

■ **Each time my husband comes home, it's like we have to start all over again.**

You do need to allow for a transition period. The much-anticipated reunion can sour if everyone is not given time to readjust. You have been the "head of the household" for a while, and your children may be confused by their father's expectation that he resume the role of disciplinarian. It's possible you may feel your territory being encroached upon, while your husband may come home to find no place for himself. Talking through these areas will help you all adjust faster with each trip.

Finally, remember to draw strength from the Lord. Allow Him to use these times to draw you closer to your children, your spouse, and Himself. Remember that parenting alone is stressful, and you do not have to be a perfect mother. While you are busy parenting your youngsters, allow God to be *your* heavenly Parent, encouraging and sustaining you with His supernatural strength.

This material is adapted from writings by Kathleen Choe of Muncie, Indiana.

8

All About
Fathers

45

Effective Fathers

. . . .

■ **I know that fathering is a daunting and complex task. I once heard it said that fathers these days often feel like a "dachshund running in deep snow." That sure sounds like me. I want to stay on track—and out of the heavy powder. How can I do that?**

Your motivation to be a good father will be greatly enhanced if you accept three important truths.

The first truth has to do with the **importance of fathering.** The Industrial Revolution exerted considerable influence on the role of fathers. Our dads and granddads and great-grandfathers left the home for the factory, and fathering in America was relegated to the distant roles of financial provider and disciplinarian of last resort. It didn't take long for social scientists to begin telling everyone that only the mother-child relationship was central to parenting; fathers were peripheral.

■ **That statement is hogwash! You mean people actually believed that stuff?**

Yes, sir. For a period of time, fathers were told to step back and stay away, and many Baby Boomers were raised by fathers who were physically absent and emotionally distant. Thankfully, the pendulum is swinging again, because fathers are *not* peripheral to parenting. They are crucial. Children need their dads. The importance of fathers is demonstrated by what occurs when fathers *aren't* in the home. Studies show that children who grow up in fatherless homes are more likely to drop out of high school, suffer from poverty, go on welfare, marry early, have children out of wedlock, divorce, commit delinquent acts, and engage in drug and alcohol abuse.

■ **That's a long list. So if I'm in the home and being a dad to my two boys, that's enough, right?**

Not necessarily. The second truth we must accept is that **effective fathering must be learned.** Fathering skills don't automatically accompany that Y chromosome your dad gave you. Hopefully, your dad also presented a good model of fathering. As you grew up, you watched him, taking subconscious notes on how a man interacts with his wife and kids. Unfortunately, with the divorce rate doubling in the last forty years, many of us grew up without any accessible fathering models, let alone effective ones.

Our society has shown that trial and error usually doesn't work in the craft of fathering. Fathers need to be craftsmen, but in order to become skilled, we must all begin as apprentices. We need to turn to other men and ask, "Show me how to do this and do it well. What are your tricks of the trade? What are your secrets?"

■ **So that's why we're seeing organizations like Promise Keepers and men's groups and things like that?**

Exactly. Men are coming up to other men and saying, "I'll walk beside you; I'll be here to help you." Fathers who do this are discovering the third great truth: **effective fathering is of overwhelming importance and often requires rigorous training, but it also bears significant rewards.**

Every father knows there are times of great pain, anguish, confusion, and inadequacy. But then there are other times, like when you walk into your children's room when they are sleeping. How do you explain it? At that moment, it's not like they are doing anything to please you. They're just sleeping. They aren't being intelligent, athletic, obedient, or witty. They're just lying there, their dark hair mussed on their pillows, their limbs tangled among pajamas and blankets and stuffed teddy bears. How can you explain what you feel at that moment, when you stand there and just stare at them?

The rewards of fathering are often those intangible moments. But just because the rewards are indescribable, that doesn't make them any less real or powerful.

■ OK, now you've got me all fired up to be a good dad. How can I be an effective father?

Ken Canfield, executive director of the National Center for Fathering, asked that same question. When he and his colleagues began their research, they first sought to identify the basic roles and responsibilities that fathers are called to perform. Then they surveyed the Bible, finding nearly 1,200 verses pertaining to fathering, fatherhood, and fatherlessness. They read the scholarly journals. Then they talked to other men.

The National Center for Fathering developed a test called the Fathering Style Inventory. From this research, they were able to identify the "effective fathers" and their "seven secrets" of effective fathering.

■ What are the seven secrets of effective fathers?

The first is **commitment.** A father's commitment to his children is demonstrated by his readiness and willingness to carry out his fathering responsibilities. Is he eager to be with his kids? Does he enjoy the fact that he is the one they're depending on?

The word *commitment* literally means to give, hand over, or entrust. The most helpful image might be of the person who walks into a bank, digs in his pocket for the money he has wadded up there, and slides it under the glass window to the bank teller. He's making a deposit. He's committing his money to their safekeeping.

Similarly, like a faithful bank customer, we need to make regular (daily) deposits into the lives of our children. What is it that we deposit? Time, energy, and resources. Commitment is the actual amount of time, energy, and resources you are willing to pledge to the task of fathering.

■ **What's secret number two?**

Knowing your child. That means you know what your children are capable of at a particular age. You know what they need for healthy growth, emotional stability, and intellectual development. You know each child's individual tastes, goals, and abilities, and you support each one in his or her unique characteristics. You also have a good idea what concerns, problems, and questions a child would have growing up in this day and age.

■ **Is there a balance here? I can see some fathers going overboard and being highly controlling.**

Of course. Some fathers can be intrusive and so involved in every aspect of their children's lives that they may not allow children much of a life of their own. The key is finding a balance between being intrusive and just plain unaware of what is going on.

Which leads us to the third secret: **consistency.** The effective father is consistent in his:

► mood swings
► presence in the family
► keeping of promises
► morality and ethics
► daily schedule
► hobbies and interests

All told, consistency is regular and predictable. Children of a consistent father know that when Dad leaves for work with a kiss and a "See you later," he means just that.

■ **What's the fourth secret?**

The fourth secret of effective fathers is that they strongly accept their role as **protector and provider** for their families.

■ **How can a father be a protector these days? We don't have lions running through our backyard.**

It means that fathers take a leadership role in dealing with any crisis that comes up. It lies within each one of us to rise to the occasion and do what needs to be done. It's striding out of the front door of your home when your child has fallen off a tree limb, fearing he may have broken his arm. You calmly tell your oldest daughter to call your doctor, and then you kneel by your son's side, brushing his hair out of his eyes. You tell him, "It's going to be all right. Daddy's here."

As for **providing,** fathers instill security by having a steady, reliable income and providing for the material needs of the family.

■ That last one surprises me. Hasn't our culture overemphasized the role of the father as the financial provider?

What effective fathers are saying is that we should not feel guilty about going to work. If we never come home from work, then we should feel guilty, but while doing our jobs and drawing our paychecks we should feel proud that we are faithfully meeting the needs of our children and dutifully fulfilling our roles as fathers.

■ I'll buy that. What's secret number five?

That would be **loving their mother.** It's cultivating a strong marital relationship with your wife. This provides children with a healthy model for masculine behavior toward women.

Your modeling of a loving marriage will influence the way your children will look at their own marriages. It will help your children develop a healthy understanding of what a husband or wife does or says, feels or thinks. It will also affect your children's decisions about whether to stick it out through the tough times that their marriages will inevitably face.

■ What's number six?

Being an **active listener.** This means that effective fathers give their children their full attention when they are speaking. But the fact is that many of us have trouble actively listening to our children. Some of us may have grown up in a home where "children are seen and not heard." Yet if you force your kids to be silent over the years, those kids won't know how to speak, let alone be heard by their father.

Too often the important tiny voices of our children get lost beneath adult noise. But there's a lot we can do to turn down the decibels. For example, we can turn off the TV and put away distractions. Most important, we can train ourselves to be slow to speak and quick to listen. We can learn to focus our attention for those times when we especially need to listen to our children.

■ **All these secrets of effective fathers are excellent. But where's the spiritual emphasis?**

Yes, that's the seventh and final secret of effective fathers: **spiritually equipping your children.** That means you feel strongly about teaching Christian values by reading the Bible with their children, having a time of worship in the home, and modeling godly behavior. They understand the spiritual aspects of their children's lives, and they work to help their children discover their own relationship with God.

■ **How do I do that? I feel inadequate when it comes to spiritual matters.**

Try to lead your family in worship at home. Family devotions don't have to be a huge or slick production. You also don't have to study and prepare a full-blown sermon for each occasion. With a deluge of published resources—more than fifty different children's Bibles and hundreds of devotional books—you shouldn't have much trouble putting something together.

Use your family devotional times to equip your children learn how to pray. Ask them if they know of anyone among their friends who could use your family's prayers. Then pray for these requests.

Remember, the goal of spiritual equipping is to give our children the spiritual resources they need to live their lives faithfully before God. Praying with them will help you accomplish that goal.

This material is adapted from The Seven Secrets of Effective Fathers *(Tyndale) by Ken R. Canfield.*

46

Daddy's Home

. . . .

■ **I just read in the last chapter that a father's duties include loving his wife and children, providing strong leadership, earning a living to support the family, and imparting spiritual values to his kids. What are some other parts of my job description?**

If you ask good fathers what makes a good dad, invariably, they will stress the importance of spending *time* with their children. Of course, that's the no-brainer answer you'd expect—and want—to hear from fathers who are getting the job done. The importance of spending time with children is a truism that needs to be repeated as much as possible. Why? Because time is a nonrenewable resource; once it's gone, it's gone.

■ **OK, spending time with kids is a great idea—right up there with ordering a hot dog at a ball game. Can you give me some ideas how to carve out more hours with my family? I'm a busy guy.**

▶ *If possible, rearrange your work schedule.* Herb is an orthopedic surgeon in Akron, Ohio. At 43, he is getting his practice established, but Herb knows the medical profession can gobble up hours in huge chunks.

"How do I spend time with my kids?" said Herb, repeating the question. "I'm not a morning person, so I've changed my hours around. That way, I don't have to go into the office right away. I can eat breakfast with my kids and take them to school. I'll start my surgeries at 1 o'clock in the afternoon and go until 7 P.M. or so."

▶ *Make dinner a priority.* Dinner is a time to reconnect. There's something about the entire family sitting around and enjoying a meal together. And in this day and age of working moms, long commutes, and kids in sports, it's no easy chore for everyone to sit down together. Eating together promotes communication, which promotes discussion, which promotes sharing, which promotes love. Did you ever notice that when you eat alone you flip on the TV? You want some sort of communication, even if it's one way.

Dinnertime together is also a great way to know what's going on in your kids' lives. Brad, a New England father, says when the family sits down at the table, he asks each child, "What was the best thing that happened to you today?"

WHERE'S YOUR TIME GOING?

Out of a 168-hour week, American men on the average devote 56 hours to work, 70 hours to sleeping, eating, and personal care, and 42 hours to leisure activities.

So, let's do a little exercise: Grab a pencil and determine how you "spent" your last twenty-four hours (make it a weekday):
▶ Sleeping _____
▶ Grooming _____
▶ Working (main job)

_____
▶ Commuting _____
▶ Overtime or moonlighting

_____
▶ Household chores _____
▶ Eating with the family

_____
▶ Leisure pursuits (exercise, reading, hobbies) _____

After you've added up the hours, ask yourself these questions:
▶ Was this a routine day?
▶ How much time did I spend with my children?
▶ What did I do with them?
▶ Was I home for dinner?
▶ Did I do paperwork while Mom bathed the kids and put them down?
▶ Did I talk with my wife?
▶ How much time was frittered away watching TV?

"Doing that stimulates talk, and everyone has to listen," says Brad. "That way, we begin the dinner conversation with a positive focus, and I try to remember something each one said so when it's time for nightly prayer, I can say, 'Thanks, Lord, for helping Jeremy pass the test.' "

In the last year, Brad has tried to spend some *unscheduled* time with his kids too. Sometimes he'll knock on the bedroom door and ask to come in and just talk. "It's amazing how kids will open up then," he says.

► *Ban the TV.* What book worth its salt wouldn't suggest this? But letting the hours vaporize into thin air because the "boob tube" drones on and on *is* a waste of time.

► *Do "Daddy Dates."* Westy, a Wisconsin father, says he can think of nothing better than taking his 9-year-old daughter out for breakfast or dinner. "She knows the only reason we're going out is so we can talk," says Westy. "We probably get as much conversation in during that one meal as we do all week. We sit across the table from each other and converse; there's a lot of questions and answers going on. These 'Daddy Dates' tell my daughter that she is very, very important to me."

A good time to start "dating" your child is around eight or nine years old. "Don't wait until he or she is fifteen years old. That's too late," says Westy. By spending individual time with your child, you build a friend-

---

THE SEVEN WORST WAYS TO SPEND TIME WITH YOUR KIDS

7. Serve as their human quarter machine at the video arcade.

6. Have the NBA playoff game on while you're playing Monopoly with them.

5. Read the paper while helping them with their algebra assignments.

4. Go to the local high school football field to practice your short irons, and have them collect the golf balls after you're done.

3. Suggest they take a nap with you on a beautiful Sunday afternoon.

2. Drive them to Cub Scouts and read a magazine in the car while the den mother instructs them on how to tie knots.

1. Take them to your office on Saturday and have them color while you work.

ship, so when the *really* big discussions pop up later (love, dating, and sex), a foundation has already been laid.

▸ *Include your children in your vacations.* You'd be surprised at the number of families who vacation *without* their kids. When Randy, a Texas rancher, and his family go on vacation, they drive. That way, Randy's certain they'll have plenty of time in the car. (Believe it or not, that's the way he wants it!) One of the kids sits with Dad in the front seat, and as the scenery passes by, long discussions ensue.

▸ *Volunteer to coach your child's sports team.* When you make that commitment to coach, it *forces* you to spend time with your children. That's the way Jeffrey, a Sacramento father, slices out hours with his four children (ranging in age from three to fifteen). He's coached baseball for eight years, from Little League through Pony League.

FOUR WORDS YOU'LL NEVER WANT TO SAY

Roy, a Midwestern professional, recalls a job that required a lot of out-of-state travel. "The first ten to twelve years after the kids were born, my work took me away quite a bit," he says. "My wife was really good about it, and she did a great job of raising our three kids. When they hit early adolescence, however, it suddenly dawned on me that I had missed out on a great deal.

"After much reflection, I did something I never thought I could do: I quit that high-paying job. Then I went out and found a new job that would keep me close to home. But despite all I did, it was too late," he laments. "No matter how hard I tried to put myself back into my kids' lives, it didn't work. They had adjusted to the point where having Dad around wasn't necessary. Now, seven years later, we're a little happier, but it's not anything like I wish it could be. I missed my chance, and *now it's too late.*"

That's right, Dad. If you're not around, your wife and children will learn to live life without you. It's as if you're the manager of the New York Yankees, but you don't arrive at the ballpark until the seventh inning. You'll find the players and coaches playing the game without you. Life goes on. Not every dad who feels he must pour his best years into his work (or has a job that forces him to travel) will end up with a lifetime of regret. But since we're given only a short time with our children, the best years to get them on our team are when they're young.

"Baseball is a real competitive sport here in California, and with a lot of competition comes a lot of pressure. There's a struggle in keeping sports in the right perspective. I tell my boys to use the talents the Lord gives them—but to have fun too. I think the lessons sports teach are good for kids because they learn about life's ups and downs," says Jeffrey.

▶ *If you can't be a coach, then cheer from the grandstands.* Max, an attorney, said he always wanted to take time to be with Max, Jr., while he was growing up, but he (Max, Sr.) wasn't the athletic type. "I didn't coach, but I went to all the Little League games, where I could encourage him. And when he started playing high school football, I was there, even for his J.V. games that started at 3 P.M. I was lucky to have a job with flexible hours."

HOW MUCH TIME SHOULD I BE WITH MY KIDS?

The answer is simple and rather straightforward: "Enough." That's the best answer because, in reality, there is no single answer.

The question is much like asking how much sleep does a person need? "Enough" is the right answer. We need enough sleep to be refreshed, alert, and to remain healthy. Of course, the actual amount varies from person to person, depending on age, workload, stress, etc.

In the father-child relationship, similar variables exist—the child's age, stage of emotional development, personality type, the ease or difficulty existing in the relationship, and the stability of the marriage and home.

Sixty years ago, children typically spent three to four hours a day personally involved with various family members or extended family, working together, discussing items of interest, and playing together. Today, that interaction has been reduced to fifteen minutes a day.

To determine how much time is "enough" for a *locking together* of your interests, attention, and heart with those of your child's, answer thoughtfully these questions:

▶ Can you name your child's best friend?
▶ Within three pounds, how much does your child weigh?
▶ What is her greatest disappointment or unfulfilled desire?
▶ Which chore does he hate the most?
▶ If she could visit anywhere in the world, where would it be?
▶ What are their teachers' names?
▶ What books are they reading now?

And finally, there's one other reliable way for a father to determine if he is spending enough time with the children: Ask the mother!

Max adds that he and his wife had made an early commitment to go to *everything* at school: recitals, sports, band concerts—you name it. "Even if the kids tell you they don't want you to show up, they really do," says the Windy City dad.

► *Make the best use of your recreational time.* It's important to exercise our bodies (we feel better when we're in good shape). Many of us enjoy the spirit of competition. Some recreational pursuits, however, take up a lot of time. Take golf, for instance. As Baby Boomers age, golf is *the* sport of the '90s. Yet when I (Mike Yorkey) play, it burns up most of a Saturday. Even if I'm a member of the "dawn patrol," I'm still not home till noon. I've decided golf is going to have to wait.

That's why I play a lot of tennis, but I've had to cut back there too. Usually, I'll play one or two mornings a week *before* work, starting at 6:15 A.M. I figure it's better to play while the kids are still sleeping than to practice my backhand after work when they're home.

► *Finally, remember that your kids are keeping tabs on you.* When 1,500 schoolchildren were asked by social scientists John DeFrain and Nick Stinnett, "What do you think makes a happy family?" the children didn't list money, fine homes, or big-screen TVs. No, the answer most frequently offered was "doing things together."

"I once saw a sign in the nursery," said Herb, the orthopedic surgeon. "It said: 'Children spell love L-O-V-E.' You can't buy your kids' affection unless you spend your time with them."

This material is adapted from Daddy's Home *by Greg Johnson and Mike Yorkey,* © 1992. Used *by permission of Tyndale House Publishers, Inc. All rights reserved; and by Paul Lewis from* Parents & Teenagers *(Victor).*

47

Father Knows Stress

. . . .

■ **I was sitting in a window seat waiting out another of O'Hare's interminable delays. I had read the complimentary newspaper and the in-flight magazine—even the Boeing 737 safety card! I was bored. So I broke a long-held habit and started a conversation with a businessman sitting next to me. Before the jet finished taxiing, I had asked him that time-honored question: "So, what do you do for a living?" I mentally slapped myself on the head. Why did I ask that question? It seems to be a real "guy" thing.**

Because it's a time-honored inquiry dating back to the days of Fred Flintstone. You asked that question so you can quickly size up your new acquaintance—and with the secret hope that he'll ask you what you do.

■ **That's because we are what we do, right?**

For most of us, much of our self-esteem and self-worth is tied up in our work. If we're a success in the workplace, we welcome the chance to let the world know. On the flip side, nothing is more debilitating than being fired or laid off. Our sense of purpose—and our ego—is deflated. That's because work is *very* important to us, as it is to God.

■ **Work is important to God? How so?**

Let's not forget that God established people on earth to work: "The Lord God took the man and put him in the Garden of Eden to work it and take care of it" (Gen. 2:15). Notice that Adam wasn't given a chaise lounge and directions to the nearest pool. Nor was Adam told that earning a living was going to be a breeze.

These two gems from Proverbs sum up God's feelings: "Lazy hands make a man poor, but diligent hands bring wealth" (10:4); and "The plans of the diligent lead to profit as surely as haste leads to poverty" (21:5).

■ **Those Scriptures aren't lost on me. I know I have to work for a living to build a future for my family. In fact, I'm being asked to work *too* much. Corporate downsizing, you know.**

If you're in that bind, then you're working for a company that believes employees must sacrifice their families on the altar of work. Sooner or later, you'll have to decide whether to continue in that anti-family environment. Yes, your career is important, but no job is worth offering up your wife and children.

■ **I'm in that situation, and I'm contemplating changing jobs. Where should I begin?**

Take it to God first. Ask Him for direction, what avenues you should pursue. Then have a friendly chat with your boss. Let him or her know how you feel. Can you do some work at home? Could you get more help? What can be done to reduce the overtime?

But don't expect corporate America to recognize how much fathers are needed at home. The employee's family life isn't part of the annual report, nor can it be measured on the bottom line. What many CEOs don't understand is that work and family is intertwined; if Dad isn't overworked, and his family life is in balance, he will be a happier, more productive employee.

■ **OK, I want to get my work life in balance. Although I'm chalking up a lot of OT, what are ways I can break loose a few more hours at home?**

1. *Understand what the most important hours of the day are.*

OK, what are the most important hours? Answer: when you're home, Dad. Or more specifically, the time period between 5 and 10 P.M., that stretch when the family can regroup, eat dinner, share their day, and talk about the future.

If you're closing that window of opportunity because you're booking extra hours or crawling along some expressway, then it's hard to perform your fatherly duties.

2. *Work smarter.*

Have you ever noticed that some people just don't work that well? They're the type who putz around doing a little of this and a little of that—and then erupt into a major panic when crunch time arrives.

What's your body clock? Are you a morning person? Or do you do your best work at night? If you get more done in the morning, perhaps you should begin working earlier in the day (if your company has flex time). That way you can get off earlier—and beat the traffic home—thus saving you even more time.

3. *Skip going out to lunch.*

More time is wasted by employees who eat out during lunchtime. Yes, it's nice to be served a prepared meal, but by the time you're seated, given a menu, order an entrée, wait for the food to arrive, eat, ask for the check, make the payment—well, say *sayonara* to a huge chunk of time. And that doesn't include the minutes lost driving or walking to the restaurant. (It's a different matter if your job description includes business lunches. Hopefully, your boss considers those events part of your eight- or nine-hour day.)

But if you're working past 6 or 7 o'clock because you and some friends lingered over lunch, then that's not good stewardship of your time. (It's also not the greatest stewardship of your finances. The tab for eating out can easily cost $25 to $40 a week.) Brown-bagging is cheaper, faster—and healthier. If you need a change of scenery during the noon hour, take your lunch to a nearby park or company picnic area. You also should consider taking a thirty-minute lunch. Quitting time is a half-hour earlier!

4. *If possible, decide where your priorities are—family or career— early in your marriage.*

The worst time to choose between family and your job is when you're thirty years old and have a couple of kids. That's when your circumstances have been positioned toward upward mobility and it's tough to put on the brakes. You will be tempted not to let the company down, which would put the family second.

5. *Think through any promotion.*

Does it mean more hours? Will it lead to more travel? Is the money worth it? What would you do if your boss offered you a raise—albeit modest—but said you might have to put in eight hours of overtime per week? Would you take it? You should role-play this scenario with your wife. Have her take the role of the boss (she'll love that!) offering you a promotion.

6. *Live closer to work, or consider relocating to a smaller city.*

That suggestion is easier said than done, isn't it? For openers, it's hard to sell a house in today's tough economic climate, and some of us don't want to live in neighborhoods close to work. Or, we like where we live. The kids are established in school, and we're active members of the local church.

But living closer to work can be a huge benefit, especially if you're burning up the miles in ninety-minute commutes. By cutting your drive time to a manageable ten or fifteen minutes, you can gain another hour or two a day. That's often enough time to see your daughter's soccer game or coach your son's baseball team. You can retrieve up to ten hours a week. Think about how many family or ministry activities you can do with that extra day! You should realize that moving to a new job—or city—is a long-range project. It might take a couple of years to make it happen. But you need to start thinking about it now.

7. *If you've got to work overtime, take a break during dinnertime.*

If you *have* to work on that sales presentation, can you do it at home after dinner? Can you catch up on your business reading *after* the kids are in bed?

■ **I know I should make the most of the hours I am home, and I know that quality family time doesn't bite me on the leg when I walk through the front door. What are some creative things I can do with the kids?**

You can walk your kids to a park, organize a bike ride, or take them for a swim at the municipal pool. Sometimes, kids will balk at doing something with Dad because they don't want to leave their friends. Invite them along too. Play catch, hit tennis balls, shoot baskets. One of the best investments you can make is to mount a basketball rim in the driveway.

And one last tip: take advantage of daylight savings time. When the days are long and the evenings are warm, you can do many outdoor activities. Don't let the sun go down without doing something together.

■ **Sometimes I feel married to my desk. I just have so much work to do and so little time. I'm frustrated because I know I should be home more with my kids, right?**

Although it's been said a million times, it bears repeating one more time. No one, when they reach the end of life, has ever looked back and said, "Gee, I wish I spent more time at the office instead of with my kids."

We only go through this season of fathering one time, so let's make the most of it. Larry Crabb, the noted family counselor and author of several books, conducted a seminar in Colorado Springs where he asked the 350 men if their own dads were good role models. Only *30* men raised their hands! Will your son or daughter raise their hands one day?

This material is adapted from Daddy's Home *by Greg Johnson and Mike Yorkey, © 1993. Used by permission of Tyndale House Publishers, Inc. All rights reserved.*

48

A Worker's Greatest Fear: Being Laid Off

. . . .

■ **I'm in my fifties, and I'm scared to death that I will lose my white-collar job the next time my company goes through its periodical "downsizing." Why do I feel so nervous?**

Because news of another corporate layoff is a regular occurrence these days. It can happen anywhere and anytime. Just ask Brian Knowles of Los Angeles. He lost his job when he could ill afford to lose it. At age fifty-four, after working nearly eight years as a department manager at one of the nation's largest life insurance companies, Brian was told he was being dumped, his department was being disbanded, and his functions re-engineered into another area. The severance package was about as good as it gets these days, and his pay continued for three months.

■ **That must have been quite a blow to get cut loose in the prime of his career.**

In days past, the fifties used to be the decade that people would peak out in their careers. Brian thought, *I've paid my dues, I've worked for decades, I know my job inside out and backwards, so I should be reaping some major blessings.* Then he found himself being designated valueless to a company that he had been loyal to for years.

WHAT ARE YOUR OPTIONS?

What can you do if you lose your job and have to get back on your feet right away? Consider the following:

1. Buy a franchise. Becoming an entrepreneur is a way many former executives have found profits and satisfaction. Instead of running someone else's business, they are now working successfully for themselves.

2. Become a consultant. Some believe consultant is a euphemism for dignified unemployment. However, many skilled professionals are finding that companies are willing to pay for their expertise as consultants, rather than hiring them. It's also a safe way for companies to screen people before offering them a position.

3. Build a portfolio career. Many people today are building portfolio careers; that is, they are earning money doing multiple kinds of work. If you happen to be a multi-talented person, this may be the way to go. Since Brian Knowles lost his job, he has earned money as a writer, an art teacher, an illustrator, a television producer, and a cartoonist. The sky's the limit, depending upon your range of talents.

4. Sell something. There is always a demand for commissioned salespeople. If you're a friendly, extroverted, personality, with a strong self-image, this may be the way to go for you. Depending upon how good they are, salespeople have no ceiling on their earnings.

Brian assumed there was probably some other reason they let him go: *I'm too old, I'm too fat, maybe I really am incompetent, or maybe they're making room for younger people who will work for less.*

Somehow, you never believe the reason given. If you're African-American, you assume prejudice is involved. If you're a white male, you assume it's female chauvinism. If you're Hispanic or Asian, you assume it's because you're a minority. If you're a woman, it's because the Good Ol' Boys Club is clinging to power.

The point is, losing your job—no matter what your age—is a traumatic experience. It's way up there on the Holmes Stress Scale. It's devastating to your self-esteem. You feel discounted, betrayed, and discarded.

For men who have worked all their lives, and who have made their careers the center of their lives, becoming unemployed is a shattering experience. It results in a profound loss of dignity. If you've managed large staffs and millions of corporate dollars, then suddenly you find yourself looking, hat in hand, for any McJob you can find, all dignity is gone.

■ Why this unprecedented jettisoning of workers?

Follow the money. It's all being done in the name of higher profits or increasing shareholder value. Companies chase capital. Capital follows profitability. Profitability means reducing the costs of doing business to the bare minimum. The greatest cost of doing business is labor. The more workers a CEO can get rid of, the more expenses are reduced and margins enlarged. It's that simple.

Corporate officers are also offered major incentives to increase profitability at the expense of jobs. Don Bauder, a *San Diego Union Tribune* columnist, put it this way: "Corporations get their big earnings gains from the cost side—slashing employment. And as companies were whacking the payrolls—and watching their stocks rise as a result—corporate chief executives were raking in bigger and bigger bucks. According to a study by William M. Mercer, Inc., chief executive's salaries and bonuses have risen 8.1 percent in the last year, the same as the year earlier. By contrast, inflation-adjusted pay of non-supervisorial Americans has been dropping since 1973."

So the rich get richer on the former salaries of those they've re-engineered out of jobs.

In 1994, American corporations eliminated more than 500,000 jobs, many of them middle-management positions. The trend is continuing through the last half of the 1990s. Between 1979 and 1992, Fortune 500 companies threw 4.4 million Americans out of work—a rate of about 340,000 jobs per year.

■ Who's getting it in the neck?

Managers mostly. In 1991, for instance, unemployment rose by 15 percent—but managerial unemployment rose a whopping 55 percent!

Another major trend that is resulting from professional level job losses is the gradual reduction of the middle class, and the growth of the poor class. Of course, the wealthy ruling classes are also getting wealthier. The average American CEO earns 175 times the salary of the average worker. This compares with an eleven-fold difference in Japanese CEO salaries.

Driven by large institutional investors who demand ever-greater returns on their investment, corporate leaders are forced to savage their work forces. If they fail to increase shareholder value, they themselves are rejected and replaced with tough-minded managers who'll get the job done. On the other hand, if they make their companies perform by producing competitive margins, they are rewarded with huge bonuses, perks, and stock options. Human nature being what it is, which way would you choose if you were wearing their shoes?

John Kinloch, of the Communications Workers of America said, "Corporations are now trying to create a disposable work force with low wages and no benefits."

■ **How low will wages go?**

We've already learned that wages haven't kept up with inflation since 1973, but what does it mean when American auto companies that have been using Mexican workers at $2 an hour start complaining that labor costs *in Mexico* are too high?

American companies are chasing cheap labor all over the globe. They can get nearly a dozen, two dozen Filipino, Chinese, or Vietnamese laborers for the price of one American. The portents of these trends for the shrinking American middle class are frightening.

Wherever possible, American companies are replacing American workers with computers—or cheap foreign labor.

Thus, the trends are:

1. Replace people with computers.

2. Get cheaper labor where you can.

3. Outsource as much as possible to cut salaries, benefits packages, and overhead.

4. Eliminate every position that isn't directly tied to the sacred Bottom Line.

So long as business conditions remain as they are, and global competition intensifies, the corporate bloodlettings will continue apace. There's no use whining about it. It's our reality. If they don't need us, they don't need us.

■ **I'm in my thirties and headlong into my career. What are the implications of all this downsizing on the traditional family?**

Very dire. It's getting harder and harder for any individual to earn a decent living and support his family as the primary breadwinner. The whole economic infrastructure of American life is undergoing massive changes. A New World Order is in formation. We are moving from a national to a global economy. The wealth of the West is being redistributed to the Third World. A leveling process is underway—except, of course, for the moneyed elite. The strong middle class upon which America was built is in decline. Times are changing.

■ What's the answer then?

Now, more than ever, God's people need to cling to the Lord with unapologetic zeal. Only God can see us through the times that are ahead. If the traditional family is to be preserved in any form, we must fight to preserve it. The forces arrayed against it are formidable indeed, and many of them are economic in nature.

With God, all things are possible. Let's face it, without God in our corner, we're lost—in more ways than one. This is the most important point of all. As the Psalm says, "Unless the Lord builds the house, its builders labor in vain" (Psalm 127:1).

Bring God into partnership in everything you do. "If the Lord delights in a man's way, he makes his steps firm; though he stumble, he will not fall, for the Lord upholds him with his hand. I was young and now I am old, yet I have never seen the righteous forsaken or their children begging for bread" (Psalm 37:23-25).

God's children must learn to trust their heavenly Father to take care of them. If we truly have faith, we'll not only survive, we'll thrive. We may undergo some refining trials, but we'll make it if we stick with the Lord.

IF YOU LOSE YOUR JOB

► **Create a life plan.** Focusing on your long-term goals will ease this temporary setback.

► **Set your alarm clock** for the same time each morning. Establish a daily routine.

► **Educate yourself** on multiple job-hunt strategies and employ as many as possible.

► **Follow a weekly schedule,** including a variety of job-hunting, family, and personal activities.

► **Recognize that job hunting** is a "numbers game"; the more doors you knock on, the better.

► **Do volunteer work** to keep productive and to learn new skills.

► **Tell everyone you know** that you are looking for work.

► **Seek emotional and financial counseling,** if you need it.

► **Don't take your job loss out on your family.** Instead, relieve stress through exercise and other constructive activities.

When we are weakest, God can be strongest on our behalf. When we fall down, it is our Father who picks us up, dusts us off, comforts us, and sends us on our way. Trust Him to do just that. He will.

■ **Can you give me some practical advice?**

Here are some basic tips:

▶ *Save money while you're working.* If and when you lose your job, you won't be able to rely on any kind of government safety net to bail you out financially. Unemployment insurance is close to minimum wage, and not nearly enough to pay the bills. Anytime you earn extra money, and claim it, your unemployment insurance is cut proportionately. You need money in the bank—and money that you can get at.

If your company has a stock savings plan, use it to full advantage. If it has a 401K plan, put all the money in it you can. That's your money—the government can't touch it until you retire, and then you're taxed at a lower rate. And, if you get desperate while your unemployed, you can get at that money by paying a major tax penalty. The point is, save all the money you can— you'll probably need every cent of it. It is biblical to save money, or to prepare for hard times. Remember Joseph in Egypt? Live out the proverb, "Go to the ant, you sluggard; consider its ways and be wise! It has no commander, no overseer or ruler, yet it stores its provisions in summer and gathers its food at harvest" (Proverbs 6:6-8).

▶ *Network, network, network!* The major way people get jobs and work today is through networking. This is especially difficult for natural introverts, but you have to do it. If you don't, you'll find yourself isolated and largely without support if you become unemployed. Study Luke 16:1-12. Think also about the proverb that says, "A man of many companions may come to ruin, but there is a friend who sticks closer than a brother" (Proverbs 18:24).

▶ *Lower your expectations.* In today's job market, no job is secure, none is for life. No matter how well you do your job, or how loyal you are to your company, you could be out of work tomorrow. Never think, "It couldn't happen to me." It could, and it might.

Don't expect your company to be loyal to you, or to care about your financial well-being. Today's spate of corporate bloodlettings have little to do with things that used to matter— loyalty, hard work, doing a good job, etc. Often bloodless corporate leaders are making decisions based on competition for capital, and preserving their own jobs, not yours. Don't expect anything of them, and you won't be let down.

▶ *Increase your marketability.* If you can make money for someone, someone will hire you. Your value to almost anyone is based on how much you can increase the size of their money pot. That can mean making money or saving money (as do accountants, auditors, actuaries, attorneys, etc.). Get good at it! Develop your marketable skills. Be able to do things employers want and need.

▶ *Bring God into partnership.* Only God can see us through the times that are ahead. If the traditional family is to be preserved in any form, we must *fight* to preserve it. The forces arrayed against us are formidable, but with God, all things are possible.

This material is adapted from writings by author Brian Knowles of Arcadia, California, and Donna Partow of Mesa, Arizona.

49

Long-Distance Dads

- -

■ **I am on the road thirty-five weeks a year, which means I must father from afar. I make it a point to call home every day. There are times when I learn one of the kids was injured, or they did well in school, and I'm not home to help or to celebrate. Afterward, I feel helpless. How can I be a good long-distance dad?**

God's role for the father as head of the home should be the norm for families in the '90s. Yet in millions of households, Dad won't be home tonight.

Long-distance fathering is a growing phenomenon. Not long ago, fathers worked on the family farm or commuted fifteen minutes to work. Today's business travel, however, sends fathers skittering across time zones. On-the-go-Dad could be breakfasting in Baltimore and supping in San Francisco before the day is out.

■ **But divorce has to play a big role in the increasing numbers of long-distance dads, right?**

Absolutely. The nation's high divorce rate means that tens of millions of fathers are legally separated from their offspring. In the 15 million single-parent homes in North America, the father is absent in nearly nine out of ten homes.

A growing trend, however, is the awarding of *joint* custody. Fathers who win custodial rights are discovering the difficulties of parenting with logistical challenges. For instance, his ex could live in Phoenix, while Dad is headquartered in Chicago.

That's why staying in touch with the kids—physically, emotionally, and spiritually—is probably the most difficult assignment a father can face. The pressure to be a good dad often results in guilt, bitterness, anger, denial, and passion.

■ **Is that why some fathers go off the deep end and even kidnap their children?**

Yes, unfortunately those incidents happen and get reported in the news, but many fathers do rise to the occasion and use their bottled-up feelings to fuel heroic expressions of grace and love. Long-distance dads can bridge the geographical boundaries and provide much of the love and support their children need.

■ **Here are some questions that run through my mind as a supertanker pilot. How much damage is my absence doing? What is my child really thinking or wanting? Things *seem OK* now, but am I just kidding myself? And finally: Is the expense of my heroic efforts to get home worth it when my child seems too small or doesn't respond much at all?**

A father named Chris began asking similar questions after his ex-wife and their toddler, Sheri, moved to a new town two hours away. "The move brought the reality crushing down on me," he remembers. "I felt my heart would break. But it also marked the point where I knew I had to turn my hatred over to Christ. Only through His help was I able to redirect my energies toward restoring a working relationship with Sheri's mom."

Rebuilding that relationship was in Sheri's best interest as well. Over those years, Chris visited Sheri once or twice a week. She's eleven now and lives with Chris every other weekend and on alternate holidays. On the weekends she doesn't visit, Chris writes a short letter. When Sheri was younger, Chris often mailed a postcard of a cute animal. Now his letters share thoughts and experiences that can only be expressed between a father and a daughter.

■ **My situation is different from Chris's. I live on the other side of the country from my son, Peter. Even though his mom sought to restrict my contact, I was determined no matter what the financial cost, I would do what I could. I telephoned weekly, and some of those calls were disasters. I could tell there were some occasions when Peter was far more interested in the TV than in talking to his dad. But I hung in there. Isn't that what you have to do?**

You've provided an important measure of stability in your young son's life. Here are some other helpful pointers for long-distance dads:

▶ *Strive for consistency.* Regular, small moments express love far better than infrequent "Disneyland" extravaganzas.

▶ *Make and sustain contact with your child's schoolteachers.* Knowing how they're doing in school will help you better support and encourage them.

   Direct contact with the school will also reveal any discipline problems and help you learn about academic achievements. This will keep father-son or father-daughter long-distance interactions more enjoyable and insightful.

▶ *Similarly, an occasional phone call* to their sports coaches, music instructors, and Sunday School teachers will display your attention to your child.

▶ *Keep your children in touch with relatives and friends* on your side of the family as much as possible.

▶ *Guard against letting those hours you used to spend with your children each week become absorbed by other activities.* Noting your child's special days or events on a calendar will keep you in touch. Ask their school and PTA to put you on the parent's mailing list.

▶ *Keep a camera handy and regularly enclose snapshots of yourself at home or at work.*

▶ *If you're not intuitively creative* about how to make notes, cards, letters, and phone calls fun and meaningful, seek out published resources and tips from other dads in similar situations.

▶ *Finally, let your separation motivate you to pray for your child in more specific ways.* Read up on the stages of development your child is passing through. Your fervent prayers can help protect him or her against the lure of life's many seductions.

■ **What happens if my ex-wife remarries and a stepfather enters into the picture?**

He may or may not do a wonderful job of guiding your children. Whatever the case, you will need to act wisely. Your sensitive involvement remains important.

Everyone knows, however, that *quality* time does not fully compensate for the loss of *quantity* time. A dedicated long-distance dad can be enormously effective in his child's life. Being a long-distance dad is never a lost cause. It's worth every ounce of energy, expense, and effort you can invest.

Your child has only one natural father. In this broken world, our Heavenly Father takes great delight in meeting giant needs with our loaves-and-fishes efforts!

This material is adapted from writings by author Paul Lewis of San Diego, California.

9

All About Marriage

50

Taking Your Wife to Court

. . . .

■ I call myself the Master of the Cheap Date. But don't get the wrong idea. I'm a CPA by trade, and I have taught finance seminars at our church and counseled couples on financial matters. Besides, I often say that there's a difference between being good stewards and being cheap, and that difference is learning how to be careful with the money we spend on food, clothing, and ourselves.

But I'm not a cheapskate. A cheapskate is one who orders the least expensive thing on the menu and then stiffs the waitress out of a tip. That's not a good witness, either. When I take my wife out each Friday night, we usually drive over to a Vons Pavilions (a Southern California upscale supermarket/deli) and order a Chinese take out platter for five bucks. Then we carry our meal to one of the two plastic tables in front of the supermarket. Invariably, church friends wave at—and razz—us as they walk into Vons. "Hey, Ronnie," yells one friend. "Got your wife out on a date, I see." We laugh, and I'm not embarrassed because we're laughing all the way to the bank.

Way to go! At least you're not as cheap as the guy who took his wife to the local blood bank on Tuesday nights. Why did he do that? Because on Tuesday nights they had a free buffet line for those donating blood. Now, that's *cheap*.

But you don't have to drain your veins to go out on a husband-and-wife date. By scheduling a regular time together, you're telling your wife that you love her and that she's special enough to court—even if it's over egg rolls and chow mein outside a supermarket deli.

■ **I've got an even better way to romance my wife. I roll up my shirt-sleeves and attack the dinner dishes. I tell Rhonda, "Honey, go sit on the couch and kick up your feet." Then I'll get the boys, and we'll clean up the dinner dishes. I tell them we're treating Mom special tonight. Let me tell you. My beautiful wife is putty in my hands after that. Are there other ways we can treat our spouses special?**

Glad you asked. But before we go into those, you should be congratulated for cherishing your wife, a concept that often gets tossed by the wayside once the honeymoon is over. Here are a few ways you can treat your spouse special:

▶ *Go shopping with her.* This is a brutal suggestion. It takes a brave man to walk through a mall hour after hour—with no end in sight. It's clearly beyond the call of duty for most husbands.

But one father said he feels like he actually courts his wife by "mall-crawling" with her. "In a humorous way, shopping isn't a great thing for me to do, but when we do it, I say, man, it's nice to be by ourselves," says Dan.

▶ *Write notes to her.* Concentrate on one area of her character that you admire, or you can express appreciation for what she does around the house and with the kids. Present the notes when they're least expected. (You'll be glad you did!)

Remembering to write a weekly note is nearly impossible. One father discovered that his wife is crazy about receiving little notes on a regular basis, so he devotes one hour every other month (after everyone else is in bed) to composing two-paragraph love letters. Then he doles them out week by week. He even uses different color pens so it won't look as though he wrote them all at once!

You can also turn the notes into a treasure hunt. Hide each one, giving a clue where to find the next note. The final note can tell her that she's invited out to dinner that night. (Be sure to arrange a baby-sitter in advance.)

▶ ***Sacrifice what's important to you.*** On Sunday afternoon, turn off that basketball game and take the kids to the local park so she can tackle that favorite sewing project. Rent *Love Story* rather than *Rambo*. Volunteer to cook one night a week—or have Domino's deliver. Carry the laundry basket down to the basement. Pick up after yourself. (Wouldn't that be a switch!) Large or small, she'll know that you're doing these things for *her*.

▶ ***Finally, make a big deal about anniversaries.*** If you know what's good for you, you better pull out all the stops for her birthday and wedding anniversaries. For Nicole's thirty-fifth birthday, I (Mike Yorkey) wanted to do something *really* special. We were living in Southern California, and one morning an advertisement for the Queen Mary popped out in the morning newspaper. Eureka!

Thoughts of spending the night in the Queen Victoria Suite and waking up to breakfast in bed danced through my head, but we didn't have anyone to watch the kids—nor could we afford it. (Besides, her birthday fell on a school night.) So I told Nicole to dress nicely and be prepared for *anything*. Some friends picked us up, and as we drove the sixty minutes on the L.A. freeways, I kept watching Nicole's face. She was enjoying every minute of the suspense! Once we pulled into the Queen Mary parking lot, we spent an afternoon tramping around the famous ocean liner. When evening fell, we topped off her birthday with an exquisite meal of *haute cuisine* at Sir Winston's restaurant. She's still talking about that adventure.

■ **My wife and I never have adventures. You can tell when the honeymoon is over for us. Communication has been reduced to "yes" and "no" answers, or it only occurs when we're trying to read each other's mind. Minor resentments build into larger ones. We've committed to too many activities outside the home, including our church. I've noticed that minor offenses or cross words are going more and more without an apology. What's happened to our marriage?**

Sounds like your romance meter is barely above zero. Any conversations between the two of you most likely revolve around the mundane: kids' school, carpools, soccer practice, getting to church on time. Neither of you are paying attention to each other's emotional needs.

Like the so-called "random acts of kindness," you need "random acts of romance." At the same time, you need to convince her that romancing doesn't mean you're looking for a payoff.

Have you bought her a surprise gift in the last decade or so? One husband, Nathaniel, has a good friend at a boutique, and he'll call her up and ask her to pick out an outfit or a pair of earrings since she knows his wife's size and taste.

But gifts don't have to cost much. One father, who doesn't have much money, says he buys his wife a single-stem rose for $2, or a little card that says she's looking great.

Another thing you can do is surprise her with a nighttime or weekend getaway. Mick, from Virginia, cooked up a little surprise for his wife's birthday one year. "I took her to a '50s-type diner where the motto was, 'If we can't fry it, we don't make it.' She thought it was really fun. Then I took her to the mall, peeled a fifty-dollar bill out of my wallet, and told her we're going to spend it on her."

THE TOP TEN ALTERNATIVES TO HAVING A DATE NIGHT

10. Going in for a prostate cancer checkup

9. Working in the yard

8. Calling Ma

7. Driving the kids somewhere—anywhere!

6. Getting a head start on the tax returns

5. Chris "Back-Back-Back" Berman and ESPN SportsCenter

4. Checking the crawl space for termites

3. Flea dipping the cat

2. Tightening bolts on the Taurus' muffler bearings

1. Installing a new gun rack on the pickup

■ **I've heard about couples who do weekend "getaways." These don't sound very practical to us, but if we are going to try it, what should we do?**

Weekend getaways involve lots of planning, and it might not work for many couples, especially those with young children. Unless you have grandparents nearby who can take the kids for a night or two, it's a tough proposition. But it can be worked out.

■ **What are some sports that my wife and I can do together?**

Bowling. Don't laugh, because it's not much of a sport, but how about joining a bowling league?

■ **You mean wear one of those goofy shirts? I had something more athletic in mind.**

Tennis, anyone? One of my (Mike Yorkey) first "dates" with Nicole was on a tennis court, and we've played hundreds of husband-and-wife matches since. (We figure if we can survive playing tennis together, our marriage can survive *anything*.)

Waterskiing and snow skiing are two recreational activities that couples can do together. For those more sedentary, we've heard of couples who love to watch high school football games together.

■ **I'm glad that works for you, but we aren't sportive.**

Then find a hobby you both enjoy, such as bird watching, strolling through art galleries, or gardening. If you can't go out, spend an evening talking to her. Does the TV automatically flip on each evening at your house? If it does, it's a huge communication buster. How about reserving one night each week for conversing with her? Make coffee or tea and sit in the den and look at each other and *talk*. It may seem awkward at first, but it can be the first halting step toward intimacy.

One Texas father has made communication Job One. "I try to share as much as I can about what goes on during the day," he says. "Both of us try not to hold anything back, and we've practiced that since we first got married."

■ **What would happen to our marriage if I suddenly started treating my wife special all the time?**

At first, depending on your track record, she'd probably think that you're after something. Then she'd probably ask you if something's wrong. Eventually, if you can maintain your good intentions, she'll start believing you've really changed.

But if your motives are wrong, it won't work. When you're above board, your wife's love for you will deepen. One man leaves notes on his wife's pillow ("though I'm not much of a writer"), sends her flowers occasionally, buys her inexpensive gifts, remembers special days and anniversaries, gives frequent hugs, and helps around the house. And every day he tells her he loves her!

■ **Dating your mate sounds like a good idea. But finances are a problem. What are some ways to make the most out of our times together?**

I (Mike) knew I wasn't doing a good job romancing Nicole. We had gotten into a nondating rut over the years, the biggest hindrance being a lack of finances since we've decided to make the sacrifice to keep Nicole at home with the kids. But after reading and hearing so much about the importance of regularly dating your wife, I figured I better get with the program. We decided to start going out to lunch three, four times a month, and it's made a difference.

Lunch is 20 to 50 percent cheaper than eating out for dinner, and if your kids are in school, you save on baby-sitting costs. Lunches are better too if you have a time crunch with kids' activities during the week.

■ **But my husband works in the city, a good forty minutes away.**

Then getting together for lunch is not going to be practical. Can you go out for breakfast or brunch on Saturday morning while some friends watch the kids? Reserve one night for yourselves?

If your children are a little older, but you don't feel comfortable leaving them alone for a long time, go to a neighborhood cafe for after-dinner coffee. The idea is to converse. That's why if you go to your local cineplex, you may see a good film, but no communication will go on.

This material is adapted from Daddy's Home *by Greg Johnson and Mike Yorkey, © 1992. Used by permission of Tyndale House Publishers, Inc. All rights reserved.*

51

The Language of Love

■ **I have to say that it's a real struggle for my wife and I to understand each other—particularly when we discuss important issues. How can we get on the same page?**

First, you need to know that males and females think and speak differently, much differently. In order for you to begin spanning the communication gap between you, you need to start using emotional "word pictures."

■ **"Word pictures"? What's that?**

Word pictures, or emotional word pictures, can supercharge communication and change lives, whether in marriage, families, friendships, or businesses. Indeed, word pictures have the capacity to capture a person's attention by engaging both their thoughts and their feelings.

Have you ever tried to express an important thought or feeling with members of the opposite sex, only to have them act as if you're speaking a foreign language? Have you ever asked, "Why can't he (or she) *feel* what I'm saying?"

Throughout history, many women have found it difficult (some say impossible!) to communicate with men. And an equal number of men have given up trying to converse with women.

■ So how do I go about creating an emotional word picture?

You must begin with an important preparatory step: deciding how you want to enrich your relationship. Do you want your words to:
    A. Clarify thoughts and feelings?
    B. Move you to a deeper level of intimacy?
    C. Praise or encourage someone?
    D. Lovingly correct someone?

■ This all sounds good on paper, but I need an example. Can you give me one?

How would you like to be a royal adviser who was called on to confront a warrior king—particularly one who recently tried to cover up both an affair and first-degree murder? The following word picture demonstrates the power to change a person's heart.

There was a once a young shepherd boy, named David, who was singled out to be a future king. When David ascended to the throne, he was known throughout the world as a fearless warrior who led his armies in countless victories. But as his fame increased, he began walking on the dangerous edge of power. Anything he wanted was in his grasp.

It was during this time, when his shepherd's heart had grown cold, that he walked onto the roof of his palace and gazed across the city of all he controlled, all he commanded. As the sun set and a refreshing breeze picked up, his eyes suddenly caught a reflection from a rooftop below. It was the last rays of sunlight, shimmering off a pool of water. Looking closer, he realized the reflection came as the water was stirred by a woman bathing.

Moving to a better vantage point, he scrutinized the beautiful woman. His pulse grew quicker; his breath, shorter. Then, his lust having devised a plan, he dispatched his guards to bring the woman to the palace. Soon enough, David learned that this striking woman, named Bathsheba, was the wife of one of his officers on the battle line.

Now, that didn't deter David. His mind was not on a faraway battle but on a conquest near at hand. So he had her brought into his private chamber for a night of forbidden passion.

The next morning, the evening's entertainment was sent back home. There is every indication the king wanted their encounter to be a one-night stand, but several weeks later, the young woman sent a private message to the king. She was pregnant with his child.

In his early years, King David had been known as an upright man. But by this time, his one error seemed to justify another, so his darkened heart devised another cunning plan.

He would send for the woman's husband, who was still away fighting, and bring him home on leave as a decorated hero. David was sure the soldier, like an average red-blooded serviceman who'd been away from his beautiful wife for months, would fill his night home with romance.

But Bathsheba's husband was several cuts above the average. Since the men he commanded were still on the battle lines, far from their wives and families, he refused the privileges of marriage.

The king was stunned that the man's loyalty to his troops was more powerful than his passions. His mind quickly scrambled for a second plan, and a crude idea struck him. He invited him to the palace, got him drunk, and then sent him home. Yet once again, he refused to go inside. Knowing the wine would weaken his resolve, he slept on the steps of his house. Unbeknownst to him, he signed his own death certificate.

Several weeks had passed since Bathsheba first announced her pregnancy, and it took a few more to get her husband back from the battle. As a woman with a shapely figure, she couldn't keep the secret much longer. Increasingly desperate, David stooped the lowest when he grasped an evil plan that couldn't fail.

Through a top-secret dispatch, he sent her husband back to the front lines and into the thick of battle. Then, following the king's specific instructions, the commanding general pulled back all his supporting troops to leave the soldier alone in the face of the enemy.

The plan worked flawlessly. With no protection and no one to stand with him, he was slaughtered in the open, alone.

With Bathsheba's husband out of the way, the king brought his one-time lover into the palace as his new wife. Overnight, a thin veneer of legitimacy covered the dark secret. In time, David's fears of being found out relaxed. He slept much easier, but he desperately hoped the general who executed his evil sentence would guard the secret with his life.

■ **But didn't the truth come out?**

Yes, it did, and here is how powerful words can pierce the heart. While King David's conscience had been in hiding, a court adviser named Nathan was given a divine charge. He was to confront David with an emotional word picture that would change the course of a kingdom and echo through the ages.

"Your Majesty," his adviser began, bowing low, "a serious problem in the kingdom has come to my attention. Sir, in your kingdom is a very poor family, who with all their resources could purchase only one suckling lamb. As this animal grew, he became a special pet and an important part of the household, having the run of the house and even sleeping with the children to keep them warm.

"In this poor family, the farmer farms lands owned by a wealthy rancher," he continued. "Recently, late in the afternoon, unexpected guests arrived at the rich man's house. A customary feast was in order. Yet the herdsmen were away with the flocks, and the only fresh meat at hand was one of the aging goats—far too tough a meal for the important guests.

"That's when the landowner looked down the hill and saw two children playing with a beautiful, plump lamb," the adviser said, pausing a moment to clear his throat.

SOME SAMPLE WORDS PICTURES

Need some help coming up with word pictures? Maybe these will spark some ideas:

► "With the job I'm in, I often feel like I'm walking on a desert trail on a hot summer day. After struggling through the heat and cactus all day, I come to the end of a path, and there's a beautiful pool of cool water. At last I'm at a place where I can drink and be refreshed. That's what it's like being with you. After ten years of marriage, I still feel that being with you is like coming upon an oasis."

► "There have been times over the years when I've faced hailstorms that I thought would turn into tornadoes. But like the shelter of a storm cellar, I can always run to you to protect me from hardship. You're as solid as a rock, and I know you'll always be there when the storm clouds blow into my life."

► "Sweetheart, when you live with a brand new, gleaming white Cadillac convertible, there's no desire to rush and drive a Yugo."

■ **And then what happened?**

"Well, go on," King David replied impatiently. "Finish your story."

"Yes, your majesty," he said, maintaining his voice at its deliberate pace. "As I was saying, the rich man saw the animal, and an idea came to him. He could butcher the lamb and not have to send a servant all the way to his own flocks. And that's exactly what he did. The lamb was slaughtered and prepared for his guests, without any thought given to the children or their parents."

Color rushed to the king's face, and his eyes flashed with rage. His feelings brought back memories, which in turn sparked deeper memories. He too had raised lambs from birth, sheltered them from harm, loved them as pets, and felt heartbroken if anything happened to them.

"As you know, your majesty, children may have the heart for battle, but they are no match for grown men. With their father away tending his fields, their cries for help went unheard. And the little boy, clinging desperately to the lamb, was slapped away like a fly.

"That night, the little children huddled in their beds, weeping to hear the music and laughter from the rancher's house above. Their hearts broke to think of other people's appetites being satisfied by the pet which—"

"That's enough!" the king shouted. "Say no more!" He jumped to his feet, livid with anger. "That man deserves death! I tell you, today he is to make restitution to that family. He is to pay them back fourfold what they lost. I want four of his best lambs to be chosen from his flocks, and I want them taken to that family—immediately," he commanded. "And then," he said with a glint in his eye, "I want that man brought to me this very afternoon!"

The large throne room had the acoustics of a Gothic church. When King David's angry words ceased reverberating from the walls, a heavy silence fell upon the room. Ears were poised with anticipation. Though the adviser never spoke above a whisper, the impact of his words crashed through the room like peals of thunder.

"Your majesty," he began, "*you* are that man! The little lamb you took was another man's wife!"

The story hit the king so forcefully and unexpectedly that he was driven to his knees. His heart, encased by adultery and murder in steel-like silence, now lay shattered by the blow of one emotional word picture. For the first time, he was forced to face the evil he had done, forced to *feel* some of the emotional trauma he had caused others.

■ **Wow, what a story! I probably won't be facing an angry king anytime soon, so what does this have to do with me?**

Ah, but you probably are aware of someone with whom you need to talk. Like Nathan, you may need to confront a problem in your marriage relationship. Or perhaps you're looking for more clarity in your communication or greater intimacy in your marriage. Or maybe you're searching for just the right words of love and encouragement for your children.

■ **Well, I've been postponing a conversation about summer vacation with my wife. I'm not quite sure how to tell her that we need to switch dates. What do I do?**

First, carefully study the other person's interests. The word picture used with King David showed an intimate understanding of his background and interests. That is, Nathan chose a story that tapped into David's experience as a shepherd and a defender of his people. By doing so, Nathan took a shortcut to the king's heart.

If you're thinking about a word picture for your wife, learn enough about her world to understand what makes her good days good and her bad days terrible. If she works at home, what are her needs and frustrations? If she works outside the home, what does she do during lunch breaks? If you look long and hard, you'll discover the interests that enable you to enter the world of the person you're trying to reach.

This material is adapted from Language of Love *by Gary Smalley and John Trent, Ph. D. Copyright © 1988, 1991, Gary Smalley and John Trent, Ph. D. Used by permission of Focus on the Family.*

52

Surround Your Marriage with Hedges

. . . .

■ **Some friends of mine came up to me and said, "Did you hear about So-and-So?" That question has become so common that I cringe when I hear it because my first thought is, Oh, no, please not them too. What a shocking disappointment to discover another Christian couple has split because one of the spouses was unfaithful. If so many of my friends and acquaintances have fallen—people I never would have suspected—how can our marriage avoid becoming a casualty?**

There's a new openness to interaction between the sexes in the workplace, in the neighborhood, in counseling—even in the church. Christians touch, speak more intimately, are closer to one another. There are advantages to this, but also grave dangers. Fear can be good. Fear is as good a motivator as any to maintain fidelity.

■ **How big then is the problem of infidelity among Christian couples?**

According to a survey of 1,000 readers of *Christianity Today*, fully 23 percent indicated that they had engaged in sexual intercourse with someone other than their wives. Twenty-eight percent indicated they had involved themselves in other forms of sexual contact outside their marriages, so it's a big problem.

Marriages are breaking up at such an alarming rate that it's hard to find someone who has not been affected by divorce in his immediate family. How many divorces can you count in your own family, including grandparents on both sides, aunts, uncles, and your own siblings?

You may not know how many of those divorces were the result of immorality, but half is a fair assumption. Women leave their husbands for a variety of complex reasons, the most minor of which—according to marriage counselors—is their own lust. Rarely do you hear of a woman who simply fell for someone who, by his sexual appeal alone, turned her head and heart from her own husband.

But men—yes, even those who would blame their frumpy, crabby, boring wives for their own roving eyes—don't really need an excuse. They will point to myriad reasons for having to leave, but it nearly always can be traced to lust, pride, and a false sense of their own strength.

A strange aspect of infidelity is that a man usually has to invent reasons after the fact. The man who once taught marriage seminars, raved about his wife, treated her right, was proud of her, now must say:

"We hid the truth. Our marriage was never good."

"In private, she was not what she appeared to be in public."

"I never loved her."

"She didn't understand me" (the oldest saw in the tool kit).

■ But aren't there two sides to every story and no such thing as an innocent party?

Those statements need examination. No, none of us knows what went on behind closed doors, and we all know how base we can be in private, compared to the image we project in public.

But if you know divorced couples, you know of examples where, if she was not innocent, the wife was certainly not guilty of anything that justified her husband's leaving her for another woman.

A man who is no prize himself will justify breaking the laws of God, breaking his promises to his wife, violating their union, and then blame it on her! Call it what you will, but a man with as perfect a wife as he could ever want is still capable of lust, of a senseless seeking of that which would destroy him and his family. If he does not fear his own

continued on page 336

INNOCENT HUMOR
by Jerry Jenkins

I worked at a camp one summer during my high school years. One week one of the women counselors, about a year older than I, shared my last name. We were not related and had never seen each other before. When we were introduced, we had not even made much of an issue over the name duplication. While Jenkins is not as common as Smith or Jones, neither it is as unique as Higgenbotham or Szczepanik.

One night after the campers were in bed, a bunch of us staffers and a few of the counselors, Miss Jenkins included, were watching a football game on television. A couple of the guys started kidding Miss Jenkins and me about being married. We were both so young and naive and insecure that we just blushed and hoped the running gag would run out of gas.

For some reason I had to leave the impromptu party before the game was over, and as I headed for the door, someone said, "Hey, Jenkins, aren't you takin' yer wife with ya? "I got this urge to show the crowd that I could be just as funny as they and that I was a good sport, so I turned and pointed at her. "No, but I want you home in bed in fifteen minutes."

I was out the door and ten feet from the TV cabin when I heard the hooting and hollering. I had not intended even to imply anything risqué. I had merely been trying to go along with the joke, and instead of speaking to the girl the way a husband would to a wife, I had spoken to her as a father to daughter.

Of course, everyone took my wanting her home in bed the wrong way, and with my reputation for enjoying a funny line, I knew I would never live it down. In fact, if I tried to go back and explain, no one would even believe me. They would wonder why I didn't want to take the credit for such a great joke. The girl was as sweet and chaste as most counselors would be at a camp like that, and the last thing I wanted her to think was that I had been inappropriate and gotten a cheap laugh at her expense.

A hundred feet from the cabin, still hearing the laughter, I knew I had to go back. When I opened the door, no one even noticed me. Something had happened on the game that had everyone's attention. I was glad to see Miss Jenkins wasn't sitting there weeping with her head in her hands. When I called her name and she looked up, so did everyone else, and the snickering began again. I wished they had been laughing at me for saying such a stupid thing, but I knew they were laughing because I had gotten away with such a saucy line.

"Could I see you for a minute?" I asked, and the room fell deathly silent. I'll never forget her response as long as I live. "I'm not too sure," she said.

It was the funniest comeback I could imagine in that situation, and I wish I'd anticipated it. If my original line had been intentional, I would still have always thought hers was better, especially on the spur of the moment.

The place erupted again, and I winced self-consciously, knowing that I appeared to deserve that. I was grateful when she bounced to her feet and followed me out into the darkness. I had the impression she knew what I was going to say.

"You need to know I didn't mean that the way it sounded," I said.

"I know," she replied.

"You do?"

"Uh-huh."

"I don't think anyone else understands that."

"Maybe not, but I do. I've seen you around, heard you be funny. That's not your style. At first I was embarrassed and disappointed, but I caught a glimpse of your face as you hurried out, and I knew."

"Your comeback in there was priceless."

"I couldn't pass it up. But I knew you were back to apologize, so I figured I could say something and apologize for it at the same time."

I laughed and she added, "We Jenkinses have to stick together, you know."

Strangely, we didn't see any more of each other after that than we would have otherwise. She had her crowd and I had mine. I had learned a lesson, though. I knew to be more careful about teasing in a flirting manner. I also learned how wonderful and forgiving and insightful some women can be. Funny too.

potential and build a hedge around himself and his marriage, he heads for disaster.

■ What do you mean by building a hedge around himself and his marriage?

Jesus told parables about landowners who planted vineyards and protected them with hedges. When those hedges were trampled or removed, ruin came to the precious possessions of the landowners. Similarly, we need to plant hedges of protection around our marriages to protect them.

Need any more evidence that there are biblical bases for planting hedges around your marriage? Psalm 89:40 implies that strongholds are brought to ruin when hedges are broken down. Job 1:10 implies that Job was so richly blessed—before God allowed him to be tested—because God had made a hedge around him, his household, "and around all that he has on every side."

We hold people and relationships much more precious than land or holdings. If we can keep from deceiving ourselves about our own resolve and inner strength, we will see the necessity for a healthy row of blossoming hedges that keep love in and infidelity out.

■ **What are some ways I can protect myself from infidelity?**

Here are six hedges you should have:

► *Hedge No. 1:* Whenever I need to meet or dine or travel with an unrelated member of the opposite sex, I make it a threesome. Should an unavoidable last-minute complication make this impossible, my spouse hears it from me first.

► *Hedge No. 2:* I am careful about touching. While I might shake hands or squeeze an arm or a shoulder in greeting, I embrace only dear friends or relatives, and only in front of others.

► *Hedge No. 3:* If I pay a compliment, it is on clothes or hairstyle, not on the person herself. Commenting on a pretty outfit is much different than telling a women that she herself looks pretty.

► *Hedge No. 4:* I avoid flirtation or suggestive conversation, even in jest.

► *Hedge No. 5:* I remind my spouse often—in writing and orally—that I remember my wedding vows: "Keeping you only unto me for as long as we both shall live. . . ."

■ **I can see how many affairs are the result of falling into our own self-made and self-baited traps. How can I keep from setting my own traps?**

Here are some things to remember:

1. *Consider first your friends.*

In a society where flirtation is the norm and an affair is commonplace behavior, you must choose and cultivate your friends carefully. Friends who treat marital infidelity lightly or tell suggestive jokes and stories are really enemies of your marriage.

Avoid them. Since many affairs take place between close friends—

couples who have had strong friendships together—loose sex talk breaks down the protective walls, piques the curiosity, and encourages fantasies. The more open and transparent the friendship, the more necessary to keep the conversation on a high level.

Many a woman has faced the double tragedy of her husband's unfaithfulness with her best friend. Without appearing self-righteous or preachy, you can always find ways to let your friends know that you consider fidelity to be very important. And, of course, your own positive actions must support this so your friends see and hear that you admire, appreciate, and love your spouse.

When anything is said in conversation that in any way makes light of marriage, you should respond with something positive in your relationship. Don't let the atmosphere remain poisoned with the doubts and negativism that gives marriage a bad press. Be more than a silent witness. Speak up for marriage—for your marriage.

2. Watch out for office romances.

It is no secret that many affairs are spawned in the office and that sexual favors often influence contracts and affect promotions. One attractive and competent secretary said she protected herself this way: "I have turned down all invitations to eat lunch with other men in our office because I valued my marriage too much to expose myself to those risks."

3. Avoid magazines and entertainment that lower inhibitions.

You know what we're talking about—the gossipy supermarket tabloids and the "Hard Copy"-type programs and the TV "soaps." In fact, it is nearly impossible to build a great marriage and be a devotee of soap operas. Their distorted drama of romance, sexuality, infidelity, and affairs encourages marital dissatisfaction.

Becoming engrossed in the sordid lives of soap opera stars is bound to result in a feeling that you're being cheated in your present marriage and that an affair would bring release from your boredom. This unrealistic fantasy increases any marriage disappointment you may already feel.

The result of this decreasing commitment and effort is further marital deterioration. This, then, further feeds the fantasy and sets you up for an affair. It's a vicious cycle. You simply cannot build a real marriage on a fantasy with imaginary characters.

This material is adapted from Loving Your Marriage Enough to Protect It *by Jerry Jenkins, Copyright © 1989, 1993 by Jerry G. Jenkins, Moody Press. Used by permission; and J. Allan Petersen,* The Myth of the Greener Grass *(Tyndale House).*

53

When Families Break Up: The Human Toll

. . . .

■ **I've heard family experts say that the word *divorce* should never be discussed between couples, but lately our marriage is in such sad shape that I'm thinking about the D-word. Would divorce solve my problems?**

Thankfully, divorce is a word millions of couples never have to think about seriously. Their marriages flow on like Old Man River, even if they run into rapids occasionally.

But for others like you, the water is bumpy for long stretches. Nearly everyone knows a couple whose marriage vows are being tossed and turned by white water. Should they opt for separate boats?

Anyone trying to decide whether they should divorce a mate is probably experiencing the greatest emotional pain of his or her life. People rarely make good decisions in such a state.

■ **But isn't divorce liberating?**

The general impression is you will have a great chance to be happy after you dump the bum or send the witch away. Studies have proven this is not the case. Divorce will affect you the rest of your life in ways you could have never imagined. For example, divorcing your mate often means divorcing your friends. If you go to church, it means facing the reality that your faith will not be respected as it once was. You will find yourself starting over.

■ What are some of the other consequences of getting a divorce?

If you have children, you will damage them in several ways. Children of divorce have been found more likely to commit suicide, become homosexuals, or indulge in promiscuous behavior. They are more likely to become problem students or spend time in jail. They tend to be insecure.

Children often lose trust in their parents. They start taking cues from their peers—who may be into drugs, sex, and rock 'n' roll. You probably don't find that desirable.

Children of divorce experience more illness, both mental and physical, than children whose parents stay together. They will be subjected to the repeated tugging of two parents fighting for their time and emotional support. The children will be compelled to take sides, even though that is the last thing in the world they want to do.

■ That's a grim picture you've painted, but aren't you overstating your case?

Marriage counselor Gary Richmond has seen a lot of these things in his counselor's office over the last twenty-five years.

Recently, a father named Bob told him how his marriage was steadily deteriorating. He no longer slept in the same bedroom with his wife. During an intense fight, Bob would leave the house, rather than stay and be berated in front of the children. Sharon, his wife, would fall into depression. She sat for hours doing needlepoint or reading the same page of the newspaper over and over again.

The two youngest children were left to fend for themselves. Cold cereal and quick snacks were their diet.

One night, Bob heard five-year-old Julie quietly call him. He stuck his head into her bedroom and gruffly asked, "What are you doing up?"

Julie reached up her arms and whispered, "Daddy, will you hold me?" Bob pulled her close and listened. "Daddy, it's just that I don't know if anyone loves me anymore," she said in a quivering voice.

Bob held her in his arms until she fell asleep, but before she did, he repeated, "Julie, I love you, and I always will."

Divorce robs children of their fondest hope—"and they lived happily ever after." Because parents experience traumatic pain during a divorce, they are often unable to help others, including their own children.

■ How will my finances be affected by a divorce?

If you choose divorce, your finances will be affected for years to come. Rarely is there enough money to go around. Both parties are usually assigned to a bare-bones existence.

Gary Richmond asked some single parents these questions: How did your standard of living change after your divorce? What was the worst financial problem you faced during the divorce? Some answers:

► "My divorce took me from comfort to poverty. I guess it's poverty when you can no longer pay your basic living expenses and you lose all your credit."

► "It seems the most of the support from my husband goes to child care so I can work. My hourly wage is low, so things are always tight. The thought of my car breaking down terrifies me. I feel stressed out just thinking about it!"

► "It was hard to leave our home and move to a rental house. We had to take in boarders to make ends meet."

► "It's been hard since the divorce. You can best describe our life as 'no frills.'"

Financial life after divorce is the pits. If you don't believe it, ask around. Your divorced friends will verify everything.

■ But can't I get a good lawyer to see that I am financially protected in divorce court?

One of the most frightening aspects of divorce is the legal system. You *will* need a divorce lawyer, and that is not good news.

Don't think for a minute that your mate will be the only one fighting for a share of the money. Wait until you see your own lawyer's bill. In California, the average couple spends $15,000 fighting for children, lawn chairs, the family dog, and the ten-year-old sedan. Lawyers are the only winners in a divorce proceeding.

"I hate being a divorce lawyer," said Dean. "I'm not going to be one much longer. I'm going back to criminal law."

"Why criminal law over divorce law?" Gary inquired.

"Everyone is out to get everyone. No one is ever satisfied. Kids are getting the shaft, everyone is lying through their teeth, and everyone's angry at someone all the time."

"What angers people the most?"

His answer was surprising. "There is never enough money to go around. Everyone thinks they are going to maintain the same standard of living, and when they don't, it really burns them. They resent paying my bills, and I feel like I'm ripping off poor people whom I helped make poor."

■ **I once read a respected and successful lawyer describe his colleagues who practiced divorce law as "the dregs of the profession." Who would want to spend their waking hours helping families dissolve?**

Consider this story. Several months ago, George came to Gary seeking counsel. His wife of three years wanted a divorce. She was leaving him no opening for reconciliation and had, in fact, filed papers. It was George's first marriage and her second.

"I don't know any lawyers," he said. "Could you pick one?"

"I think so," Gary replied. "If your case is simple, you can get a lawyer just starting out and save a lot of money. Do you own a home together or rent?"

"Rent."

"Do you have any assets that you obtained during your marriage? A car, boat, savings, stocks, or bonds?"

"The only thing we have is a car worth about $2,000."

"Are any of the children yours, or are they hers from her previous marriage?"

"All hers."

"Well, George, your situation is very simple. Anyone could handle it. Get an inexpensive lawyer and give your wife the car."

"Isn't that like handing her a thousand dollars?"

"Not really. If you decide to fight for the car or your share of it, you will spend that much anyway. Say your lawyer costs $125 an hour. If you go to court and your case goes past the lunch hour, your lawyer will likely charge you for the whole day. That's $1,000. Even if you win, you won't win anything. If you lose—which is likely, you'll lose $2,000."

George's last question was, "How much do you think this will cost me?"

"If you don't fight for anything, you should get out of this for under $300."

Gary didn't hear from George for three or four months. When he did, he was shocked to find he was embroiled in a horrendous legal battle. It seems his lawyer, Benedict, was able to stir George's emotions to the boiling point and goaded him into fighting for the $1,000 equity in the car. One thing led to another and a war broke out, replete with restraining orders, court dates, and dozens of lawyer and client conferences. As Gary had predicted, George lost the car and spent $7,000 doing it.

Benedict charged him $140 an hour, so the bill ballooned quickly. Have you ever seen a lawyer's billing sheet? Every time you phone the office and talk to him, the meter is running. Every time he calls the courthouse to schedule a hearing, the meter is running. Every time he dictates a letter, the meter is running. Every time he appears in court on your behalf, the meter is running—including the time he spent driving to court!

The sad truth is that if you decide to divorce your mate, you will need a lawyer and a judge. You will be paying lawyers by the hour, so it is in their best interests to prolong the proceedings. The judges, on the other hand, are hard-pressed for time, so your case probably won't be given the time needed for a fair and prudent decision. The judges may also be sick and tired of hearing two people verbally cut each other to pieces.

Don't count on justice in the divorce court. It may happen, but don't count on it.

■ **Yes, but when the divorce is over I can go on, free from the influence of the person who brought so much pain into my life.**

That seems reasonable, but it never works out that way. If you have children (and 70 percent of those seeking a divorce do), you will be *forced* to talk to each other. You will arrange child visitations, vacation plans, holiday schedules, and inform each other when the children are sick or have some special problem.

Children are the surest way to "get" the former spouse. Even though children should never be used in this way, it seems impossible for divorced parents to resist the temptation. If something happens during your period of care, you will probably be called irresponsible and inept.

You may have to ask why the support payments are late—or nonexistent. If you remarry, you are sure to have some well-meaning friend address your new spouse by your old mate's name. You will need their signature for some piece of unfinished business. It never ends. *Never!*

■ **I know in the Bible that it says that it's not good that man should be alone. I'm in an abusive situation, but if I divorce my husband, I'm afraid I'll be so lonely.**

Loneliness *is* a problem. Gary Richmond remembers the time when Gail came to his office one day seeking counsel. Her story was a journey to hell and back.

"I was a pastor's wife; he's not a pastor anymore, and we're now divorced. He's been calling and writing lately and says he wants to get back together."

"And you're wondering if that would be possible or wise?"

"Yes, that's the question."

"What led to your getting a divorce?"

"Jack and I were married for twenty years when I discovered that he was having an affair. I was deeply hurt and confronted him about it. I asked him how he could commit adultery and still call himself a Christian. This really struck a sharp chord. He slapped me and pushed me down on the floor. Then he screamed at me. This type of thing happened frequently, and Jack became progressively more violent. Jack is still in that relationship, and they've been living together for four years now."

"He's living with the other woman and has been writing to you about getting back together?"

"Yes, that's right."

"Aren't you a little skeptical?"

"Well, yes."

"How can you even be considering taking him back?" Gary asked with genuine amazement.

"I'm very lonely," she offered.

"Gail, let me recount to you what you have just shared with me. Jack has sustained a long-term affair, repeatedly hit you, and lied to you over and over, so there is no way you can trust him. Are you telling me that your loneliness is harder to endure than that?"

"Sometimes."

Gary couldn't think of anything to say. He had never been that lonely.

■ So is divorce ever appropriate? Will I be sinning if I file for divorce?

This is a tough one. What matters is what God thinks. He has promised His Holy Spirit to convict us of sin if we're sinning. A good rule concerning sin is: "When in doubt, don't." If there is a shred of doubt that you are violating God's will, then you will lose nothing by waiting to make the decision. You will certainly win God's approval, not to mention peace of mind. Don't make this decision quickly. Give God the time to move in your situation or make His will clear to you.

There will be critics to the following list, but many pastors and counselors believe there are three legitimate causes for divorce:

1. Adultery
2. Abuse (physical to spouse or children)
3. Abandonment

■ Is there a Scripture substantiating your position that physical abuse is a legitimate reason to divorce your mate?

No direct Scripture exists, but consider the following related passage:

Husband, love your wives, as Christ loved the church and gave Himself up for her, that He might sanctify her, having cleansed her by the washing of water by the word, that He might present the church to Himself in splendor, without spot or wrinkle or any such thing, that she might be holy and without blemish. Even so, husbands should love their wives as their own bodies. He who loves his own wife loves himself. For no man ever hates his own flesh but nourishes and cherishes it, as Christ does the church, because we are members of His body. For this reason a man shall leave his father and mother and be joined to his wife, and the two shall become one flesh. This mystery is a profound one and I am saying that it refers to Christ and the church; however, let each one of you love his wife as himself, and let the wife see that she respects her husband. (Eph. 5:25-33)

This passage allows no room for physical abuse. Perhaps author Lewis Smedes spoke rightly when he said, "This is not to say that God approves of divorce; it is only to say that He sometimes disapproves of its alternatives more than He disapproves of divorce."

But let's say your situation is difficult—very difficult. You may have biblical grounds for divorce. It would still be in your best interest to consider a reconciliation. Even if it doesn't work out, you would have the knowledge that you did everything possible to maintain this sacred human relationship. For that, you will obtain peace of mind and the respect of those who know you best.

■ But aren't second marriages better than first marriages since both partners know what went wrong?

If you choose to divorce with the thought that love is better the second time around, you need to know that second marriages have a less than 30 percent chance of surviving five years or more. A third marriage has less than a 15 percent chance of survival.

It could be that you have a legitimate case for divorce, but you need to know that being divorced is so devastating that you must face its consequences squarely as you make your decision. Fixing your marriage may be easier than breaking it, although at this moment you find that impossible to believe. You owe it to yourself, your mate, your children, your friends, and God to carefully explore this issue. If you give God an inch, He'll take a mile if you're willing to go along for the ride.

This material is adapted from writings by Gary Richmond who directs the single parents ministry at First Evangelical Free Church in Fullerton, California.

54

Becoming One

. . . .

■ **Why aren't more marriages successful? In the past few years, there have been thousands of articles, books, films, videos, seminars, and workshops on marriage. It seems like there are enough resources out there for couples to get their acts together.**

Good question. Dennis Rainey, National Director of the Family Ministry for Campus Crusade for Christ, has himself given thousands of marriage seminars. From his experience, couples who are trying to become one need to ask themselves three questions:

1. Are you and your spouse a part of the family of God?
2. Are both of you allowing Christ to control your entire lives?
3. Are both of you allowing the Holy Spirit to guide and empower your lives?

Rainey says that unless you can answer yes to all three questions, you will lack the power to build your home with the oneness God intends. His ideal plan is that both partners in a marriage know Him personally.

■ **But I know Christ. I'm a Christian.**

Yes, but are you experiencing Him to the fullest, especially within the bonds of marriage?

Dennis Rainey says for the longest time he used Jesus Christ as a spare tire. When he had a "flat" (or crisis), he would pull Christ out of his trunk and run Him for a couple of days, maybe two or three hundred miles, whatever came first. But when the crisis was over, guess where Christ went?

■ **Right back into the trunk.**

Exactly. When Dennis realized that He was more than a spare tire, he began treating Him like a hitchhiker. So Dennis let Him in the car with him, but he let Him ride part of the way. Dennis didn't expect Jesus to be a permanent passenger.

Then it dawned on Dennis that if Jesus Christ was his Savior *and* Lord, He wouldn't be satisfied with being a spare tire or a hitchhiker. He wanted to drive the car! That's when Dennis gave his total life to Him. At that point, Christianity changed from just being a fire insurance policy to the abundant life we hear so much about.

■ **When we got married a year ago, we had expectations of how the relationship should work. An unspoken assumption is that we would meet each other halfway, kind of a "You do your part, and I'll do mine." That concept sounds logical to me. Is it?**

Couples who use the "do you part, and I'll do mine" philosophy are destined for disappointment because it is *impossible to determine if your mate has met you halfway.* So many times in a marriage, both partners are busy, overworked, tired, and feeling taken for granted. The real question isn't who put in the hardest day's work or who had the most pressures or the most hassles. The real question is: How do we build oneness here instead of waiting for the other person to meet us halfway?

■ **Do you mean that if one of us is always "keeping score," we will never become one in our marriage?**

Now you're getting it. Many marriage partners unknowingly base acceptance of his or her spouse on performance. Performance becomes the glue that holds the relationship together, but it isn't really glue at all. It's more like Velcro. It seems to stick, but comes apart when a little pressure is applied.

In addition, giving is based upon merit. With the "meet-me-halfway" approach, you might give affection to your spouse only when you felt she earned it. If she keeps the house running smoothly and meets your expectations, you might drop her a few crumbs of praise only when you would hold up your end by getting home on time, keeping the house in a reasonable state of repair, or working in the garden.

■ I can see how I bought into this "50/50" thing with marriage. What's the solution?

The biblical plan for marriage states, "I will do everything I can to love you, without demanding an 'equal amount' in return." This is a 100/100 plan of unconditional acceptance, which builds oneness instead of isolation.

If marriages are to succeed and become havens of oneness rather than dungeons of isolation, we must do more than add a few godly touches to the world's 50/50 plan. The 100/100 plan calls for a total change of mind and heart, a total commitment to God and to one another.

The Holy Spirit can fill marriages, too. In Ephesians, Paul mentions one other result of being filled with the Spirit, and, as he does, he moves into a discussion of family life—marriage and parenting. Immediately after telling us to be filled with the Spirit, to sing, make music in our hearts, and to always give thanks in everything, he says, "Submit to one another out of

---

"THE FAITHFUL COUPLE"

In Yosemite National Park, giant redwoods can be found in the Mariposa Grove. These forest giants can be forty feet in diameter.

At the base of one tree is a sign that says, "The Faithful Couple." It seems that fifteen hundreds years ago, two trees had sprouted as seedlings on the forest floor about fifteen feet apart.

The first seven or eight hundred years together, the two trees had grown individually, but as they got larger, their trunks grew closer and closer together. Sometime around the age of eight hundred years, the trunks had touched and they began the process of fusing together as one tree.

Those two giant redwoods becoming one is a perfect symbol of a godly marriage. As two people grow *upward* in their relationship with God, they grow *together* as one—a faithful couple—but each with his or her own identity.

reverence for Christ" (Ephesians 5:21). Obviously, a clear result of being "filled with the Spirit" is to have a submissive spirit. Men and women are to submit to each other and to serve each other's needs.

In marriage, there is to be *mutual* submission where a man denies himself in order to love his wife as Christ loved the church. He is still the leader, but he submits his life to his mate. Any husband who is living out Paul's instructions in Ephesians 5 could never treat his wife as a second-class citizen or with chauvinistic disregard for her feelings. That is the farthest thing from Paul's (and God's) mind.

This material is adapted from Lonely Husbands, Lonely Wives *by Dennis Rainey, © Word, Inc., Dallas, Texas. All rights reserved.*

55

Making the Most of the Second Decade of Love

. . . .

■ **We've been married seven years, and I've been thinking about the future of my marriage. Can you tell me what married life will be like ten or twenty years from now?**

Although you're very busy these days, take a moment and look into the not-too-distant future. Maybe your future looks like this. . . .

Your eyes blink open in the darkened room. As you roll over, you check the red numbers illuminated on the nightstand. It's 7:17 A.M. Another Saturday morning.

*But this one is different: You're waking up with no children in the house. Besides a few days here and there, it's the first time **that** has happened in twenty-three years.*

What makes this day even more unique is . . . they won't be back.

The nest is empty.

It's just you and your spouse.

Together.

Alone.

As you turn back over, you catch the sleeping silhouette of the person you said "I do" with so many years before. Time has passed quickly. Your mind flashes back through footage of dozens of memories.

*The kids **were** your life. Did you even have a life before kids?*

Now they're gone, and it's just the two of you.

That first Saturday morning in an empty house could be a sad reminder that you're stuck in a marriage that didn't quite turn out as you'd planned. In the first years of marriage, it was just the two of you. Waking up to bad hair days and asking your spouse not to kiss you until you swished Listerine was fun! Remember?

Now you're in the child-rearing season of marriage. Your kids have filled your life with purpose and scores of Kodak moments. You finally understand what your parents did for *you*—and how God's plan for replenishing the next generation makes perfect sense.

■ **Yes, but kids have also increased the pace of life. We're busy like never before: Doctor visits, car pools, sports, music, and homework have run us down. We can't wait until the kids are in bed so we can enjoy twenty minutes of relaxation before hitting the sack—and starting all over in the morning. But I haven't had a meaningful conversation with my spouse in a week. Will that ever happen again?**

The fact is, marriage is also a high-maintenance item. Everyone needs the reminder that couples need to invest in the relationship *before* the kids leave home.

Have you heard the historical terms "Dark Ages," "Reformation," and "Renaissance"? Well, they're handy in creating a word picture of where your relationship is or where you want it to be.

Most marriages begin with lofty goals, partly because newlyweds have time—and energy—to build their relationship brick by brick. The onset of the parenting

---

THE TOP 10 SIGNS THAT YOUR MARRIAGE MAY BE IN THE "DARK AGES"

10. Your most significant conversation in the past week had something to do with pizza toppings.

9. Your spouse gives you all the mail addressed to "occupant."

8. You think there's nothing wrong with your marriage.

7. The last time you went on a date, McDonald's had served only 4 trillion hamburgers.

6. You were watching your favorite sitcom and never noticed that your spouse left the room.

5. "What was that, dear?"

4. "Flowers? What are those for?"

3. Your Parcheesi game night was the most excitement you had in months.

2. You insist that your wife call you "sir."

1. When you see a couple kissing in public, your first word is, "gross."

years, however, causes many couples to shift their focus and energy to the kids. Nearly all parents derive great satisfaction during the twenty to thirty years of child-rearing, even though the romantic side of marriage is often put on hold.

When the children are younger—and totally dependent on the parents—marriages often go through what we call the "Dark Ages." No, not *everything* is dark. (Remember, kids bring incredible joy to a marriage.) But many couples aren't able to put much time into each other. Careers are advancing, homes are being furnished, and the kids are getting plugged into school, sports, and church activities.

These are crucial years for a couple. In fact, the median duration of all U.S. marriages that end in divorce is *seven* years. The reason: Like most newlyweds, the partners began the marital years with a wrong or incomplete picture of marriage. From there they moved quickly into the Dark Ages, and before they knew what hit them, they were bailing out.

This is the point where a relational "Reformation" needs to take place, or the Dark Ages will continue. Many couples, without a clue of how to make things right, can't see a way out of the parenting maze. The result? They live a marriage of convenience, or they divorce and find someone else.

We think it's possible for marriages to achieve a rebirth *before* the children leave home. Actually, it must! If the day comes when the kids are gone, and you wake up staring at someone you're not excited about spending the rest of your life with . . . you may not have the desire to rekindle the marriage flame.

■ **What are some ideas to get our marriage moving in the right direction during the second decade?**

▶ *Keep in mind your dating schedule.* If a couple of weeks have gone by and you and your spouse haven't done *anything* together, it's time to get out of the house, even if it's just for pie and coffee at Denny's.

▶ *Make a point of talking every day for at least ten minutes.* If your children are still small, you won't be able to "find" the time—you'll have to carve it out.

▶ *Take up sports or hobbies you can do together.* Bicycling, tennis, golf, and bowling are just a few sports couples can do together. Or you can develop common interests in collecting, cooking, or volunteering.

► *Relearn walking.* The twilight walk, especially during the summer months, can be a wonderful time to talk—and exercise!

► *Serve together in your church.* This is a way to kill two birds with one stone by serving *and* spending time with your spouse.

► *Each Sunday evening, share your daily schedules for the coming week.* Not only will you each feel more involved, but you can schedule some time for each other.

► *If you can tell something is bugging your spouse, ask him or her about it.* Slowly draw out your spouse. Ask gently but directly, "Is anything bothering you, Honey? I'd like to hear about it."

► *Even if you've been watching TV together, turn it off before going to bed.* A small trickle of conversation can turn into a river of exchanges between you and your spouse.

► *Remember the three C's: communication, compromise, and consideration.* Compromise is the cornerstone of marriage, but it works best when both sides have aired what's bothering them. In order for give-and-take to work, offer to hear what your spouse has to say first.

Finally, heed this advice a father gave one of his adult sons: "Treat your wife with as much courtesy as you would a friend, even a stranger. If you can treat her like a best friend, you'll be fine."

This material is adapted from The Second Decade of Love *by Greg Johnson and Mike Yorkey,* © *1994. Used by permission of Tyndale House Publishers, Inc. All rights reserved.*

56

When You're Dealing With Infertility

. . . .

■ **How many times have I seen the television commercial for in-home pregnancy tests in which a young, happy couple wait expectantly for the stick to turn blue? For my husband, Bill, and I, the stick has always remained white. No tears of joy or congratulatory hugs. No oohs-and-ahs from two sets of proud grandparents. No gentle cooing of a newborn, no satisfying feeling of a tiny, sleeping babe cuddled in my arms. Why do I feel so awful?**

You've done a nice job capturing the emotions that many infertile couples feel. For more than 5 million baby-boomer couples, the stick has always remained white. Many of these couples delayed trying for a child until their mid-to-late thirties when their biological clocks were nearing midnight. As any family doctor will tell you, it's more difficult to get pregnant in your thirties.

■ **Tell me about it. My husband and I are dealing with the knowledge that our bodies have not cooperated in a quest to bring a child into this world. Not that we haven't tried. For my part, I've endured six surgeries and years of having my private life invaded by ovulation test kits and timed sexual relations. I've seen my infertility doctor over 200 times, trying to deal with two ovaries that produce eggs that refuse to be fertilized. I've undergone daily** injections of fertility drugs, resulting in enormous medical bills and tons of stress. The end result: nothing. My doctors offer little hope except to turn to donor eggs or sperm injection. Neither option left us with a feeling of peace.

It's interesting to live in a culture where millions of couples spend a lot of energy trying *not* to get pregnant. And when a pregnancy occurs, all too many rush into abortion clinics to snuff out the "inconvenience," never giving much thought to the innocent life growing inside the womb or how much a pregnancy would mean to a childless couple. How many couples wish they could erase the words they had ignorantly prayed early in their marriages: "Oh, God, please don't let me be pregnant. I'm not ready."

■ **For years, I've comforted friends with this passage from Scripture: " 'For I know the plans I have for you,' declares the Lord, 'plans to prosper you and not to harm you, plans to give you hope and a future. Then you will call upon Me and come and pray to Me, and I will listen to you. You will seek Me and find Me when you seek Me with all your heart' " (Jer. 29:11-12). But now that we've battled infertility, that verse has lost much of its hope for me.**

Say out loud that last part again—the part where it says

HELPING CHILDLESS COUPLES TRUST

Even amid the high-tech baby-boom generation, millions of infertile couples are left with empty arms. Searching for hope, they eventually realize they need the very God they may have initially thought had abandoned them. They also need the support of concerned family members and caring friends. Granted, you do run the risk of hitting a raw nerve, setting off an angry explosion, or witnessing a gush of tears, but *take the risk*. Let them know you don't fully understand, but you *do* care. Here are a few suggestions to help you reach out:

▶ **Pray for them.** Committing to pray for the couple is the most powerful and meaningful act of support. It is wisest to pray for their acceptance of what lies ahead, the strength to cope, and a renewed sense of purpose. Pray that their spiritual eyes and ears will be open as they seek the Lord on the moral and ethical dilemmas that plague infertility. Pray that their marital bonds will be unbreakable as they endure the hardships of treatment and work through their grief.

continued next page

"when you seek Me with all your heart." Think about it. Are you trusting medical science more than Him? Perhaps in your struggle to understand your inability to have a baby, you have gone to great lengths to make God look like the good guy by seeking every new medical treatment and blaming repeated failures on the doctors. Deep down, you may have been trying to protect God—and yourself.

Keep assuring yourself that God has a plan for you. If He has chosen you and your husband to be childless, then you can serve Him in other ways. Be willing to accept that. Rest confidently in the One who has promised to supply all your needs according to His plan.

■ Is there a "cause" for infertility?

Causes are most often hereditary in nature. Such conditions as sexually transmitted diseases or prior abortion can lead to infertility, but in a vast majority of cases, a couple does nothing "wrong" to bring about their problem.

■ What are the chances of eventually conceiving?

According to Dr. Joe McIlhaney, a noted Christian infertility specialist in Austin, Texas, and frequent "Focus on the Family" radio guest, at least 50 percent of those seeking infertility treatment will eventually conceive. Because of improving medical techniques, this success rate will increase.

> ► **Assure them of God's love.** Scripture reassures infertile couples, many of whom ask, "God, are You punishing me?" "Do You think we'll be bad parents?" "What did we do to deserve this?" Infertility may be a matter of healing, surrender, or timing, but certainly *not* judgment.
>
> ► **Point them to God's faithfulness.** As an intimate friend or close relative, you have the advantage of knowing your childless couple well. Help them to focus on times when God proved faithful. This reassures them that God is aware of their present situation, and that His faithfulness is unchanging.
>
> ► **Extend an understanding touch.** A knowing touch, a warm smile, or a heartfelt hug will reach deep into their pain, producing bits of healing. Touch also banishes those awkward moments when you are uncertain of what to say.
>
> ► **Remember, there is more to their lives than childlessness.** Yes, infertility is a major life crisis, but there are more dimensions to a couple than their status of parenthood. Inquire about other areas of their lives. The childless couple must know that God has a special plan for them—with or without children.

■ But conceiving is expensive, isn't it?

Fertility treatments can be very costly, and corrective surgery is $10,000 and up. Health insurance usually does not cover all the costs.

HANDLING THE HOLIDAYS

The holiday season—along with Mother's Day—is the most difficult period of the year for infertile couples. Watching boisterous nephews and nieces frolic around the house before everyone sits down for the Thanksgiving meal can be a real blow. Christmas hurts even more: No stocking hangs from the mantle, no ornaments for the baby, no presents under the tree. Nativity scenes celebrating the birth of the Christ child can also trigger conflicting emotions.

If you have an infertile couple in the family, here are some ideas on how to help them through the holiday season:

▶ **Encourage the couple to participate in family activities.** Don't lace them with guilt if they choose to opt out, however.

▶ **Avoid offering false hope.** Don't say, "Maybe the Lord will give you a special gift this Christmas, and you'll be pregnant."

▶ **Plan a dinner out or a festive game night during the holidays—adults only.**

▶ **If the infertile couple seems to enjoy your children, invite them to celebrate Thanksgiving or Christmas with you.** Your children may be a wonderful outlet for their parenting desires.

■ What's the worst thing someone can say to a friend going through infertility?

Don't joke about the subject. Your comments may hit a sour note. Don't offer advice unless it's asked for. If a couple is trying to have a child, they are almost certainly well aware of the steps that can be taken to improve fertility.

Above all, remember the wisdom of Proverbs 17:17: "A friend loves at all times." Be a good friend—and a sensitive one. Know that infertility can cause great emotional strain, and that many conceal their stress well.

If you suspect a friend is struggling with the problem, think of the little things you can do. When you sense your friend's mood is low, call on the telephone for a chat. Or send a note that just says "Hi." Pray for your friend. Show the infertile couple your Christian love—with actions more than words!

This material is adapted from writings by Andrea Stephens of Covington, Louisiana, and Becky Foster Still of Duarte, California.

10

All About
the Civil War
of Values

57

Constructing Guardrails

· ·

■ As kids grow up, parents choose the roads and paths their children will take. We select the safest roads, especially ones with good guardrails. But now the curves are more treacherous. Our kids are just about in the teenage years, and yes, my husband and I want to transfer more responsibilities onto their shoulders. We want them to leave home one day with their faith intact—driving the straight and narrow, so to speak. How can we ensure that they will seek out roads with firm guardrails?

During my (Mike Yorkey) first trip to Switzerland fifteen years ago, I was introduced to fast *Autobahns* and curvy mountain passes. The two-lane highways carved into the sides of the mighty Alps are narrow, exhilarating, and superbly engineered. For some stretches, a ribbon of steel guardrail was all that separated our car from the highway and the bottom of the valley thousands of feet below. But I felt safe. My father-in-law, Hans Schmied, had been driving in the Alps since World War II, and I knew the guardrails were designed to keep our car on the pavement.

Toward the end of my stay, Nicole (my wife) and I borrowed the family sedan for a two-day trip to Italy. We aimed the auto for the imposing Grand St. Bernard Pass—first crossed by Roman legions centuries ago. After an hour of switchbacks, hairpin turns, and seat-of-the-pants driving, we reached the summit of the Grand St. Bernard and a border stop. After a routine passport inspection, we began our descent into Italy. My mind quickly picked up three things about Italian roads:

- ▸ They don't have any painted lines.
- ▸ They do have potholes.
- ▸ They don't have guardrails!

Well, not guardrails like we're used to. On the more treacherous curves, the Italians dotted the edge of the road with stone blocks, each about a foot high by a foot wide. About the only thing they'd do is rip off your oil pan cover if you went careening over the cliff.

Ever since that trip, I can see why parents want roads with solid *moral guardrails* for their children—guardrails engineered to keep the family's standards inside a protective railing.

■ So how do I go about constructing those guardrails for my family?

How good are you at digging post holes and bolting on heavy-duty sheet metal?

Not the greatest? Well, too bad. Because at various times with your children, you'll have to dig, cement in, and bolt together *protective* guardrails for your kids. When your children hit the teenage years, you could be putting in a lot of overtime on the family road.

A day will come when your children will want to peer over the edge. For many, a quick glance will suffice. For a few oth-

---

OUR VIEWING HABITS

- ▸ The average American household can now receive thirty-one channels; 68 percent can receive at least fifteen; 25 percent get seven to fourteen; and only 7 percent can choose from seven channels or less.
- ▸ In 1989, 92 million households owned TVs. Sixty-five percent of those have more than one set.
- ▸ More than two-thirds of TV households own VCRs.
- ▸ During the 1988–89 TV season, people had their sets on an average of seven hours and two minutes a day.
- ▸ The average child will have watched 5,000 hours of TV by the time he enters first grade and 19,000 hours by the end of high school—more hours than he will spend in class.

—*Sources:* American Demographics *and* Time *magazines.*

ers, that won't be enough; they will want to floor the accelerator and see how fast they can drive through the curves.

For many of us, it's tempting to make the protective guardrails one-lane wide. That way we can be *sure* our kids aren't near the edge of the cliff. But, as mentioned before, we won't be able to protect them forever.

That's why it's the parents' responsibility to teach their children to think critically and "Christianly" about popular entertainment. When TV shows, movies, music, magazines, and videos enter the home, they all need to be evaluated from God's perspective. That means we help our kids ask questions, from an early age, about the new Arnold Schwarzenegger movie, the latest Tupac Shakur release, or Calvin Klein jeans advertisements. We don't just give them the answers (our guardrails), but we take the time—and it will take more than a few hours—to help them discover where *their* guardrails should be.

As we mentioned earlier, if a child owns his moral guardrails, he'll try harder to stay inside them. If he's borrowed *yours*, he's more apt to make bad driving decisions—and bust through that guardrail.

■ **What are some practical ways I can teach my kids to learn discernment?**

Here are some ideas:

► When you're watching TV or a video together, talk through what you're seeing during the commercial breaks (or after the video is over). If you've exposed your kids to a lot of good things, the bad things were self-evident.

► Be sure to explain the

QUOTEBOOK

► "Childhood is no longer perceived as a time of innocence. Indeed, the steady diet of TV violence, sex, and social problems insures that kids are not innocent any more. Children are now viewed as competent and sophisticated. This view can lead the parents of teenagers to feel that it is unnecessary for them to provide limits, guidelines, and supervision."
—*Child psychologist David Elkind in* Psychology Today

► "In 1991, the three networks displayed more than 10,000 sexual incidents during prime time; for every scene depicting sexual intercourse between married couples, the networks showed fourteen scenes of sex outside of marriage."
—*An American Family Association study*

consequences of following a certain lifestyle of an actor or musician that's in the news.

► During your family devotional time, use Scripture to reinforce good moral character, comparing it to something you'd seen on TV lately.

► Draw the line at horror flicks, "horny teen" films, and R-rated violence. Those films can stick with impressionable youngsters for months, if not years.

► Talk a lot about the choices you made in your lives; choices of standing up for what was right. Tell your children you expect them to make godly choices.

■ **About that last comment. How can we get them to make those godly choices?**

Our society has raised a generation of baby boomers *without* well-developed consciences. Though all men are given a conscience at birth (Rom. 1), a child's upbringing can either bury it or reinforce its value. Two of the most essential characteristics we can pass on to our children are a love for the work of their conscience, and the knowledge that the Holy Spirit lives within.

Building a sensitive conscience means we have to demonstrate *honesty*. If you've ever given back the extra change the sales clerk gave you—in front of the kids—they will not forget it.

Or, you can take the family's tax return and walk your child through it. "You see this column here?" you point out. "This is the place Uncle Sam trusts me. I could fudge a little bit, and they would likely never find out. But you know what? That's not right. God would know, and I would too. Three hundred extra dollars isn't worth not being able to sleep at night. Besides, if God thinks we can use $300 extra, I believe He could give it to us without cheating to do it."

The son will learn two lessons: First, even though his dad was tempted to cheat—and knew he could get away with it—he chose not to defraud the IRS. Second, it's God who provides what we have, and He uses only honest means to give it to us.

Also let your children see you exercise some self-discipline, a value that's better *caught* than taught. When our children watch us use the TV flicker when one of those "jiggle" shows begins, or when they hear us discuss why we're not going to see the latest movie everyone is talking about, they will ask themselves *why* Dad and Mom feel that way. But children don't need a sermon from us, either. Seeing us calmly make the right choices, and offering some commentary along the way, will be enough.

■ **Let's talk about the TV. It seems like the family TV is always on as "background noise" in our home. It's real hard for us to turn it off when company comes over. We even have three TVs in the home, so different family members are watching different shows in different rooms. How can we get a handle on the "one-eyed box"?**

What's going to happen when you start getting 500 channels? Yes, TV has quite a grip on your household. Do you ever wonder how your parents lived *without* TV?

That's a tough question, but the TV has become so ubiquitous, so all-encompassing, that many families can't imagine what life would like be if the dumb thing wasn't on from 4:30 P.M. until 11 o'clock every night.

But TV *can* be limited, and for some families, it means breaking long-ingrained habits. Here are a few ideas for accomplishing that daunting task:

▶ *Use the chart system.* Photocopy a weekly chart that has the agreed-upon number of hours your children can watch on weekdays. (Weekends could be different.) After each program, the kids color in their chart in thirty-minute segments. You could pay them a nickel a minute for every minute they *don't* use.

▶ *Have a "matching" system.* Make an agreement with the kids that for every minute they read a book, they can watch one minute of TV. And every minute of reading the Bible can "buy" three minutes of TV.

▶ *Learn to discern together.* On the average, children see 20,000 commercials a year. As an experiment one night, whenever you watch TV together, write down on a sheet of paper what product a commercial is trying to sell. On the other side, write down their method. For example:
• Bud Light—young guys and gorgeous girls.
• Cadillac—older celebrity.
• Barbie—groups of girls having a party in glamorous clothes.

This teaches kids to recognize the real purpose behind TV, which is reap advertising dollars.

▶ *Develop a bedtime reading habit early.* When the kids are young, always read to them before lights out. As they get older, let them keep the light on while they read themselves. This idea also fosters a love for books.

▶ *Use the VCR.* With your own VCR sitting on top of the TV, you get to be your own network. Don't like the latest offerings from NBC, CBS, or ABC? Fine. Tape some of the good shows from the History Channel. Looking for some sitcom laughs without being bombarded by double-entendre jokes? Then tape the old "I Love Lucy," "Mayberry, RFD," or "Leave It to Beaver" shows now in syndication.

You can also rent or buy prerecorded videos, especially those offering solid Christian entertainment. The "Last Chance Detectives" and "McGee & Me!" videos for kids (produced by Focus on the Family and Tyndale House) have been runaway successes. More and more Christian bookstores are renting videos suitable for the entire family. Check them out!

■ **I know movies are powerful and appeal to the senses. These days, we have teenage kids, and we use the dinner table to talk about the latest films and ask each what he or she had heard. I tried to point out that if the movie was based on a book with a bad moral to it, the film probably wasn't any good either. What are some other things I can point out?**

Most of the advice for picking a good movie is contained in Chapter 60, but here are a few tips to get you started:

▶ *Talk about new films in your Sunday School class.* "Has anyone seen the latest Michael Douglas film? Is it all right?"
▶ *Read movie reviews in newspapers and magazines.* Even though reviewers aren't writing to a Christian audience, you can certainly find out a lot about the film. The reviewers will often talk about how gory the movie is, how a certain sexual scene stayed in but the movie still earned an R or PG-13 rating, or why this movie is "controversial."
▶ *Realize that today's movies are tomorrow's videos.* The time

between theatrical release and the Blockbuster video outlet is shrinking; it's sometimes less than three months. Exercise the same "I-want-to-know-what's-in-this-movie" mentality on anything being brought home.

■ **OK, my parents hit the roof every time I wanted to buy a Jimi Hendrix or Rolling Stones album. Jimi and Mick were no role models, but they seem like choir boys compared to the degenerate lifestyles of today's rockers and rappers.**

My teens are in public school, which means they are probably aware of every group that's getting a steady rotation on MTV or the hit radio station. I can sense there is a subtle pressure for my kids to keep up with the conversation. In fact, when I objected to one of those group's music, my fifteen-year-old son said, "What's wrong with it?"

Because music is so personal, your response may determine the quality of your communication for the next few years. If you want to see some fireworks, say something like this: "Look at those guys. They look like girls!" or "I can't understand the words," or "If they're on MTV, they must be evil." All you've done then is to reveal your prejudices and age. Such a statement may end the argument once, but because the logic is weak, you can expect more clashes in the future.

■ **So what should I say?**

Try this out: "So, you want to buy Madonna's new CD? Well, let's go down to the record store and listen to it. That way we can check out the lyrics together. We can also discuss what her message is and see if it's something you really need to be pumping into your brain."

In that case, expect a brief tussle. Your children might think you don't trust them. But your comments show you're open-minded and fair.

If you should discover the music's garbage, calmly remind them of your responsibility to God to protect their spirits and their brains. Tell them that one day they'll be making their own choices about music, but that day hasn't arrived yet.

■ **What's the score on contemporary Christian music? I didn't have Christian artists when I was growing up, but I hear there's a big Christian music industry these days.**

There are diverse opinions on this subject. Some parents don't believe that music can be Christian if it has a 4/4 beat. In other words, *it has to be old or slow if God likes it.*

That logic is faulty. If your children enjoy music, go ahead and introduce contemporary Christian music to your kids. There are tons of quality Christian groups and singers in all genres—even Christian heavy metal.

■ **Speaking of metal, my son already has quite a collection of Slayer, Def Leppard, and Guns 'n' Roses. I know this is not good for my son's mental health, so what do I do?**

Youth culture specialist Bob DeMoss recommends parents discuss the lyrics of *all* their kids' music. If the music doesn't meet the family standard, offer to buy back their tapes at half price. Then go with them to the music store and pick out some good Christian alternatives.

The battle over the boom box doesn't need to be divisive. It does, however, call for prayer, open discussion, and an early strategy to deal with this powerful medium.

58

How to Choose a Good Movie

. . . .

■ A few years ago, I went into my local video store to find something suitable for Friday night family viewing. As a parent who cares about what goes into the family VCR, I try to avoid movies that are unsuitable for my children, as well as myself.

I went to the children's section and spotted a film I thought I recognized, but I wasn't sure. Entitled *The Golden Seal,* its cover had a cute little seal with a fair-haired young boy hugging it. It looked like a good family film, but it wasn't rated. The video cover said, "A delightful nature tale about the plight of a golden seal and how it affects the humans around it. Beautiful photography in a fable the entire family will enjoy."

That night, we popped the corn, popped in the video and, within minutes, my ears were popping. Obscenities and vulgarities were coming into my living room, into my six-year-old son's and ten-year-old daughter's ears—much to my horror and disgust. Off went the video.

Upset, I returned the video the next day and chastised the owner for not placing a warning on the video cover. He eventually did, as I noticed later a little message on the box, "Contains bad language: probably a PG-13 rating." Why is it so hard to find a decent movie?

Several lessons can be learned from your experience, and if you incorporate them into your mental checklist the next time you stroll into a video store, you'll have a much better chance of making the good decision.

The word "unrated" on the *The Golden Seal* video jacket should have sent up a red flag. Unrated means unknown. You had no idea what you were getting. Now, with *Stripped to Kill, Part II*, it would be obvious what you were renting—a movie with loads of violence. However, borderline titles, such as *The Golden Seal*, are not so clear-cut.

In some states, videotapes that are sold or rented do not have to display the rating given to the movie by the Motion Picture Association of American (MPAA) when it was shown in theaters. Although the MPAA ratings leave much to be desired, they are better than nothing.

HEADING FOR THE VIDEO STORE

Here are some more tips for renting a good video:
► **Listen to word of mouth.** What are your Christian friends saying? Perhaps your Bible study group could discuss suitable films and come up with a list.
► **Consult resources that review movies from a Christian perspective.** *MovieGuide: A Biblical Guide to Movies and Entertainment* is a biweekly newsletter that reviews Hollywood's latest releases. Christian film critic Ted Baehr is the publisher.

John Evans of Dallas publishes *Preview Family Movie & TV Guide*, which reviews films and TV series from a Christian perspective.
► **Know what you want to rent before you walk into the video store.** If you are
continued next page

■ **I've always thought that parents could rely on the MPAA ratings. You mean we can't?**

Unfortunately, the G, PG, PG-13, R, and NC-17 ratings provided by the MPAA are arbitrary, as the video store owner indicated on *The Golden Seal* box when he wrote: "probably a PG-13."

■ **But isn't the MPAA supposed to protect kids and help parents?**

You've got to be kidding! Many people believe the MPAA is a government-rating service or an independent agency designed to protect moviegoers. It is not. The MPAA has been set up by the motion picture distributors to help market their movies. It has no regulatory status. The ratings are merely a sugar pill to make parents and individuals believe that impressionable youth are being protected.

In fact, ratings are *rarely* enforced by the movie theaters. In 1995, minors had no problem seeing *Showgirls*, a NC-17 flop posing as a skin flick. Besides, the MPAA has no enforcement power or procedures. The distributors use the ratings to attract an audience and to pretend they are concerned about the youth of our country.

A few years back, Robert Redford asked for an R rating for his movie *Milagro Beanfield War* because he thought that it needed an R to attract an adult audience since it contained no sex, violence, or excessive language. The Billy Graham Association's World Wide Pictures asked for a PG rating on *The Prodigal* because they felt that it would attract a wider audience, but that film was as pure as the driven snow.

The MPAA has consistently refused to clarify their rating process so that families and individuals would know what the ratings mean (for instance: R=nudity and violence, PG-13=language and violence, and so forth). The MPAA refuses to *quantify* its ratings (in other words, tell you *how many* times something is bad in the movie) because it uses the ratings to attract an audience—just as a used car dealer uses signs like "Top Value" and "Best Buy" to hook a buyer. The MPAA system can actually confuse the real content of the film, rather than clarify.

browsing, head for the "classics" or "musicals" sections. Movies made before 1963 stand a better chance of being good.

▶ **Rent videos at a Christian bookstore.** Although few Christian bookstores do rent videos, you're sure to find something good at those that do.

▶ **Stay away from horror movies as well as teen "sexploitation" films.**

▶ **Don't be afraid to rent foreign films, even ones with subtitles.** Lately, many foreign films have had the most penetrating biblical messages. Not only are such films as *Babette's Feast, Repentance,* and *Manon of the Spring* entertaining, but they have the most to say to Christians.

■ **Why can't we rent "airline" versions of movies—films with all the nudity, profanity, and excess violence edited out?**

Great question. In the future, the Dove Seal may be part of the answer to the MPAA ratings. Pro-family organizations and individuals are working with Hollywood to produce specially edited videos that excise all the objectionable ingredients such as profanities, nudity, and obscenities. But these folks are running into problems with studios and directors who want to protect the "integrity" of their films.

If and when these family-edited movies make it to your local Blockbuster store, they would be available along with the unedited version.

■ **I'm getting the picture. I'm really on my own in the video store. What are some questions I can ask myself?**

Even with an MPAA rating, discernment is crucial in choosing a videocassette. Movies are loaded with messages. The biggest questions is: What is the movie's premise? You can often find the premise on the jacket of the videotape. Remember this: You often have to read between the lines.

Does the premise agree—or conflict—with biblical concepts? For example, *The Accidental Tourist* was a popular movie a few years ago. Starring William Hurt, it was nominated for several Academy Awards. The premise of this popular film, however, was that adultery leads to happiness. That premise is abhorrent to God and aggravates the tremendous marital problems confronting us today.

On the other hand, *Chariots of Fire* had a powerful premise: Should a British Olympic sprinter run on the Sabbath?

ADDRESSES

MovieGuide
P.O. Box 190010
Atlanta, GA 31119
(800) 899-6684
Suggested donation for 26 issues: $40

Preview
1309 Seminole Dr.
Richardson, TX 75080
(214) 231-9910
Suggested donation for 24 issues: $30

■ **I remember that film. It was great to see Eric Liddell stand up for his faith. He was a hero—a positive role model. How come we don't see many heroes today?**

Hollywood has this strange idea that nobody wants to see heroic figures on the silver screen. And then a film like

Forrest Gump is released and everyone is surprised that it becomes one of the top-grossing films of all time.

But there are heroes and then there are heroes. *Henry V* tells the story of a young Christian monarch who gives God all the credit for victory. Contrast that to the hero in all the *Lethal Weapon* movies—a totally despicable policeman. In one film, he congratulates his partner when his daughter stars in a commercial for condoms.

■ **What gets me these days is that whenever a man of the cloth is portrayed in a film, he's usually a creepy character.**

Welcome to the all-purpose villain of the 1990s: a minister or person of faith. Hollywood delights in portraying moral people as nerds, prudes, kooks, and psychopaths. Pro-lifers are depicted as cold-blooded killers. Believers are personified as evil, weak, insincere, obsequious, rotten, and foolish. *Born on the Fourth of July* portrays Christians and patriots as warmongers and fools. In *Ministry and Vengeance*, the minister is a vengeful killer. (What else? That's the title of the movie.)

■ **The reason our family watches very few mainstream films is because the way love is portrayed. Why all the sex—especially the premarital kind?**

Most movies reduce love to one-night stands, tedious ordeals, or homosexual liaisons. But love is at the heart of the Gospel. Who can forget the godly mother in *Eleni* standing in front of a firing squad to save her children? *Driving Miss Daisy* showed that human friendship does not have to be coupled with the obligatory sexual relationship.

Unfortunately, the family is also under attack—and has been for some time. All too often, the children steal, swear, and indulge in promiscuous sex. The parents lose all control. While played for laughs, the films lack any sense of moral perspective.

Whenever a couple is shown in bed, four out of five times they aren't married. Little wonder: 87 percent of the media elite feel adultery is OK. Films are a rationalization for their own conduct and an attempt to drag the rest of us down to their level of immorality.

■ **What's a good, bottom-line statement about picking a good film?**

Ask yourself, "Would I be embarrassed to sit through this movie with my children or Jesus?" When we are alone, we often deceive ourselves regarding the true nature of a movie; however, if we imagine that our children or the Lord are with us (which He is), then the movie's faults stand out clearly. If we ignore the faults in a movie we are watching, then we will slowly be conditioned to condone, if not accept, a non-Christian point of view.

■ **Although I love watching movies, sometimes I feel like throwing up my hands. Any closing thoughts?**

Remember, the motion picture medium is not bad per se. Movies are tools for communication. Like any tool, they can be used for good or for evil. A hammer can be used to build a church or to crack a skull. Movies can uplift (*Squanto*) or degrade (*Pulp Fiction*).

Films are often viewed with suspicion by the church. It's true that too many movies are filled with nudity, profanity, and immorality. They deserve our condemnation since we are called "to flee immorality" (1 Cor. 6:18). On the other hand, Christians should support entertaining, uplifting movies, such as *The Hiding Place*, if only for the reason that our support will cause producers, who are primarily interested in making money, to make more wholesome movies.

Trying to ignore movies has proven to be counterproductive. Rather than bury our heads in the sand, Christians should be careful about which movies we support at the box office and in the video store. If Christians redirect their entertainment dollars away from immoral entertainment and toward moral movies, Hollywood will take notice, and we'll have more to pick from the next time we want to see a film.

This material is adapted from writings by Ted Baehr, publisher of MovieGuide.

59

MTV-Shaping a Generation

∎ **Not long ago, I was channel surfing and I stopped on MTV—the Music Television channel. I started watching this one video. The lead singer, his body stripped to the waist, was covered with rivulets of sweat. Standing in the middle of a deserted, run-down warehouse, he beat his chest like a modern-day Tarzan. This time, however, he wasn't interested in saving Jane, because in a nearby room an attractive—yet obviously frightened—young girl awaited her fate. It occurred to me that a rape was in the making, and millions of kids were watching every move. Is this what passes for normal fare on MTV?**

Afraid so. Where else but on MTV can the Stone Temple Pilots be given an international platform to sing about the joys of rape, as they did in their video you watched? MTV is where your teens can watch Snoop Doggy Dogg rap about how great drugs are, or voyeuristically ogle Janet Jackson, Madonna and Robert Kelly as they bump and grind their way through simulated sex acts.

MTV, since its inception in 1981, is one cable network where all the self-promotional hype is true. Yes, MTV is a cultural force. People don't watch it. They live it. MTV has affected the way an entire generation thinks, talks, and buys.

That's why parents of teens and elementary-age children should not dismiss MTV as a "generational thing." With more than 231 million households in some 75 countries wired to it (CNN is only in 100 million households worldwide), MTV is perhaps the leading contributor to cultural decay in the world—and they're proud of it.

■ **Well, that may be fine and dandy, but my kids don't watch it.**

Parents who think teenagers in the church are beyond the reach of MTV's video tentacles are in for a rude awakening. The sad truth, according to the Barna Research Group, is that Christian baby busters were *more likely* to have watched MTV during the past week (42 percent) than their non-Christian counterparts (33 percent).

■ **Who are these Beavis and Butt-head cartoon characters? They make Bart Simpson look like an overachiever.**

MTV first introduced these animated juvenile delinquents to the world in 1992. Stuttering their way through life, these misfits get excited about lesbian sex, watching people urinate, and joking about perverted sex. Even the occult gets a thumbs-up (Butt-head: "Is this like, satanic music?" Beavis: "No way. It's not cool enough.").

When Beavis and Butt-head

ANY ALTERNATIVES?

There's no need to sing the blues. Today, programs such as "Lightmusic," "CCM-TV," "Real Videos," "Signal Exchange" and "Night of Joy" have become regular favorites of the un-MTV generation. All total, more than 100 contemporary Christian/Gospel music video outlets exist nationwide.

The programs seek to help teens celebrate life with a new song in their heart. From Steven Curtis Chapman, Carman, and Michael W. Smith, to Cindy Morgan, DC Talk, and the Winans, alternative video viewing is now possible compliments of the four leading Christian networks: Faith and Values Channel, the Family Channel, the Inspiration Network and the Trinity Broadcasting Network.

In an aggressive move, Z-Music launched this genre's first twenty-four-hour Christian music network in 1994. Check with your local TV guide or cable provider for times and listings for all of these music video alternatives.

Remember: Your cable system does not *have* to carry MTV as part of its basic cable package. Several cable companies around the country have pulled the plug on MTV, so let your cable operator know how you feel!

started playing with fire (Butt-head would hold an aerosol can while Beavis flicked a lighter under the spray), the episodes ignited a host of young copycats from Sidney, Ohio, to Sydney, Australia.

Yes, Mom and Dad, MTV is going to continue to push the cultural envelope, whether you like it or not. And if something blows up in their face, like Beavis and Butt-head's penchant for pyromania, they will shift the blame onto parents' shoulders. Michael Medved, a Hollywood film critic and author of *Hollywood vs. America*, said, "There is absolutely *no excuse* for MTV to be present in the home. It is 100 percent negative."

■ What will a teenage boy who spends endless hours watching MTV learn about the opposite sex?

Well, he will master a few pickup lines, but after that, he will discover that there are no "average-looking" women in the MTV universe. Rather, women are glamorous, well-endowed, and very skimpily dressed. Women also have body parts ready to satisfy a guy any time of day or night. But you gotta play safe, because there's a nasty virus out there called HIV. If you use a condom, however, you'll be playing safe and smart.

Probably the most destructive message reinforced by MTV music videos is this: Women actually *want* to be raped. They're *dying* for it. When they say no, they really mean yes.

Let's put it this way: No MTV video has ever put the virtues of modesty and fidelity in a good light or displayed a lady with the qualities of Proverbs 31.

Also conspicuously absent is the celebration of sex within marriage. (Now there's a concept!) Reminder: If MTV gets regular airtime at your house, remember that the girl you wouldn't want your son to bring home is already appearing on the screen in your living room.

■ So, what can parents do to regain the upper hand?

In order for parents to help their teens get unplugged from MTV's electronic hold, here a few things you can do:

> ► *Set the standard.* A critically thinking teen has a firmly developed sense of right and wrong—and prefers wisdom over

foolish thinking. Use dinnertime to instill a love for the Scriptures in your home by having your children take turns reading God's Word. Then, apply what you've discussed to the current MTV lineup.

► *Tune in, don't tune out.* A critical thinker understands that all music, media, and entertainment are *not* harmless fun. As a parent, watch what your teens are watching. Listen to what they're listening to. You'll be in a better position to help them make sound, biblically-based entertainment choices.

► *Love what God loves.* A visually literate teen, once he or she understands the message of a musician, will desire to honor the Lord with the choices he or she makes. Taking the lead with the choices you make will give them the courage to do the same.

■ **OK, you've got me convinced. But why do millions of parents invite MTV to spend the night, allowing their teen to wade through this mire of mindlessness in the first place? Isn't there anything more constructive to do with our time? Are we that bored as a nation?**

Several years ago, MTV took a swipe at the older generation with an ad campaign built around the theme: "MTV: Some People Just Don't Get It." These days, many families have "gotten it." They've witnessed the negative impact of music videos on their children and have decided enough is enough—and pulled the plug on MTV. You can do the same by having MTV blocked from your home. One phone call to your cable company will set things in motion.

And what better way, to borrow another MTV slogan, to free your mind.

This material is adapted from writings by Bob DeMoss of Colorado Springs, Colorado.

60

Learn to Discern

. . . .

■ **Our local cineplex has eight movie screens. On one hand, it's great to have so many options, but on the other hand, the management is sloppy in its enforcement of NC-17 films. In fact, they don't make any attempt to stop kids under the age of seventeen from walking into those movies. What can we as parents do?**

At the moment, not much. You see, Jack Valenti, president of the Motion Picture Association of America, changed the rules of the movie rating game a few years ago to include a new category: NC-17 (no children under seventeen permitted).

Here's how the game works. Producers of X-rated fare have their soft-core pornographic films reclassified to the less-threatening sounding NC-17. In turn, theater owners around the country feel better about booking skin flicks in their "family" multiplex cinemas.

Enter the children during the Saturday matinee. "Hi, I'd like a ticket to see *Beethoven III.*" No problem. Junior buys a ticket to see this movie, but the clever child can wander into any film playing at this multiplex cinema, including those rated NC-17. Here's where the fun begins. Somehow it's our job to make sure that kids don't play the revolving door game when they go to see a movie.

■ **How do we achieve that goal?**

We can't count on the theater owners to pay for security guards at the door to NC-17 films, and we can't take them to court when children do get in. This, of course, is because the rating system is only a *suggestion*, not the law. There are no legal teeth to "no children under 17 permitted." It's just a guideline. Bet you didn't know that!

■ **Since we can't apply legal pressure to the theater management, what can we do?**

Begin by writing a letter of concern to the owner. First, encourage him to stop carrying NC-17 rated films, citing the problems we've discussed. Next, if he won't consider dropping NC-17 titles, ask him to outline what, if any, steps he will take to keep minors from viewing these shows in the future. Allow him several weeks to respond.

If you don't hear back or you are dissatisfied with his answer, consider "going public" with your concern. Describe your behind-the-scenes efforts to resolve this problem in a letter to the editor or an "Op-Ed" piece for the editorial page. Depending on how aggressive you want to be, you may consider sharing your concern with local PTA, church, and civic groups. Calling for a boycott of your local cineplex will bring economic pressure to bear. Although picketing is a lot of work to coordinate, it can be an effective tool.

■ **My child has been after me to buy him a Sony Walkman-type portable tape player with headphones. A lot of his friends have one, but I'm not sure it's a good idea. What would you recommend?**

As a society, we manage to play music virtually everywhere—in the car, waiting at the doctor's or dentist's office, standing in line at the grocery store, or relaxing at the restaurant. Music is inescapable. Department store executives have learned the secret of keeping shoppers shopping by playing "feel good" Muzak (you know—"elevator music").

Then came the invention of the Walkman in the 1980s. Now we can take music with us everywhere we go, and millions of Americans do just that. Don't laugh, but since the development of the portable cassette player, several companies have marketed waterproof sets that some teens actually use in the shower!

The problem with Walkman-type players is not their portability, however; it's with the headphones. Safety considerations while wearing headphones is a genuine concern. Walkers, joggers, and bike riders cannot hear the sound of oncoming cars. Many ski areas have banned Walkman players because skiers were crashing into each other—they couldn't hear another skier bearing down on them.

More ominously, nor can anyone anticipate the footsteps of a would-be assailant. This aside, there's no debate that their usage keeps the overall noise level down in the home—a real plus for you. But at what cost? Your child has created a private world that only he can experience—one that excludes you.

■ **I know. Shouldn't I want to listen to what they are hearing?**

By all means. But you should keep headphones off-limits for children through their junior high years. One ploy to waylay potential hostility at this mandate would be to offer them assistance so that they can buy a decent stereo or portable tape player with speakers. Your goal through these formative years will be to instill in them a love for the best in music by listening together as a family.

When your children reach the high school years, allow them to purchase a headset, if they wish. Remind them that they still must uphold the family standard. Explain that you are trusting them to use their best judgment in the music they will be selecting. And, reserve the right to pull the plug if they begin to spend too much time by themselves apart from the family routine.

Extended isolation is to be avoided. On the other hand, part of being a teenager is to be at a stage in life when pulling away from the folks to establish their individuality is a natural step before leaving the nest. Some privacy and isolation is permissible. You can keep the balance by spending plenty of "nose to nose" time throughout their adolescent years.

■ **What are some ways I can teach my kids to "learn to discern"?**

Parents have a great deal of moral leverage over their children. The next time you see your child glued to the tube, sit down and watch with them. Your very presence, even in silence, will instantly make them view the program through different eyes.

If you decide to point out why some programs are destructive, absurd, silly, or wasteful, don't do it a preachy way. Offer good reasons for your decisions, instead of "this is bad" or "this is good." The same can be done with rock music or video games. Modeling and quiet reasoning at home will help your children think more skillfully.

■ **I try to set a standard and encourage the family to make good entertainment choices. Unfortunately, my husband is not particularly supportive. He doesn't think there's a problem with allowing our kids to listen to what they want or to watch whatever they like on the video player. How can I gain his support?**

There are two primary reasons why some spouses shirk this responsibility. First, they don't understand how warped the entertainment landscape has become in recent years. The common reaction of the "live and let live" parenting approach goes something like this: "Give me a break; I survived the '60s with all of its permissiveness and drug experimentation. Things can't be any worse than that—and I turned out OK."

Actually, things are pretty bad, much worse than the excesses of the '60s. Today, we have gangsta rap, suicide lyrics, and drug use widely promoted. Frankly, your husband is undereducated on these matters and suffers from denial.

You need to request *Plugged In*, a newsletter produced by Focus on the Family. Each month's issue provides timely information on the latest in pop music—the good, the bad, and the ugly. (Write Focus on the Family, Colorado Springs, CO 80995, or call toll-free 800-232-6459.) Let him look at a few issues. With time, he'll come to see that the problem is bigger than he may have assumed.

Another reason your spouse may be shirking his responsibility is a heart condition. When someone's heart is not sensitive to the things of the Lord, it will be less offended by the slick suburban smut that Hollywood serves us day after day. It could take a lot more than a videotape or this book to turn him around. Your best bet is to commit him to prayer on a regular basis. Pray that he becomes the man of God, the spiritual leader that God intended. You might want to solicit the help of a prayer partner. True, it would be great to have his support as you work on the matter of appropriate entertainment for your home. But that should come naturally when he's cultivated a deeper love for the Lord.

One more suggestion: If you decide to ask him to be compliant on the matter of a family entertainment standard (before his heart is right), time your discussion when the children are not present and avoid confrontational, "holier-than-thou" tones.

■ **On two occasions I've allowed my eight year old to go to a friend's house for a sleep-over party. Both times the parents of that home permitted the youngsters to rent movies which, in my estimation, were highly inappropriate for the kids. How can I ensure this doesn't happen again and still allow my son to maintain social contacts?**

Staying up all night, telling stories, laughing, and wrestling till you're so tired even the floor feels comfortable—truly, there's nothing quite like sleeping at a friend's home when you're a kid.

For obvious reasons, hosting the overnight at your place provides you with the advantage in controlling their activities. You should consider opening your home on a regular basis for your children's friends. Before rolling your eyes at the thought of entertaining someone else's little monsters, it doesn't have to be that much more work for you. Make a deal: If your kids want to have a sleep over, they have to clean the bathrooms and vacuum up afterward!

■ **Yes, but I was wondering what to do if my children are invited over to a friend's house!**

Oh, yes. You're going to have to make a phone call—a phone call that gets easier every time, but is still difficult nonetheless. Just telephone the parents and ask what movie is going to be shown that night. If they ask why, reply that you want to be sure your children are not exposed to films that don't meet the family standard. If the video is a bad one, you should pull the plug on the sleep over, as difficult as that might be. But kids will get over their disappointment, and that lesson will stay with them a long time.

■ **I am a divorced mother with three children. When the children are with me, I make sure that we carefully select good**

TV shows to watch. If we have the money to rent a movie, I'm pretty picky about what we'll tolerate. Overall, I think I'm doing an OK job. But the problem is when the kids are with their father. Not only is he unsupportive of these efforts, he's even hostile to them. Is there any way I can control their media diet when they are at his home?

Any attempt to control the media consumption in his home will probably fail miserably. Furthermore, you're walking a delicate line because you should avoid badmouthing the ex-spouse to the children. Instead, try this "backdoor" approach.

First, befriend a couple whose marriage you respect. Arrange to have them over for dinner. Before they arrive, explain that your kids would greatly benefit by seeing a father who shares your high standards. The objective is to let them see that not all daddies have permissive entertainment standards.

You may want to have them over on several occasions before attempting to cover too much ground. This would provide time for familiarity and trust to be developed between the couple and your youngsters. Some of the most profound influences in a child's life are heroes other than their parents. Take courage! You don't have to go it alone. God can use the example of another couple to help share your burden.

■ **Our junior higher announced that her school will be hosting a dance next month. What concerns me is that the music the disc jockey has played in the past was at times highly sexual and inappropriate for young teens. What, if anything, can I do? I remember going to a school dance when I was a teen, so I'm not totally against her going.**

Call the school and talk to the school administrator in charge of the dance. Express your concerns, and then ask if there is a dance committee, which should include a few like-minded adults. Ask the dance committee to screen the song list and the lyrics. Also tell the other adults what you've heard about the DJ in the past, noting that if the DJ wants future business, then he'll have to respect the process.

■ **My children ride the school bus every day. It's a thirty-minute ride, so the bus driver allows the kids to play tapes on their portable "boom boxes" on the way. Most of the music, from what the children have told me, is OK. But on a number of occasions, they've come home virtually in tears over the lyrics they've heard. They've asked the other kids to turn it down, but they were ridiculed for doing so. I don't think it's right that my children are subjected to degrading lyrics on the public school bus. What can be done?**

Back when disco was the rage, it was certainly disconcerting to have a six year old walking the house singing, "Do ya think I'm sexy, and you want my body. . . ." In these rap-filled days, a six year old repeating the words of Snoop Doggy Dogg would have his mouth washed out for a month.

Kids on a school bus are singing today's lyrics, and you have every right to be concerned. If it really is a problem on your children's school bus, ask your kids what songs are being played, and then go to the local record store and see if the lyrics come with the CD. (They usually do. Gutter-mouthed singers are proud to flout convention and use four-letter words and graphic descriptions of sex in their songs.)

Once you have a page or two of lyrics in hand, ask to see the school principal. Showing her the lyrics should produce the desired change in playing music on the school bus.

■ **When our school loosened its dress code, permitting greater latitude in their campus garb, it wasn't long before wearing a T-shirt was the popular thing to do—particularly shirts sporting various music groups. My wife and I refuse to allow our children to own T-shirts by certain offensive bands. Our kids insist that they are not into the music (telling us they like the art design), so they see nothing wrong in wearing the shirts. How do I handle this one?**

Sometimes teens forget they become a "walking billboard" for the musicians they plaster on their bodies, even if they are into only the artwork. If your teenagers don't believe teens notice or care what each other is wearing, have them wear a "His Pain—Your Gain" or "God's Gym" T-shirts to school. (Note to parents: This is also what's known as "three-second evangelism.")

Ask them, "What kind of reaction did get from your classmates? Did your friends *agree* with your message? Did the picture of Jesus crucified get them talking?"

If that argument doesn't work, make the point that when a fan buys a band's T-shirt, he is economically supporting the group—and probably their alcohol and drugs habits as well.

■ **My son is in ninth grade at a public school. Yesterday, I learned one of the history teachers showed** *Schindler's List,* **Steven Spielberg's Holocaust epic. While I understand the subject matter was pertinent to my child's understanding of the Nazis' cruel effort to exterminate the Jews, this film was also rated R with numerous sex scenes and disturbing violence. Was I right to be upset by this?**

Certainly. If your child's teacher wanted to show a movie on the Holocaust, there are probably a half-dozen excellent films and videos on the market. For instance, Herman Wouk's *The Winds of War,* which ran as a miniseries on ABC, captured the same emotion of the death camps without the gratuitous nudity. The violence, while disturbing, was not graphic.

Regardless of the teacher's "good intentions," no student should be required to watch a film with the inappropriate material typically found in R-rated films. You should bring the matter up with the teacher and the principal. Even if it was an exception, it reflects poor judgment. Those images, quite frankly, could cause nightmares for your impressionable child. (Incidentally, you're more likely to get a sympathetic hearing if you've previously applauded the teacher and the administration for the good things they've done.)

Urge the school to notify parents before the showing of feature films in the future, including those rated PG or PG-13, since some could contain indecent language and sexual situations. In fact, if the movie is rated PG-13, you can be sure there are a few f-words and s-words, and the camera will be in the bedroom—guaranteed.

If the school insists on showing inappropriate videos, then you should insist on optional activities for your son or daughter.

■ **My daughter went on a church youth retreat for the weekend. When she got home, she mentioned that part of their entertainment was watching a movie each night. It seems that all of the movies this youth minister brought along were R-rated. We spoke to him about this because we don't believe he used good judgment. He dismissed our concerns, stating that we were just too conservative. Furthermore, he told me if we didn't like the programming at youth retreats, we should go find another church. How typical is this kind of attitude among youth ministers?**

Actually, it sounds like you bumped into one of the exceptions rather than the rule. Most youth pastors are deeply grieved over the trashy movies and music that target teens. In fact, more often than not, youth pastors lament that it is the *parents* who are permissive, even lax, when it comes to the entertainment allowed in the home. They feel unsupported in their efforts to instill proper values about music and movies with the teens they've been asked to disciple.

But in your situation, you ran into a bad apple. Since your concerns were rebuffed by him, you should go over his head and talk to your pastor.

■ **We're trying to instill a discerning spirit in each of our family members. Like Rip Van Winkle, we've been asleep far too long, and we recognize something must be done. But is teaching our household the principles of "learn to discern" the end of our journey?**

It seems every time we see the signs of social responsibility emerge from the entertainment industries, another deviant product from Hollywood floods the marketplace with its pollutants. Ask yourself these questions: What are we trying to do, anyway? Wipe out *all* evil influences in America during our lifetime? How about 50 percent or 25 percent? Would we settle for a 10 percent reduction of immoral activity?

Scripture provides the answer. Jesus said, "You are the salt of the earth; but if the salt has become tasteless, how will it be made salty again? It is good for nothing anymore, except to be thrown out and trampled underfoot by men. You are the light of the world" (Matt. 5:13-14). Our mandate while on earth is to "occupy" until the Lord returns. Since He's already won the battle, we're essentially in the "salt and light" business.

This material is adapted from Learn to Discern *by Robert G. DeMoss, Jr. Copyright © 1992 by Robert G. DeMoss, Jr. Used by permission of Zondervan Publishing House.*

11

All About
Difficult Family
Problems

61

A Father to the Fatherless

. . . .

■ I stared mutely at my friend, a numbing fog seeping into my brain. "Paul is dead," Sue repeated. "Something happened while he was water-skiing. He died instantly when the boat ran over him."

My husband, Paul, was gone. Dead. He will never come home again, I thought. My mind raced—sixteen years of marriage, three precious sons, a future without him—before my brain shut off with the blessed anesthesia of shock.

First things first, I told myself. I called each of my three children downstairs one at a time to tell them, my oldest first and then the next. They sat in the living room and cried. I didn't—until later. I felt out of my body, observing myself and everyone else from a corner, somewhere near the ceiling.

Then the phone rang. Sue took it. The Sunday School committee was meeting to choose officers for the coming year. Even though we had lived in Texas for only two years, they wanted to nominate Paul to be president of the class. Soon after Sue told them the news, the house began to fill with shocked and tearful friends.

The phone calls started pouring in too. I had calls to make to my family in North Carolina and Paul's in Florida. Arrangements for the memorial service—date, time, what type of casket, who would conduct it—passed by in a blur.

That night as I lay in bed, the hymns and Scriptures I had

learned as a young girl ran through my mind like a self-winding tape. In spite of my shock, their meaning was crystal clear. Later on, the agonizing pain of grief settled in for its necessary stay. I've never been so grateful to know the Lord as I was then.

Your belief in God's sovereign hand on your family's lives and His perfect love are often the only answer to the "whys" following a tragic death. With God as your foundation, you knew that a long road stretches ahead of you, a young widow with three children.

Keep in mind that in the Psalms that the Lord describes Himself as a father of the fatherless, as a defender of the widowed and orphaned. And James 1:27 says this: "Religion that God our Father accepts as pure and faultless is this: to look after orphans and widows in their distress and to keep oneself from being polluted by the world."

■ Isn't there something in the Old Testament that commands us to care for the fatherless?

Yes, and judgments for failing to keep that command are mentioned nearly forty times. The Hebrew word for *fatherless* indicates that these children were actually called orphans, even with a surviving mother. In the Hebrew culture, a widow was totally dependent on her family and society for economic support.

Today, women have rights to property, access to the job market, and greater social mobility. Yet rarely is the young widow left with the financial resources to remain a stay-at-home mom. She must reenter the work force and learn to juggle the demands of home and work. Similarly, many divorced and single moms must raise children in a fatherless environment.

■ Where should new widows look for help?

The first responsibility falls to the men in the family—uncles and grandfathers. The men in the family should be "available." At the same time, your children may urgently want to know what will happen if you should die. You should assure them by making arrangements with relatives to become the new guardians.

■ But our relatives live halfway across the country, so it's not

practical to have close contact with them. What should I do?

This is where the church needs to step in. Your family in Christ can meet your needs in tremendous ways. Youth pastors, Sunday School teachers, and Christian camp counselors can emerge to meet special needs.

For instance, the youth workers can take your children to local football games or drop by for a quick game of backyard basketball.

Neighbors and friends can also be great resources by pitching in and baby-sitting so you can escape for the evening. This could also be an excellent opportunity for your children to observe the love, respect, and gentleness of a happily married couple.

Male teachers and coaches also have strong opportunities to father the fatherless. What a high calling! Male teachers can serve as exhorters, disciplinarians, encouragers, and role models.

Coaches have the delicate job of spurring their charges to do the best they can while not applying too much pressure to win. In addition, fatherless children watch a coach's every move.

■ **I'm worried that when my children get older they won't know how to work because they haven't seen a father slug it out from 8 to 5 every workday.**

When a teenager takes that first part-time job, a father seems more necessary than ever. Fatherless children don't hear their dad talk about the highs and lows of work, how they relate to supervisors and employees, or the importance of a good attitude. Employers can teach the fatherless a proper work ethic and reinforce the values Mom is instilling at home: punctuality, good manners, and tenacity.

■ **As a young widow, what else should I know?**

Mothering the fatherless is a unique, difficult calling, but you can learn, adapt, and trust in God to fill in the gaps. Of course, you should pray for energy, wisdom, and strength each day. You should pray for trustworthy men to fill the fathering needs you cannot. You should continue to read the Word of God, learning from the model of a perfect Father dealing with His imperfect children. Then you can rest confident that He will father your children with a love beyond any imaginable.

This material is adapted from writings by Terri S. Speicher of Dallas, Texas.

62

Dealing with Disabled Children

· ·

■ **A dear friend of mine just gave birth to a son with Down's syndrome. She asked her doctor for some advice, and he simply told her, "Just take him home and love him." Then he turned on his heels and left her alone. As a friend, what can I do or say?**

Although the doctor's advice was appropriate, he was too abrupt in walking away without talking it through more. Some doctors have been very insensitive to mothers of mentally handicapped newborns, referring to other children as "mongoloids," or "too handicapped to take home."

As for yourself, you may have to deal with some preconceived notions about people with disabilities. Life is not hopeless for the developmentally disabled and not all that different. Your friend's son has red hair, a batch of freckles and an endearing, dimpled smile. He has hopes and dreams and a wonderful ability to form thriving relationships.

The greatest obstacle to being handicapped—or challenged, or disabled, or whatever label we may be using this year—is not the condition, but the stigma society still associates with it. The truth is, we are valuable because of who we are, not because of how we look or what we accomplish. And that applies to all of us, including the disabled.

■ **That's a good speech, but it must be very difficult on the parents.**

You're right. Carlene Mattson of Laguna Beach, California, gave birth in 1979 to Jeff, her second son. She was still in the recovery room when the on-duty pediatrician stopped by. Instead of coming to her side, he stood at the foot of her gurney.

"Your son has ten fingers and ten toes, and his plumbing works," he began. Carlene braced herself, because the doctor's tone told her that a "but . . ." was coming. "But he has Down's syndrome."

But since that initial shock, Carlene wishes someone could have told her what a treasure she had been given upon the birth of Jeff, instead of hearing horror stories about institutionalized adults. She remembers the excitement on Jeff's face the first time his father fingered his favorite song on their piano, or the winsome way he asks Mom to close her eyes before giving her a gift.

Jeff is thankful for the smallest kindness, and he sees beauty in things we miss, even in the way a flock of birds uniformly take flight. Several years ago, Jeff played in a special Little League for kids with disabilities. After many seasons of watching from the bleachers and rooting for his big brother, Jeff's opportunity finally arrived. When he raced out of his bedroom, fully suited up, he announced, "Mom, now I'm a real boy!" Though his words pushed Carlene's heart to her throat, she assured him that he had always been a "real boy."

■ **My first grader is having problems recognizing or writing letters. I fear he may be learning disabled. How should I seek help?**

1. *First, have him tested by a school pyschologist.*
   Public schools have psychologists available who can test children for learning disabilities. This is not the same as putting your child in therapy. A school psychologist has several tests to determine academic aptitudes and learning problems. If you are home schooling or have your child in a private school, you have to go to a child psychologist to have him tested.
2. *Your child needs to take three tests:*
   an I.Q. test, an achievement test, and a personality test. These tests will start to pinpoint your child's need.
3. *Get special instruction through your school or private tutor.*

Again, this is for when you suspect that your child has a disability that is causing him to process information incorrectly.

■ **We're a hurting family. But we're reluctant to "dump" our troubles into the laps of friends when we socialize. What are some ways we can talk about our problems without "casting our burdens" on good friends?**

Thank you for your sensitivity. You're right: No one wants to hang around with folks who are constantly complaining about their lives or a difficult family situation—such as a disabled child. But let's say your elementary school-age child was run over by a car while riding his bike and he nearly died. *Of course* that is something you will want to share with your friends—and *should.* If you're facing a tough family situation, here are a few things you can do:

- ► *Ask for prayer.* Be specific in your prayer requests, since people prefer to personalize prayers. When friends and family let you know that they are praying for you, you'll feel an added boost of support.
- ► *Talk freely about your pain, but don't go overboard.* It's cathartic to get things off your chest, but be sensitive. You don't want to lay *all* of your burdens and troubles in the laps of long-time friends.
- ► *Ask for tangible help.* If you are going through a crisis, you *will* have needs—such as having someone look after the kids while you're off to medical visits and consultations. When good friends ask *you* what they can do, this will be of great benefit.
- ► *Seek out professional help when necessary.* Even though you may not want to see a counselor, talking to an experienced Christian counselor who isn't emotionally involved can often be of great benefit.

■ **My ten-year-old boy is just getting back into the swing of things after missing six months of school from a serious illness. What are some things to keep in mind?**

No one knows your child as well as you do, so be ready to be an advocate on his behalf. You can't assume other parents or his teacher will understand your child. If your child has a special need, it's up to you to tell other adults what it is.

Be sure to check out the classroom environment. If your child is in a wheelchair, are the aisles wide enough to allow him to participate in various activities? Observe the teacher in action. Does she understand the limitations of your child's disability?

Know your legal rights. You have the right to be part of every meeting school officials have about your child. If he is older, he can be there too. You should receive quarterly progress reports. If the staff does something new, you have the right to evaluate it for a month instead of the usual three months.

Encourage the people who work with your child, by making it a habit to tell your child's teachers, coaches, and therapists how much you appreciate their help. At the same time, be flexible toward friendships. You son or daughter may choose friends that you wouldn't select, but learn to trust their instincts. We are all blessed with different personalities.

On the home front, find ways to have fun. Have a "family sleep over" in the living room with sleeping bags, an armful of videos, Domino's pizza, and fresh popcorn. Or, you might plan a long-awaited weekend away at a nearby city with a motel and pool.

■ **My child has Down's syndrome, and like Carlene Mattson's son, he wants to be a baseball player *soo* bad. How can I solve this problem creatively?**

If your child wants to play T-ball or Little League, look for a noncompetitive league that reaches out to children with disabilities. But if your disabled child doesn't play sports, be sure to celebrate every little victory. Winning a spelling bee or getting an A on a big class project should be marked with a special day! Some families have a bright red "You Are a Special Person" plate that the "special child" can eat from at dinner.

■ **Although my mentally handicapped son is doing great in school, I can't help but hear unkind remarks uttered behind his** back. I'm glad he doesn't hear them, but I sure feel wounded when I catch them.

You've got to ignore them. You can't have a "prevent defense" for every person who speaks first and thinks second. Don't let unkind remarks sap your energy.

■ **For me, it's not the rude comments or playground taunts that bother me—it's wondering where God is in all of this. What spiritual element can be brought to bear?**

Medicine can't promise whether your child will get through a life-threatening illness, but by facing the future with faith—remembering that you have seen God through the worst of your trials—you will know that He can be trusted.

It's all part of living with the unknown. No one—not even the fittest Olympic athlete—has any guarantee for a healthy tomorrow. If you fret about what lies ahead, you'll waste the energy you need to get through today.

This material is adapted from writings by Carlene K. Mattson of Laguna Hills, California; Charting Your Family's Course *(Victor) by Eric Buehrer; and writings by Ann Biebel of Monument, Colorado.*

63

Attention Deficit Disorders

. . . .

■ **How prevalent is Attention Deficit Hyperactive Disorder (ADHD) these days?**

It's estimated that 5 percent of school-age children are characterized by this condition.

■ **Can you list some symptoms?**

Certainly. Psychologist Mark Gang, Ph.D., of Fairfield, Connecticut, specializes in assessing children with ADHD. He lists five common symptoms:

> ► *Poor, sustained attention.* These children get bored 50 percent faster than the average child. Thus, it is difficult for them to concentrate for long periods of time.
> ► *Impulsive, with poor delay of gratification.* In other words, they don't think; they just act. They often interrupt, find themselves in dangerous situations, and don't follow directions.
> ► *Behavior often characterized by hyperactivity.* These children move in quick, abrupt, and often disruptive bursts. But it's interesting to note that although this term is commonly used to characterize this disorder, it is only *one* in five core symptoms

and is present in 70 percent of the children—not 100 percent. Thus, it is possible to have a child who has attention deficit disorder *without* hyperactivity.

► *Diminished rule-governing behavior.* They have difficulty following through with instructions, becoming easily focused on something else. Their tendency to be consumed by the moment interferes with the completion of the task.

► *Great variability of performance.* Just when you think you have these children figured out, they display an opposite tendency. Such children are commonly labeled as lazy in the classroom when the teacher discovers they can make A's one day but slide back into Ds and Fs the next. These children are consistently inconsistent.

■ **It sounds like a couple of those symptoms fit my child. What should be my next step?**

Begin by taking him to a trusted pediatrician, who can begin ruling out any medical conditions that can create similar behavioral patterns.

■ **What do you mean?**

For example, lead poisoning—which at times has symptoms very much like those displayed by the ADHD child—can be identified by a simple blood test.

■ **But isn't psychiatric help in order too?**

You're right. Once other medical conditions have been eliminated, it is imperative to find a psychologist *whose specialty includes ADHD.* If the professional has a limited understanding of the disorder, you may find you and your family sidetracked down a frustrating path.

■ **What other kinds of treatment are available to my child?**

First of all, ADHD is managed, not cured. Treating ADHD will not make it go away. Your child's inattention, overarousal, distractibility, and difficulty in keeping rules are inborn behavioral characteristics.

■ **So you mean these qualities will stay with him throughout his life?**

Treatment can improve a child's chances for avoiding many of the long-term problems associated with ADHD. There is every reason to believe your son or daughter can have a productive life. But this objective will require long-term help.

■ **What sort of treatment are you talking about?**

Usually treatment will need to be multifaceted. For example, medication may be used to help control some of the child's inattention and overarousal. Yet medication does not give the child the skills to organize note cards for a term paper, or to make friends.

■ **It sounds like having an ADHD child can be tough on a marriage.**

Parenting an ADHD child is an overwhelming task. The statistics on marriages that don't handle the pressure are frightening. However, you can keep your marriage intact while struggling with a very demanding child.

Make a real effort to work as a team, sharing in the responsibility. It's important not to place blame for your child's condition, but rather to support each other as you attempt to reestablish harmony in the family.

■ **Give me some ways to do that.**

Be sure to take time off together. You need it more than any average couple! Make time for yourselves as individuals too. You may find that taking turns in giving care so the other parent can take even a simple walk will help.

NEED HELP?

If you are wondering whether your child has ADHD, or how you can get help, contact CHADD for a referral to professionals in your community. The address:

CHADD
499 NW 70th Ave.
Suite 308
Plantation, FL 33177
phone: (305) 587-3700.

■ **What kind of answers might I expect from God when I pray that my ADHD child be healed or changed?**

We can start with the assumption that there is nothing too difficult for God to change. The relationship we have with Christ gives us permission to come boldly before Him with our every request (Luke 11:9; John 15:7).

But God does not promise that *all* of our requests will be answered by an immediate change in circumstance. Scripture gives us a balanced perspective about faith. The faith that allows a parent to pray for the healing of a child, and yet continue with sufficient grace to deal with the problems of daily living, is no less faith than that of a parent who utters a similar prayer and finds an immediate resolution of the problems.

These are both answers to prayer. The second is more immediate and more in line with our expectations. But they both reflect God's love and grace.

■ **How can my church help out?**

First of all, take the risk to share your burden with others in the church, so they can help carry the load (Gal. 6:2). There are practical ways your church should be able to help—baby-sitting, referral recommendations, respite care while Mom and Dad get a break, safe and secure day care, and guidance from the church staff for the spiritual training of your child.

This material is adapted from writings by Sandra Doran of Attleboro, Massachusetts, and The Hyperactive Child *(Victor) by Dr. Grant Martin.*

64

Helping Heartbroken Friends

. . . .

■ **What do you say when a friend is weathering tough times?**

First off, you have to know that dreams die hard. Dave Biebel knows because twice his have been smashed to bits. The first time was in 1978, when his three-year-old son, Jonathan, died from an undiagnosed genetic illness. Since the moment the boy was conceived, he had loved that boy more than life.

For eight years, Dave struggled to put the pieces of his world back together. Then in 1986, his second son, Christopher, became brain damaged and nearly died from the same genetic disease. With angry fists, he screamed out to a God he thought had forgotten his name.

Many others are drowning in the same kind of pain. With their lives in shambles, they feel few others care or understand. They look at married couples or pastors or Christian friends and conclude that their lives are completely together. But a closer look would reveal the truth: Some estimate that one of every three people who fill the church pews on any Sunday morning are crying out for help.

These people are often hard to spot, because they arrive all dressed up and bravely masked to fit in with everyone else. But look into their eyes, observe the stress in their faces, and see the tension in their bodies. When they speak, listen for the real meaning behind their words.

Beyond all the nice clothes and perfect hairdos, you'll hear a simple longing: "Won't somebody please just be my friend?"

■ OK, I see your point, and I want to help. How do I get started?

We need to approach others and show them the love of Christ. Think back to the last time you were desperate. Did you have the courage to step out and *ask* for help? Probably not.

Pain is pain, and once you've coped with it, you can help someone else through theirs. It's true that victims of sexual abuse or widows understand one another best, but it's *not* true that we have to have been sexually abused or widowed to help those people toward wholeness. Sure, we won't fully understand their specific situations, but we understand *pain*, and the Lord is calling us to reach out. You and I may be the last friends these hurting people will look to for help.

■ But what can we do for a person in pain? What should we say when we don't have answers? How can we point a friend toward the path of healing?

There *are* no easy answers, but these guidelines will help you reach your wounded friend:

> ► *Share in the person's loneliness.* Rocky's world fell to pieces ten years ago when he leaned over to pick up something and injured his spinal cord. He then became paralyzed below the waist. Because his illness wasn't job-related, the family struggled to stay afloat financially.
>
> For weeks, all Rocky could do was stay in bed. He couldn't even use the bathroom without help. As he lay there helpless and depressed, he also felt abandoned by God. But when his friend Glenn came to visit, Rocky's spirits improved.
>
> "When Glenn came by, he didn't *say* anything," Rocky explains. "He didn't preach sermons or tell me how I should be feeling. Instead, he climbed up on my bed, wrapped his arms around me, and we both cried. After he left, I felt like I'd been bathed in love."
>
> Your hurting friends need to know you care. The best way

continued on page 408

THE DEATH OF A CHILD

Some dear friends from church recently lost an infant son from SIDS—Sudden Infant Death Syndrome. What can I say to my grieving friends?

The loss of a child, whether by death or when an adoption goes haywire, is one of the most devastating tragedies a couple can endure. They need the comfort that a Christian family can provide.

The first thing to do is not avoid your friends. The most painful event in their lives has just taken place, and they need your concern and prayers.

How then should I express my concern?

"I'm sorry," "I care," or any words sensitive to their pain will be just right. Statements such as "It must have been God's will" (no matter how theologically sound) are not helpful.

But most of all, express concern by being a good listener. Grieving parents need to talk about their loss. Don't hesitate to ask gentle questions. They may want to get out the photo album and remember him. Be attentive in that situation. Some parents, however, feel they can't tell the story one more time. In that case, your presence is enough.

Don't be afraid to touch. A despondent person needs a physical expression of sympathy. Often, a hug says what you can't.

What are some things I can do to assist in practical ways?

Preparing meals, running errands, and baby-sitting other children—especially the latter—are appreciated when a person is involved in any crisis.

If you can help financially, offer to do so. All too often, medical insurance doesn't cover everything, and for those who were trying to adopt, that process requires great amounts of money—money that is seldom returned when the adoption falls through.

How long do parents usually grieve?

For those of us not closely involved in the crisis, our lives resume quickly. But the grieving parents continue to feel the loss for months and even years. For the year following the tragedy, mark your calendar with the child's birthday and the anniversary of the loss. On those days, send a thoughtful card or perhaps make a phone call. These acts will mean much to your friends, especially as it gives them a chance to talk about their child again.

to demonstrate that is to *be there*. From other "friends," that person will hear a lot of words—sermons, Scriptures, platitudes, exhortations, easy answers. From you, let your friend hear the sound of silent caring.

Most of the time, silence is welcomed by a person in pain. He or she may just want to sit and cry with you or stare out a window. But if you insist on having something to *say*, these statements work best: "I love you," "I care about you," or "I hurt with you."

When your friend finally wants to talk, be a good listener. Forget trying to fix either your friend *or* the problem. Only God can mend a broken heart. But you can learn to listen and ask questions that help the person talk through the pain.

If your friend says something like, "I hate God," regard that as a gift: Your friend is trusting you enough to be completely vulnerable. Fight your inclination to judge or preach. Instead say, "I really appreciate you for sharing such deep pain. Help me understand how it feels." Remember: It is a privilege to have a window into your friend's heart.

▶ *Understand your friend's emptiness.* After Dave Biebel's son died, he tried to keep serving God. He preached, taught, and counseled. He stayed busy in order to fill the emptiness. But it didn't work.

After his second son, Christopher, became ill and almost died, he gradually started to depend on alcohol to dull his pain. The more he drank, the more he needed. Dave struggled to restrain himself, but the desire was too strong. He knew in his head that only Jesus could satisfy his emptiness, yet he didn't want to let go of the pain. Surrendering seemed to mean letting God win, and he was too angry at Him to allow that.

One fall day, Dave was in the Colorado Rockies near the Continental Divide. He had climbed to 11,500 feet when he noticed the incredible blue sky, and he began thanking God for it. This led to a dialogue with the Lord in which he gave back to Him each thing he'd been holding on to—his self-imposed sadness, guilt, anger, bitterness, family, and career. Dave gave up everything, until He asked him for his alcohol. He realized then that he couldn't face a day without a drink, and he was in trouble.

He wishes he could say that he had an instant victory, but anybody who has struggled with demon rum knows it doesn't give up its grip easily. The harder he tried fight it with his own strength, the more he needed it to muster the courage to take up the battle again.

But as Dave sat in church one Easter Sunday morning, he thought, *Either Jesus died and rose or He didn't. If He did, then the power that raised Jesus from the dead is available to me.* He knew at that moment that he *couldn't* fill his emptiness with anything but Him. That key unlocked a whole new life for Dave.

Every heartbroken person has felt emptiness similar to what Dave felt after Jonathan died. Not all try to fill it with alcohol, but many use wealth, fame, power, hobbies, recreation, or illicit relationships. In every case, each will be disappointed. They will see that intimacy with God is the only thing that satisfies.

■ What's my role as a friend then?

Your role is to discern when your friend is taking this detour and to become his or her fellow traveler. Without preaching or nagging, encourage repentance by putting your arm around your friend's shoulder and explaining that life *is* hard and unfair. But it doesn't stop there: Your friend, whether Christian or not, probably senses there's something more out there. Tell him or her that the "something" is really *Someone*, and that the "more" is an eternal joy that takes the place of temporal happiness.

■ What's another way I can reach out?

Allow your friend to heal on his or her own terms. After her grueling divorce, one of Judy's friends told her that because all things work together for good (Rom. 8:28), her sadness was selfish and displeasing to God. At a time when her heart was bleeding and she needed a listening ear, she felt guilty and thought even her Heavenly Father was not happy, accusing her of wrong.

Christians like Judy's friend make such statements because they think every problem must be spiritualized. But these people are answering questions hurting people aren't asking. Their solutions are irrelevant and even damaging. Broken people allow these "friends" an open door into their pain. When they spout off such spiritual answers, they violate that trust.

Suppose a man's wife ran off with his best friend, leaving him devastated. The man calls his pastor for consolation, but the pastor shows up with a copy of *Five Steps to Living the Victorious Christian Life* and pushes the hurting man to work through it point by point. Though he probably wouldn't stop the pastor from sharing the booklet, the man probably wouldn't risk sharing his strongest temptation—suicide. The wounded husband doesn't need formulas or fixing. He needs someone to sit with him and cry until he runs out of tears.

As you support your friend, remember that you will never be able to satisfy that person's need for intimacy with Christ. *Do* provide a listening ear, but don't become that person's only reason for living. Your friend may need to depend on you heavily for a while, but you should gently help that person understand the need to find fulfillment in the Father.

And remember: You do not have the power to change the course of a person's life. The Lord is using you as a tool to show your friend His love. The power lies in God. The same Father who helps you handle your heartache is the same Father who can mend the broken heart of your friend.

This material is adapted from writings by David Biebel, a minister and the director of communications for the Christian Medical and Dental Society in Colorado Springs, and from writings by Cynthia Culp Allen of Corning, California.

65

What Makes a Dysfunctional Family?

■ **One of the bywords of the last ten years has been dysfunctional. Bookstores are full of buzz words like codependency, shame and guilt, compulsive addiction, and the "wounded child within." Although my father was an alcoholic, I've been working hard to steer away from thinking, I'm codependent. My family was dysfunctional. I can't do much to change the way I am. Or am I stuck?**

People can learn how to counter the knee-jerk reaction that comes out of the lifestyle they learned as children. But people can't change if they continue to tell themselves they are dysfunctional and, therefore, stuck.

Every person or family is functional to some degree. A dysfunctional family, however, is operating without certain things that are necessary to everyone's sense of well-being and feelings of self-worth. When a family is functioning well, it will be meeting basic psychological needs by obeying certain rules for living together successfully.

■ **What are some of those rules?**

The first is to be firm but fair. Parents often vacillate between authoritarianism and permissiveness. Authoritarians tell the child, "My way or the highway." Permissive parents say, "Have it your way,

Honey. Can I drive you anywhere?"

Both approaches leave children feeling unloved, insecure, not belonging anywhere, unapproved of, and unrecognized—and operating in a dependent, irresponsible way. Both approaches erode children's self-image or sense of self-worth. When used to extremes, both approaches lead straight to a seriously dysfunctional family.

Within the firm-but-fair approach, however, is a great deal of flexibility—and freedom to fail. Children have freedom to think, ask questions, and disagree with parents. Children have freedom to feel angry, frustrated, sad, afraid, and so on. They have freedom to express their feelings in an appropriate way.

The firm-but-fair approach acknowledges children's anger—"I can see you're upset"—and then works out a way for them to express that anger in a nondestructive or nonabusive way: "If you want to scream, you'll just have to do it in your room. When you calm down, you can rejoin the rest of us and we can talk about it."

■ **Like Rodney Dangerfield, I don't get any respect from my children. How can I gain that respect?**

The key is not to demand respect. To gain respect from your children, you have to treat them with respect. In other words, respect is a two-way street.

Let's say your teenage daughter Krissy was kidding around with you, but she crossed a line when she called you a moron in front of several of her friends. Most parents would promptly dress her down— really let her have it—and let her know "that kind of language isn't necessary, young lady."

Yes, your daughter hadn't shown respect, but at the same time, you hadn't been respectful of her by raising your voice. You might go to her room and say, "I'm sorry, Krissy, I shouldn't have yelled at you in front of your friends. Honey, you know I like to kid around, but you went too far."

Kids won't forget your conversation.

■ **My Sweet Sixteen daughter, Lark, just got her driver's license. What should we do if she hurriedly backs into a tree at the end of our driveway? She's not a very experienced driver.**

If Lark comes through the front door upset and crying because she's dented the car, remain calm. Now's not the time to scream and threaten to take away her license or her keys. As Lark sobs, Dad should come over, put his arm around her, and say, "Honey, accidents happen. It's just metal. It can be fixed as good as new."

Then Dad works out a deal with his daughter. He gets the car fixed out of his own pocket (the bill was $200) because his insurance policy has a $500 deductible. Then he arranges for Lark to pay him back over the next six months.

To be firm but fair always allows for failure. When children feel they can never fail, they're hampered and become afraid to try, risk, create, grow, and learn. When parents are understanding, they can turn a failure into a good learning situation.

■ **I know that it is vital for parents to love their children unconditionally, although it isn't always easy. While none of us can love unconditionally all the time, how can we demonstrate real love?**

Real love means we're kind and compassionate while also firm and fair. In fact, we can't have real love for our children without reasonable, healthy limits to guide and nurture them.

"Aren't limits conditions?" a parent may ask. Limits don't put conditions on your love; limits help channel your love and give it the substance that makes it real and lasting, not artificial and temporary.

The trick is to invoke the limits without making your children feel you don't love them. Every child needs plenty of hugs, followed up with plenty of talk—kind words, loving words, appreciation, and encouragement.

■ **What's a big mistake many parents make?**

Parents fail to realize that how they live each day speaks volumes about what they really value. The choices they make, the words they use, the TV pro-

> **BASIC NEEDS OF FAMILY MEMBERS**
>
> ► To be loved and accepted.
> ► To be secure and relatively free of threat.
> ► To feel a part of a group.
> ► To be approved and recognized for the way in which one functions.
> ► To learn independence, responsibility, and decision-making.

grams they watch, the way they treat others, the way they obey or disobey the law—all are sure-fire communicators of what they think is really important.

This material is adapted from writings by Dr. Kevin Leman of Tucson, Arizona.

66

Grandparents Picking Up the Pieces

. . . .

■ Mary and I dreamed of what life would be like when the last of our four teenagers moved out. We had it all planned: We would buy a cabin in the northern Michigan woods and spend weekends snowmobiling—just the two of us.

Then sixteen-year-old Kaitlin, our youngest child, announced she was pregnant. We soon found we were to be more than grandparents—we would be Mom and Dad again. We adopted Nathan when our unmarried daughter decided she could no longer care for him and moved out. We shuffled our work schedules to avoid day-care costs, and the money we had saved for a vacation cabin now pays for Nathan's preschool.

"I wouldn't give him up for anything," my wife told me, "but there are days when Nathan's playing the flute too loudly or romping with his dog through the house that I feel a smidgen of resentment. This isn't how I planned it to be."

So much for baking cookies and occasional baby-sitting. For us, grandparenting has turned into a twenty-four-hour-a-day job.

Thank you for sharing your story with us. You are among the increasing number of grandparents who are being recycled. According to 1990 Census Bureau statistics, nearly 1 million grandparents are raising grandchildren by themselves. This means approximately 5 percent of American families represent a grandparent raising a grandchild.

■ What are some of the challenges that grandparents raising grandchildren can expect?

Grandparents are raising grandchildren today in a different world from that of their birth children. They didn't have to deal with drive-by shootings, condom distribution in the schools, or a culture that is increasingly turning its back on biblical principles.

That's why grandparents need classes that will arm them with the same survival techniques that young parents learn. Hospitals, community colleges, and social service agencies are recognizing that need and offering support in these areas.

In addition to parenting classes, grandparents raising grandchildren need social service agencies to step in with respite care, discipline training, and counseling for children from abusive backgrounds. If you or someone you know needs help, contact local senior-assistance groups. They have different names such as Seniors Rights or Council of Aging, but every county has an office for seniors.

■ Can these grandparents get financial assistance, or are they all on their own?

WHO ARE YOU?

▶ Grandmothers represent about 60 percent of those raising grandchildren, while 40 percent are grandfathers. Fifty-seven percent of such households are in the South, and the rest are evenly divided between the Northeast, Midwest, and West. About 40 percent live in non-metropolitan areas.

▶ The majority—68 percent—of grandparent caregivers are white, 29 percent are black, and 10 percent are of Hispanic origin.

▶ Legal arrangements involving grandparents raising their grandchildren vary. Some are legally in charge of their grandchildren through adoption, custody, or guardianship. Others take on parenting responsibilities informally with their child's approval. Grandparents take legal steps to gain custody of their grandchildren for two major reasons: To stabilize the relationship with the child; and they believe they need legal status in order to access benefits and services for the child like health insurance. The latter reason may or may not be true. Many of the public benefits for the child may be available without legal custody of the child.

The most significant monetary help for a grandparent raising a grandchild comes from Aid for Families with Dependent Children (AFDC), which varies from state to state and is never enough. For example, in one state, AFDC pays $349 for one child, $440 for two.

Grandparents raising grandchildren can apply for AFDC funds by filling out a form at their local Department of Social and Health Services office. If a retired grandparent has legally adopted the grandchild, he or she may apply for Social Security benefits. For information on Social Security or supplemental Social Security benefits, contact the reference department of your library or your Social Security office.

■ **What about discipline problems? Isn't it hard for tired grandparents to keep up with the antics of little ones?**

Discipline can be a difficult problem for grandparents raising grandchildren because they are often dealing with children who have suffered physically or emotionally. After all, these are often children who lived in abusive homes for months or years before coming into the grandparents' home.

Keep in mind that most grandparents raising children again are beyond the typical child-rearing years. They range in age from their late twenties to their early nineties. For older individuals, serving as parents again can exact a serious toll on their health as they try to keep up with the demands of parenting.

RESERVOIRS OF KNOWLEDGE

Grandparents, whether they are being "recycled" as parents or acting in their God-given grandparenting role, are reservoirs of knowledge and experience. We should invite them lovingly to share and enrich our lives and the lives of our children.

The next time you see your parents, tell them that you would like to record some of their memories for posterity. Turn on the camcorder (borrow one, if you must) and ask questions. For example, have them talk about their recollections of their parents and grandparents, where they went to school, what it was like living during World War II, and places they have lived. If appropriate, ask them to share their testimony and what God has meant to their lives. Telling how faith has impacted their lives can leave a tremendous impression on the grand kids.

■ **What do these grandparents need most?**

Grandparents who are parenting grandchildren need prayer. Several million grandparents are doing this remarkable work at great personal sacrifice to the dreams they had for their later years.

Consider the story of Tina and George, who received their grandson Michael when he was three years old.

"Our daughter, Samantha, never bonded with her son," says Tina. "We watched our grandson living without maternal love and got a hold of him every chance we could. Finally, after Samantha went through several drug rehabilitations only to go back to her same abuse habits and live-in situations, we took Michael for good. We legally adopted him last year. We are in our late sixties, but having Michael brings joy to our lives. He's a good boy, smart as a whip. At six, he's doing fine in school. We feel blessed to have him in our home, and we will give him the best possible future."

That's why few parents can refuse to help out when they see their children or grandchildren in great need. Besides, to do so would deny Scripture. In 1 Timothy 5:8, Paul writes, "If anyone does not provide for his relatives, and especially for his immediate family, he has denied the faith and is worse than an unbeliever."

■ **How can you find support groups?**

To offer help to grandparents like these, individuals have formed grandparent support groups across the country. Some groups have newsletters alerting members to new legislation, needed resources, encouragement, and success stories. Most grandparent support groups are grassroots organizations running on a financial shoestring of donated funds. Some of these are:

▶ Adoptive Families of America (612-535-4829) answers legal questions about adoption.
▶ Grandparents Rights Organization (810-646-7191) is a nonprofit clearinghouse that offers a monthly newsletter for $35 a year informing its readers about state laws and the availability of support groups.
▶ Grandparents Raising Grandchildren Inc. (817-428-2625) is a support group whose aim is "to make the world a safer

place for those children whose birth parents are unable or unwilling to assume the legal and moral responsibilities of parenthood; and to educate ourselves on the legal aspects of custody, visitation, adoption, and the legal rights of all parties."

▶ The American Association of Retired Persons (AARP) sponsors an information clearinghouse called the Grandparent Information Center (202-434-2296) to help the growing number of grandparents raising grandchildren. The Center—at 601 E Street, NW, Washington, DC 20049—was established with a three-year, $300,000 grant from the Brookdale Foundation Group, a philanthropic organization in New York. Their aim is to work with grandparent support groups and other national and community-based groups that deal with various family services. The AARP provides information on support-group locations in specific areas, suggestions on where to look for help, welfare benefits, and other issues important to grandparents raising grandchildren.

▶ Should you have an interest in starting a support group in your area, you can contact Ethel Dunn at National Coalition of Grandparents (608-238-8751).

This material is adapted from Grandparenting by Grace *(Broadman & Holman Publishers) by* Irene M. Endicott *and* Heaven Help the Home *(Victor) by Howard Hendricks.*

67

When Your Child Is an Only Child

. . . .

■ **For a variety of reasons, more and more children are growing up without a brother or a sister. Why is that?**

Consider the story of Carol Kent. She never intended to be the mother of just one. As the oldest of six preacher's kids, she was well-schooled in baby-sitting, nurturing, and cooking for a whole tribe. She married, taught school for four years, and then became pregnant. Nine months later Jason Paul Kent burst into their lives on a Sunday morning in October. Though the labor was long and excruciating, the reward was a perfect miniature human being with little ears, a tiny nose and rosebud lips.

Carol fell in love. Awkwardly holding J.P. in her arms, she turned to her husband, "Honey, look at him. He's *sooo* beautiful." Outside the window she saw the sun dancing across the red and orange leaves. God's creation was celebrating with them.

Carol didn't know it then, but it was the *last* time she would give birth to a living child.

■ **So Carol was never able to bring a baby to term again?**

That's right. When J.P. was 5, she became pregnant again. She was excited, but life was busy. She was speaking at women's groups and retreats. Her husband, Gene, and she decided to keep the pregnancy a secret for a short while.

Some strong cramping began, but she ignored it. One morning, severe cramps racked her body. Within minutes, she lost her second child to a miscarriage in a bathroom.

Carol's first response was devastation, but the news got worse: She and her husband would never able to conceive again. She finally understood there would be other times (perhaps many) when she would not be able to explain away infertility, pain, and disappointment.

A choice had to be made. Though Carol grieved, she knew she had to move on. Even though Carol could never have another son or a daughter, she could still celebrate and enjoy the child God had given her.

■ **What are some of the other reasons why couples are having only one child?**

Certainly the rise in working women is one reason. As more and more women enter the workplace and pursue careers, conceiving children takes a backseat. When a child does arrive, the couple decides their family is done because Mom had to return to her career. In addition, more and more mothers are waiting until their mid- to late-thirties to have their first children, and they are less prone to have a second child.

■ **How prevalent are families with one child?**

One in five American women at the end of the childbearing years has one child, twice the number ten years ago. But there are many famous and talented people who are only children, such as Charles Lindbergh, Albert Einstein, Indira Ghandi, and Franklin Roosevelt. But the

> **A POSTSCRIPT**
> **by Carol Kent**
>
> What's the toughest part of raising an only child? Releasing him or her into the adult world and letting go. After all, he's my only child. My emotions are still fragile these days, and it's hard to walk past his bedroom. The house is silent without the laughter of a teenager and basketball practice in the driveway. I worry that an unworthy woman may steal his affection, and on certain days my heart aches with the pain of separation. But I'm learning to trust God and turn fear into faith.

greatest irony is that Dr. James Dobson, the acclaimed expert on the family, was an only child!

■ **Are you saying that only children are disproportionately represented among high achievers: scientists, astronauts, star athletes, Pulitzer Prize winners, celebrated composers, actors, and actresses?**

Not necessarily, but there is a perception that only children are selfish, anxious, and egotistical, that they have problems making their way in the world. Some say that only children always have to be the center of attention, and that they are spoiled rotten.

■ **We are determined not to raise such a child. How can we keep from doing that?**

- ► *Open your home for "sleep overs" with other children—frequently.* Let your son have his buddies come over. It will give him a sense of "belonging" even though he doesn't have any siblings. Sleep overs also allow you to supervise activities, select videos, and be a spiritual influence to many young people.
- ► *Go to family reunions as often as possible.* Let him see and experience a large extended family who values him. Try to keep his "love tank" full.
- ► *Adopt a family.* If you live far away from grandparents, find an older couple in your church or neighborhood to include in your family activities.
- ► *Let go of total control and perfectionism.* Don't worry about matching clothes and a perfectly groomed appearance.
- ► *Give rewards for reading books.* Loneliness will be less of a problem to a child who loves reading.
- ► *Take the phone off the hook for the first fifteen minutes after your child comes home from school.* If you are on the phone when your son gets off the bus, you may miss an important opportunity to hear about his day. He will come in filled with excitement and anxious to talk about the challenges or perceived injustices of his day. If you are too busy to listen, you will be the loser. Those "fresh-from-school" reflections are never recaptured at the dinner table.

► *Set realistic goals for your child.* Many "onlys" tend to be perfectionists to meet parental expectations. This can cause incredible frustration for a child trying to work beyond his or her maturity or ability level.

► *Celebrate a good report card without suggesting the child was capable of "all A's."* Report card day can be fearful for children. Parents of "onlys" have an uncanny way of expecting their children to achieve better grades than they did. Some parents are masters at "miming" approval or disapproval with their eyebrows when the grades come out.

► *Expect your only child to be a child, not a miniature adult.* There may be occasions when your son is the only child at your dinners with friends and acquaintances. Although he may enjoy talking with "big people" and entertaining the group with his "adult" responses and grown-up behavior, don't rob your son of something he can have only once—a childhood!

► *In the teen years, choose your battles carefully.* Learn to make major issues *only* over things that are immoral or illegal. When you waste your energy on the small stuff, you will have no clout left for important concerns.

This material is adapted from writings by author and speaker Carol Kent, who is founder of Speak Up with Confidence. She and her husband live in Port Huron, Michigan.

68

Raising Staircase Children

. . . .

■ We're in our mid-forties with four children ranging in age from nineteen to eight. For my wife, Landi, and me, it's time to start thinking about grandchildren—not babies of our own. But over dinner at Denny's recently, Landi announced to the whole family that she is pregnant.

I looked over at my wife as if to say, Isn't that the most ridiculous thing? But she was nodding her head up and down. "Yes," she said in a weak voice. "I am pregnant! I took a home pregnancy test this morning, and I'm still in shock. . . ."

I wasn't the only one who was surprised. Our two oldest girls were absolutely mortified. They wondered how in the world we could do such a thing. They ran into the rest room, sobbing. Now that my wife and I are about to do an Abraham and Sarah impersonation, what kind of parenting challenges lie ahead of us?

Some difficult ones. You are about to become parents of "staircase children"—children with wide age differences. But if you keep these six important points in mind, these should be the best years of your lives:

> **1. *Don't turn your older children into permanent baby-sitters.***
> You'll probably have to fight a natural tendency to do this.

After all, you may wonder why you should go out and *pay* a baby-sitter when you've got some built-in sitters right there in your house. But relying on the older ones to baby-sit whenever you need someone is unfair to them, and it can make them resentful.

Should you *never* ask your older children to baby-sit? No, but you need to respect their time and their wishes and not force them into a role they don't want. If when they were small you occasionally hired a baby-sitter, do the same for the younger ones.

2. View all of this as an opportunity to show the older children how much work and responsibility it takes to raise a child.

Many young people have romantic ideas about what babies are like. They don't understand the expense, the time, the total involvement that a baby requires of his or her parents. Your children should get a good picture now. They will realize that a baby is not a toy or a pet, and that wisdom will be invaluable when they consider starting their own families.

3. A "late-in-life" baby gives you another chance to get this parenting thing right!

Do you remember when your first child was born? She came home to "Welcome Holly" banners and a beautifully decorated nursery stocked full of bright, shiny, sterile, and of course, educational baby toys. She also came to a house heated to 104 degrees because you wanted to protect her.

That's normally the way it is for a firstborn child. *Handle with care*. You act as if the child were made of expensive crystal that will break if you look at it the wrong way!

Your new child will come home to a house that is pretty much business as usual. You know now that kids are pretty tough. You won't worry about sterilizing the teddy bear before you let your infant hold him!

You will probably lighten up in a number of ways with your younger children, and there is nothing wrong with that as long as you don't swing too far in the opposite direction. (Some people are much too strict with their older children and much too lenient with their younger ones.)

4. Birth order really is a science, and you should know as much about it as you possibly can.

Any child who is at least five years younger than his next oldest brother or sister is likely to have the characteristics of a firstborn. If you understand how the various birth orders react and relate (read *The Birth Order Book* by Dr. Kevin Leman), you can save yourself a lot of trouble!

5. *Your older children can serve as godly role models for the younger ones.*

You can fully expect that your new child will be strengthened by the example of their older siblings' Christian witness, and that they will walk with God all their lives.

6. *It really is natural, when you're in your forties, to think that all the other mothers and fathers look like teenagers.*

OK, you can admit it: You're getting old. You both know that before long, PTA meetings will be past your bedtimes. You're likely to be a little less tolerant of your child's music by the time she reaches her teen years, but the good news is that you'll be able to just turn down your twin Miracle Ears!

Please understand that people are going to come up to you and ask, "Isn't grandparenting wonderful?" and you're going to have to say, "She's our *daughter,* not our *granddaughter.*" But that's all right. Don't take offense. Besides, you'll get to know how Abraham and Sarah felt having a child in their old age, and they felt terrific!

■ **We have staircase children, but it's because we're a blended family. I was divorced with teenage children, and my wife had two preschoolers. What advice can you give us?**

These days, many families with staircase children are more likely to be from blended families—not older parents. Divorce and remarriage have made families with teenagers and toddlers a common occurrence in the '90s.

In Dr. Kevin Leman's book *Living in a Step Family,* he describes how last-borns can be rebellious, critical, temperamental, spoiled, impatient, and impetuous. Naturally, last-borns are not taken very seriously because they're "not big enough to do anything," or at least not anything right. In short, babies have to live in the shadow of those who were born before, as their older siblings tend to write them off.

The child's first steps, first successful tying of shoelaces, first *anything* is more likely to be met with polite yawns or comments like, "Oh, will you look at that! Little Thadius has learned to do a somersault. Remember when Timothy did that?"

Without realizing it, these parents have sent little Thadius a dis-couraging message: *Your older brother has already done what you think is so special.*

Blended families need to make sure that last-borns don't slip through the cracks, that they still receive the same love and attention that the older brothers and sisters received during their childhood years.

This material is adapted from Dr. Kevin Leman's writings, including Bringing Up Kids without Tearing Them Down *(Focus on the Family).*

69

Blended Families

■ **I know it takes more than good intentions and wishful thinking to successfully blend families. Our first holiday season is coming soon, and I'm really apprehensive about what's going to happen.**

So was Lonni Collins Pratt when she and David walked down the aisle five years ago. It was the second marriage for both of them as their first marriages had ended in divorce.

Between them, they brought five teenagers to their new family. Lonni had two daughters, Shelly and Andrea. Although David's three children, Mike, Scott, and Michelle, lived with their mother, they spent weekends and holiday periods with Lonni and David.

The first Christmas, as you would expect, was a disaster. The boys didn't like their gifts. The girls bickered, and one wanted all her presents returned. Shelly called Michelle a brat. They ended the evening with most of them in tears.

When the next holiday season arrived, Lonni wasn't expecting much. As if to downplay the event, she prepared tacos and chili for Christmas Eve dinner. When they all sat down at the table, David led the family in prayer.

"Thank You, Lord, for our children," he began, "and thank You for this chance to celebrate Your love as a family. Help us to understand and be patient with each other. Thank You for the gift of life in

Jesus. Happy birthday."

Silence followed, then Shelly poked Scott. "At least it was short," she chortled. "You should hear him pray when you guys aren't here. He prays for everything but the food."

It suddenly dawned on Lonni that David's children had never heard their father pray. He had committed his life to Christ *after* the divorce.

David's short prayer broke the ice. Before tearing into gifts, they strung cranberries and made popcorn balls. Then came the presents. After a few minutes, the sound of ripping paper ceased. Scott had found the bottle of bubbles. The other kids quickly unwrapped their similarly shaped gifts. The bubbles had been David's idea.

Within minutes, their nearly grown children, all five of them, were chasing each other around the house, blowing bubbles and laughing like little kids. That's when Lonni knew their two families had finally blended.

■ **You're not suggesting that I go out and buy bottles of bubbles, are you?**

Do whatever it takes to get your two families pulling from the same string. Trying to blend families is a difficult task, but it's becoming a more common occurrence these days.

■ **How common are blended families?**

One out of every three Americans is either a stepparent, a stepchild, a stepsibling, or some other member of a stepfamily. According to the Census Bureau, the number of children living with their biological mother and a stepfather increased 13 percent to 6 million between 1980 and 1985 (the latest figures available), and the number

---

SPECIAL THOUGHTS FOR BLENDED FAMILIES

In a family where children and adults may be adjusting to new living arrangements, different routines, and a lack of privacy, the need for respect becomes paramount.

► Do you knock before entering a room?

► Do you show respect for the parent who is not in your home?

► Do you allow items such as mementos from the other parent into your home?

► Do you practice thoughtfulness and common courtesy with the other parent or family?

living with a stepmother and a biological father increased 2 percent to 740,000. Undoubtedly, these numbers are even higher today.

■ **I just married Rick, and he has two high-school-age children from a previous marriage. I have one son who is in elementary school. It looks like Rick's girls are going to live with us through the end of high school. What should I be prepared for?**

Well, for starters, you better get a second telephone line into your home. But seriously, your battlegrounds will be the usual between mothers and daughters: dating, school, curfews. What will make life tough is that the young teens will probably challenge your authority as a parent right from the start—even in unimportant matters. For instance, if you ask one of them to remove her books from the kitchen table, she might bark, "You aren't my mother!"

■ **That's exactly what my stepdaughter yelled at me last week, but we weren't arguing over library books. Rick's seventeen-year-old daughter wanted to go to an after-game party in which the parents weren't going to be home, and I said she couldn't go. "You aren't my mother!" she screamed, and in a way, she was right. But I still felt it was the right thing to do—telling**

THE BYLAWS OF BLENDING

1. Plan the strategy of the merger. When two families come together, every member must be considered.

2. Put a family agreement in writing. Rights and responsibilities, limitations and rewards, every facet of home life that can be anticipated should be noted and signed by everyone.

3. Practice reevaluation. Daily routine tends to wear down good intentions. A regular family council is a good preventative for deteriorating attitudes. Embarrassment and put-downs should be disallowed; all assets and liabilities must be shared.

4. Clarify authority and access to it. Families vary in their organization according to temperaments and abilities, but everyone needs to understand who is in charge and what to do with problems, criticism, and dissatisfaction.

5. Employ the tool of family worship. Nothing smoothes relationships and nourishes a home more than a time of common adoration of God and prayer for needs that everyone shares.

her that she couldn't go to that unchaperoned party.

You did do the right thing, but you, as the stepparent, are going to have to rely on the biological parent's authority until a solid relationship is established. When a stepparent walks in the door and demands immediate authority, he or she is asking for trouble. Experts say it takes at least two years before a child even *begins* to accept the stepparent.

Next time you find yourself telling your stepdaughter she can't go a party, have your spouse back you up. If he's not home, then he may have to talk to his daughter on the phone directly. After that incident, you may start saying things like, "Your father would like you to clean your room." "Do you think Dad would like you to watch this movie?" or "Did your father tell you it was OK to go?"

You will need to rely upon his established authority until your stepchildren learn to trust you.

■ **The task of blending our families has been even more difficult than we had imagined. What are some ideas for my husband and me to keep in mind?**

1. *Make your marriage a priority.*

If it's the second marriage for both of you, then you probably know that the odds of second marriages lasting are even lower than first marriages.

Before or shortly after your wedding, sit down with each of the children and explain to them that, next to God, your marriage will be given top priority. Of course, you will need to assure them that you will love them as always, but you are adding the new responsibility of loving a spouse too.

2. *Find a church that is supportive and understanding.*

Does your church have a Sunday School class for remarried couples? You'll find it helpful to listen to others talk about their teenage children and the problems of raising them in a stepfamily. It will be a comfort to know that other parents and children struggle with the same problems. No, you aren't a bad parent, and no, your children aren't rotten.

While some couples will have to deal with condemnation from church members for divorce and remarriage, count your blessings if your church restores you in loving forgiveness. No wonder statistics indicate that most single adults leave the church after a divorce because they feel judged and condemned.

The old African proverb is true: "It takes a village to raise a child." It is never more true than in the case of stepfamilies. The church needs to be that village.

3. *Seize every opportunity to establish trust.*

Blended families move toward unity one tiny step at a time, and each movement is a miracle. Individuals who think they can go into a household and snap everyone into line will soon completely dismantle whatever is left of the family.

God has given us unique opportunities to prove our trustworthiness. But we have to be looking for them with one wet finger lifted to the air, waiting for the breeze of divine opportunity.

4. *Know that relationships grow with time.*

Much of what binds a family is found in the history of living and loving together. As a stepfamily, you must build your history, bit by bit, from the ground up.

In small ways, try to make your support concrete for your young-adult children. Make every effort to be a sounding board for summer camp, college, classes, special trips, and summer employment. While not investing less time in your marriage, make it one of your top priorities to encourage your stepchildren. You do that by attending their band and choir concerts, plays, baseball games, graduations, and award ceremonies. You do that by dropping by and buying a frozen yogurt dessert when your stepdaughter lands her first "real" job at TCBY.

Gradually, you will notice your family coming together. It will never look like a traditional family, but you've already accepted that.

This material is adapted from writings by Lonni Collins Pratt of Lapeer, Michigan, Parenting with Intimacy *(Victor) by David and Teresa Ferguson, Paul and Vicky Warren, and* Heaven Help the Home *(Victor) by Dr. Howard Hendricks.*

70

And One in Heaven

....

■ **When friends and well-wishers ask me innocently, "How many children to you have?" the question always throws me for a loop. Is it because I had a miscarriage several years ago?**

Most likely. Christine Greenwald, a wife of an ordained minister, hears that same question quite often, and her usual happy answer is "Three children. Two boys and a girl." But inwardly—and sometimes outwardly—she adds, "And one in heaven."

Christine experienced a miscarriage early in her third pregnancy. Since then, she and her husband have been blessed with a healthy baby, but grief has left its mark on their hearts. They are now well tuned to the pain of other couples who are bereaved as they once were.

Christine was numb with disbelief, and full of guilt over her lack of tears after she returned home from that sad trip to the hospital. She should have been grateful for the numbness—the merciful buffer of shock. She didn't know that month after month of anguish lay ahead—anguish complicated by the fact that many people are uncomfortable in dealing with the profound sense of emptiness that may follow even the very early death of an unborn child.

■ **Is that because we don't know what to say?**

Offering consolation to any bereaved friend is difficult. The special circumstances surrounding a loss in pregnancy often leave well-intentioned comforters feeling especially awkward.

Current figures from the Pregnancy and Infant Loss Center in Wayzata, Minnesota, indicate that nearly one million families each year experience a loss in pregnancy. Consequently, almost everyone knows someone who has had this experience.

But statistics don't lessen the lonely ordeal of losing a much-wanted child. That loss may be intensified in the increasingly common scenario of first-time parents over thirty who fear that the lost pregnancy might have been their "only shot" at having a family.

■ **What do those who have walked through their own maze of grief and frustration have to say regarding miscarriage? What kind of compassionate understanding is best?**

First, allow the parents the right to grieve. While it is normal for some couples to sustain a loss in pregnancy—especially a very early loss—with minimal emotional distress, other couples will go through a period of mourning. In most cases involving a miscarriage, no funeral or memorial service is observed, usually because there is no body.

Without the formal rituals of bereavement to "legitimize" their sorrow, these couples may experience guilt in addition to the normal stages of grief—denial, anger, bargaining, depression, and acceptance. "Do I have a right to grieve for a nameless child I've never even held?" they ask.

Well-meaning comforters may unwittingly contribute to this guilt by making cheerful statements like, "You're young, you can try again," or "It's probably for the best." Such comments, in effect, deny that a life has been snuffed out, or imply that the baby who died is a "non-person." The death of an unborn child is an irreplaceable loss, and we need to respect the fact that victims of miscarriage have the right and the need to grieve in their own way.

■ **How much time should these parents grieve?**

Experts on death and grief agree that it may take a year, more or less, for most bereaved persons to come to terms with the death of a loved one. Even then, the grieving continues, but on a less-intense basis.

Recovering from the physical effects of a miscarriage usually takes the mother from one to six weeks. While a couple may quickly resume an outwardly normal routine, friends and relatives can best help by remaining alert to their feelings and sensitive to their readiness for outside help, if it seems warranted.

Some couples may benefit from participation in a hospital or church-sponsored support group for those suffering from a miscarriage. These have been organized all over the nation, and a listing of support groups in your area can be obtained by writing and sending a self-addressed, stamped (55 cents) envelope to:

The Pregnancy and
Infant Loss Center
Suite 22
1415 E. Wayzata Blvd.
Wayzata, MN 55391

Judy Prawdzik, a delivery-room nurse and advisor to a bereaved parents' support group in Pennsylvania, volunteers another suggestion that comforters can make when the time is right. She says that all couples who have miscarried should be encouraged to schedule a post-miscarriage visit with their physician. This will provide an opportunity for the couple to ask the many questions gnawing at their peace of mind.

■ What type of questions are asked in this type of setting?

Usually, parents are looking for answers to such anxious queries as: "Would the baby have lived if I had gone right to bed?" or "Did I cause the miscarriage by lifting the box that day?" and "What happens next?"

Above all, remember to offer listening ears, thinking-of-you cards, occasional casseroles, baby-sitting, and cleaning help in the weeks and months following a loss. These loving gestures will acknowledge your friend's need for time to grieve.

■ **Where's Dad in all this? Do husbands grieve when their wives miscarry?**

Understandably, more attention is focused on the physical and emotional state of the mother. But a father has his own feelings. Concern for his wife and lingering cultural expectations of "the strong, silent male" may cause a husband to bury his grief, only to have it surface later under the guises of job stress or marital tensions. Christine Greenwald's husband, Gary, will never forget the loving pastor who approached him after their miscarriage and said, "Everybody's worried about Christine, but how are you doing, Gary?"

■ **Sometimes people who experience a miscarriage are looking for spiritual comfort. What can I say in this department?**

Early in the grief process, glib use of biblical quotations can come across as "canned comfort," lacking understanding of the parents' need to express their feelings. At this stage, even the most devout couple may be blaming God—consciously or unconsciously—as the cause of their sorrow.

Gentle reminders of His love for little children (Matthew 18:4-6; Matthew 19:13,14), His watchful care over each of His creatures (Matthew 10:29-31), and His empathy with Mary and Martha when Lazarus died (John 11:1-36) will help them to focus on God's loving kindness and sustaining presence.

Later, when the parents have reached the stage of accepting their loss, the truth of Romans 8:28 will offer its ageless hope: "For we know that all things work together for good to those who love God, and who are called according to His purpose." That's reassurance to live on!

The material is adapted from writings by Christine Willett Greenwald of Findley Lake, New York.

71

When Homosexuality Hits Home

■ I felt deceitful about sneaking into my son's room, but I was worried. My sixteen-year-old son, Tony, had begun staying out all night, and I didn't know even the names of his new friends. Maybe he's written down some names and phone numbers, I thought. His wallet was on the dresser, and I found a slip of paper inside. As I hurriedly scribbled names, Tony walked in.

"Whaddya think you're doing?" he yelled, his eyes blazing. I flushed with embarrassment, but I kept my voice calm.

"Tony, I want to know where you are. When you don't come home, I've got to know who to call."

Tony argued for several moments. Then he dropped the bombshell.

"Well, you know I'm gay, don't you?"

My mouth went dry, and my mind froze. Tony filled the silence with details. Three months ago, he'd been hitchhiking home when a school counselor picked him up and seduced him. Now he has accepted his "new" identity and was getting to know other homosexuals.

"And, Mom," he concluded, "I've found the man of my dreams. Everything's going to be all right now."

I wanted my life to end. My child had confessed a sinful lifestyle. Now what?

The discovery that a child is involved in homosexuality can be a greater trauma than his death. Barbara Johnson knows; she experienced both.

In 1968, Barbara's second son was killed in Vietnam. Five years later, her oldest son died instantly when a drunk driver hit his car head on. But June 1975 brought what she describes as the cruelest blow of all: The day after her third son, Larry, graduated from junior college as class president and recipient of the "Most Outstanding Student" award, she discovered a stack of homosexual magazines in his room.

"A terrible, roaring sob burst from me," she recalls. "Never before had I felt such a combination of shock and panic."

■ **That's exactly what I felt. Shock was soon replaced by other emotions. Fear: What will people think? Bewilderment: How could this happen in a Christian family? And guilt: Where did we go wrong?**

You can expect severe stress symptoms to follow, including panic, shortness of breath, insomnia, and migraines. One woman lost all her hair within a week of discovering her son's homosexuality.

The pressure increases when families feel unable to share their problem. "I knew my pastor would never understand," said one mother. "He once said homosexuals couldn't be saved."

Another mom was a minister's wife. *How can I ever be involved in church leadership again?* she wondered.

■ **I know it's really going to be tough dealing with my son's homosexuality. My husband and I are in a crisis mode. How should we be responding?**

Your first reaction may be to disown the child, but victorious parents and professional counselors have other advice.

But from the outset, you need to love unconditionally. Reject the sin, not the person. "It's our job to love our kids," says Barbara Johnson. "And it's God's job to work in their lives. Condemnation doesn't work; only conviction from God can bring change."

One mother recalls the moment when her son confessed his homosexuality. "His head was tilted, his mouth twitching. I knew he was saying, 'If you reject me, I don't know what I'll do.'" A child's confession is often a cry for help. Although their homosexuality is news to the parent, he's usually struggled in silent agony for years.

■ Is loving the person an endorsement of the sinful lifestyle?

No. Jack, a former homosexual, remembers his father's words to him years ago: "Son, you are my flesh and your mother's, and we want to help you. Come talk to us anytime."

"Today," says Jack, who's happily married with two sons, "I know my parents' unconditional love is what brought me through."

■ Are there ministries for homosexuals, to help them leave the lifestyle?

Yes, there are, but many men and women living the homosexual lifestyle have never heard of a way out. They need to know "ex-gay" ministries around the country can offer help (see sidebar). Most of these ministries are staffed by former homosexuals, such as Phil Hobizal of Portland, Oregon.

"As a teen, I didn't see any other choice," he recalls. "My psychologist told me to just accept it." When Phil found Christ in 1978, his hopelessness changed. "I knew God was real, and that He could change my sexual desire."

■ Is there conclusive evidence to prove homosexuality is inborn?

"There is no such thing as a 'natural' inclination toward homosexual involvement," says Dr. George A. Rekers, professor of neuropsychiatry and behavioral science at the University of South Carolina School of Medicine. "Instead," says Dr. Rekers, "there are adverse situations in a child's life that can lead to homosexual temptations." Such factors may arise within the family. Many homosexual men, for instance, never sensed warmth and acceptance from their fathers. Others lived with controlling, hostile mothers. Other significant factors include peer rejection, homosexual molestation, same-sex experimentation, exposure to homosexual pornography, and the absence of healthy sex education.

In lesbians, a lack of bonding with the mother often leads to a feeling of isolation from her own gender ("I never felt like a girl").

That lack of sexual identity can also result from her father not having affirmed her femininity. Another common factor in lesbian development is sexual trauma. "At least 85 percent of the lesbians I talk to have been victims of abuse," says Darlene Bogle, a counselor in the San Francisco area. These issues, although deep-rooted, are not too much for God to handle. He is "the God of hope" (Rom. 15:13).

WHERE TO FIND HELP

Exodus International
P.O. Box 2121
San Rafael, CA 94912
(415) 454-1017

Information on ex-gay ministries in North America and overseas. Literature and support groups for those overcoming homosexuality, plus additional resources for parents.

Spatula Ministries
P.O. Box 444
La Habra, CA 90631
Directed by Barbara Johnson. Offers resources for parents, including literature, tapes, books, and monthly newsletter.

Also:
Desert Stream
12488 Venice Blvd.
Los Angeles, CA 90066-3804
(310) 572-0140

His Heart Ministries
12162 E. Mississippi Ave.
P.O. Box 12321
Aurora, CO 80011
(303) 663-7778

■ **I have to confess that I am struggling with guilt after discovering my child's homosexuality.**

All parents make mistakes. It's only when our kids mess up that those mistakes come back to haunt us. Anita Worthlen raised her son alone and recognizes the struggles of single mothers of sons. But she reminds parents that even when circumstances are less than ideal, family factors don't *cause* homosexual behavior. Each child makes a conscious decision to pursue whatever temptations arise. Entering the gay lifestyle comes from the child's decisions—not the parent's failures.

■ **My regret is that I was never home to raise my son, who followed a homosexual lifestyle for a number of years. How can I undo the past?**

God wants us to turn that burden over to Him. He will replace the guilt with His peace.

There's still time to restore your relationship with your son. It's never too late.

■ How can I start to heal from this traumatic time?

Seek God daily. Mary Lebsock, a Denver mother, climbed out of depression's hole by recording Scriptures on a cassette tape, leaving enough silence in between to repeat them back. Those verses became her "spiritual breakfast" each morning.

"The Bible gives us important promises," says Mary. One of her favorites is Acts 16:31: "They replied, 'Believe in the Lord Jesus, and you will be saved—you and your household.' " Other parents cite Jeremiah 31:16-17; 1 Samuel 1:28; Proverbs 22:6; or Jeremiah 29:11.

■ How realistic is it to expect that my child can leave the homosexual lifestyle?

Thousands of men and women have come out of homosexuality. However, for most of them, healing has been a long-term process. Most former homosexuals report that victory is a process of day-to-day discipleship. Temptations may sometimes occur, similar to a Christian previously addicted to alcohol or gambling.

One former homosexual, now married, remembers his early struggles. "Even two years into my Christian walk, I fell back into homosexual activity. I'd secretly been holding onto homosexual desires and had isolated myself from other Christians."

Afterward, he repented of his actions, confessed to a Christian friend, and kept pushing forward. In the eleven years since, he's learned more about the grace and mercy of God and has not fallen back into homosexual behavior.

You should also commit your loved one to God. Prayer is the strongest weapon parents have against their child's homosexuality. "I was able to put my son on God's altar when I realized I can't change him, but God can," says Mary Lebsock, whose son is still involved in homosexuality. "I've committed him to the Lord, and I'm at peace."

One father turned his son over to God with the prayer, "Do whatever it takes to bring him to Yourself—even if it means death." Then he let his son know he'd be there whenever he needed him—day or night. Eventually, his son did leave the homosexual lifestyle, although he is now HIV-positive.

Barbara Johnson knows from her own experience there is hope. "God can take your trouble and change it into treasure," she says. "He offers you an exchange. It's your sins for His forgiveness, your tragedy and hurt for His healing, and your sorrow for His joy."

This material is adapted from writings by Bob Davies, executive director of Exodus International in Seattle, Washington.

72

Living Together: What's a Parent to Do?

. . . .

■ **My grown daughter, Debbie, is living a loose life. Last Christmas was a disaster. She arrived in a bad mood, and it felt like the only reason she dropped by was to collect her gifts and have a nice meal. She left before dessert was served when her latest live-in lover picked her up. My husband and I are at a loss to handle this situation.**

You're right to worry about adult children who choose to cohabit, since the situation carries many spiritual, moral, and emotional risks. Unfortunately, it's usually only the parents who can see the numerous pitfalls of sex outside of a lifelong, committed, monogamous relationship. Even the very real threat of HIV and other sexually transmitted diseases is all too often ignored by young adults; they think those tragedies only befall *others*.

But even without the threat of disease, the couple's choice to live together has jeopardized their future. According to David Larson, M.D., of the National Institute of HealthCare Research, couples who live together before marriage have an increased tendency to divorce, paralleling the rise in the divorce rate over the last twenty years.

Quoting several studies of thousands of couples, Dr. Larson also reports that the marital adjustment is better among those who have *not* lived together before marriage than among couples who did. In fact, statistics show that cohabiting couples abuse each other more often and more severely than dating couples or married couples.

■ **Yes, I can see how cold research would show that living together is not a good idea, but I'm an emotional wreck each time Debbie introduces my husband and me to her latest "significant other." I've experienced many negative emotions: anger ("How dare Debbie treat us this way!"); humiliation ("What will our friends think?"); and finally, hopelessness ("Things will never change"). I can't believe how much emotional pain we are suffering.**

It's probably time you and your husband seek out the services of a Christian therapist. What he or she might tell you is that you are grieving the daughter you lost, the one you dreamed you would have, but don't. You will need time to work through your feelings.

The therapist will also review the emotional turmoil of Debbie's teen years, and how you stayed true to your biblical beliefs. You always made it clear that sex outside of marriage is wrong. Obviously, Debbie chose to disrespect your teachings. When she turned eighteen and took off on her own, at least you know that you did all you could.

THE POWER OF A GODLY MOM

A study by two university researchers, publishing in *American Sociological Review*, indicates that parental attitudes toward marriage and cohabitation do affect children's behavior.

Young women whose mothers do not approve of cohabitation are more likely to get married and less likely to "live together" with a boyfriend. However, a young woman whose mother thinks cohabiting is acceptable is statistically more likely to do so.

Young men, in contrast, appear to make their decisions more independently, and thus are not as likely to be influenced by their mothers' beliefs.

—Family in America *magazine*

■ **I'm a hurting parent too. I have two adult children who were raised in a Christian home and a Bible-believing church, so they knew where I stood on the issue of premarital sex and "shacking up." Despite that, my children have both chosen to live with their girlfriends. They knew where I stood when** they announced the news to me. "Mom, I know you're not happy with this," said one son. How should I handle this?

In a way, that's great that your adult children are at least *talking* to you about their situation. Deep down, they *know* they are not in God's will. Continue to keep the door of communication open. Continue to express your love for them, but be honest in expressing your disappointment in the lifestyle they have chosen.

Continue to make your home open to your children, which will keep the lines of communication open. But on overnight occasions, insist on separate sleeping quarters, just as you would for every other single male and female guest. If they ask why, give them this reply: "There are just some things I won't allow in my house."

■ **I'm a pastor of a small-town church, and when my son, Phil, moved in with his girlfriend, the news set tongues wagging. My wife, Betty, and I have prayed through feelings of shock, hurt, disappointment, and anger. Then I began wondering what my congregation would think. How could I proclaim truth from the pulpit while a family member was living in sin?**

Good question, but dealing with the issue head-on with your congregation is the way to go. Continue to make it clear where the "line in the sand" is drawn. At

JOB DESCRIPTION

A liberated woman . . .
Pays 1/2 the rent
Shops for food
Cooks the food
Washes the dishes
. . . and gives her
lover sex.

Dusts the furniture
and vacuums carpet
Scrubs the bathtub
and sinks
. . . and gives her
lover sex.

Picks up socks
and underwear
Washes socks and
underwear
Puts away socks
and underwear
. . . and gives her
lover sex.

A liberated man . . .
Pays 1/2 the rent
Changes light bulbs.

—*Melvin Hasman, author of* Spiritual Life in the Good Ol' USA the same time, you do not want to disown your prodigal son. You can still love your child without loving his decision. Don't allow your son's lifestyle to destroy your relationship with him. Choose to build bridges instead of walls.

When children are involved in sin, they aren't thinking rationally. Their sin natures are sticking out all over, and their lives are like a snowball: little problems soon turn into big ones. Their snowballs will soon roll downhill faster and faster, creating a bigger and bigger mess.

The snowball may have to crash before God can do His work. Often it takes a crisis—financial, emotional, or spiritual—before the situation will change. Parents can't stop their grown children's decisions; *they* just have to keep praying and trusting. And blaming yourself won't help.

■ Yes, but I feel like such a failure as a parent.

Parents can do all the right things—you know, "Train up a child in the way he should go" and all that. But eventually, it comes down to the choice of the individual. It's natural for you to blame yourself for your son's or daughter's decision, but they made the choice to live outside of God's law.

■ Do adult children, like modern versions of the Prodigal Son, eventually come back to their early training?

Every family situation is different, but in many cases, the adult child becomes convicted by the Holy Spirit and returns to the Lord. Parents who have experienced this joy say they hung on to this verse from Philippians 1:6—"He who began a good work in you will carry it on to completion until the day of Christ Jesus."

God knows what it will take to bring a wandering child back to Him. Never underestimate His power. Continue to proclaim that God's Word is true and unchanging.

This material is adapted from writings by Cynthia Culp Allen of Corning, California.

Epilogue: Thanks, Mom and Dad

I (Mike Yorkey) would like to close *The Christian Family Answer Book* with this letter by Myra Holmes. It's a letter that I hope my daughter, Andrea, can write to me one day:

Thanks, Mom and Dad

Dear Mom and Dad,

I know I don't write you often, but I just have to after watching the "Oprah Winfrey Show."

You see, Oprah brought on a panel of parents who had told their teens it was okay to have sex with their boyfriends or girlfriends—but it had to be under their roof and when the parents were home. That way, mothers and fathers were providing a "healthy" environment for "safe sex."

As I listened, I thought back to your adherence to God's rules over the years. I'm glad I listened. *Thank you* for giving me the strength to make sound choices as I was growing up. Every time I encountered peer pressure or personal temptation, your influence was there.

You were there the night my college friend—I'll call her Kelsy— told me she had given away her virginity over spring break. Even though she had already sought God's forgiveness and promised she'd wait until marriage for the next time, I felt betrayed. If Kelsy could do it, why should I bother holding onto my high standards? I felt as though I was the last person on our Christian campus who was still holding out for God's best: sex only in marriage.

But even as I struggled with the peer pressure, I remembered it was okay to be different. You taught me that. Remember seventh grade? That awful, gangly year when the ninth-graders on the bus teased me because I carried my books home each afternoon—in a *book bag*, of all things? You hugged me and told me it was *their* problem, not mine.

Later, you encouraged me to stand up for my faith in Mrs. K's English class my senior year. She usually had us read books that showed characters making decisions without considering right or wrong. Anything that even hinted of Christianity was ridiculed in her class.

One day, she hovered over my desk. "Do you believe in Absolute Truth?" she asked, daring me to defend my faith. The rest of the class snickered. I was in a no-win situation. If I answered what I believed, I'd be ridiculed. If I answered what she wanted to hear, I'd compromise my faith. But I stood my ground that day and every one thereafter, including the time she scorned my decision to attend a Christian college ("You'll be brainwashed" was her stinging comment).

When I told you what she said, you replied that you were proud of me, and that deep down, Mrs. K would respect me and my beliefs. Apparently she did; I still received my A.

Later on, when I thought I was the last virgin on campus, I still knew it was okay to be different.

When Kelsy told me, "Don't make the same mistake—it's worth waiting for," she was only echoing your words. You were the ones who first taught me that sex was too beautiful, too wonderful to waste on anyone but my husband.

In fifth grade, when our class studied "Family Living," you took the time to lovingly answer my questions. You also told me what the textbooks neglected to say: God said sex was only for husbands and wives.

You never wavered on that. I always knew where you stood. One newspaper columnist recently boasted that she gave her teen condoms in their Christmas stockings. She reasoned that since they were going to do it anyway, she wanted them to be "safe." I'm glad you never did that. The peer pressure was always tough enough without my parents giving me mixed messages.

Having high morals—and being up front about it—didn't make me exactly the most popular young woman on campus. I thought of you when I was eating pizza in the dorm—just me and my roommate—on the night of the big Valentine's Day Banquet. I was lonely and wanted to feel sorry for myself. Perhaps that handsome football player would have asked me out a second time if only I had kissed him and showed some physical affection. But then I remembered what you taught me about love.

Growing up, you showed me what it's like to love someone unconditionally: even when I picked every last one of your daffodils; even when I flushed a comb down the toilet.

I watched both of you love each other unconditionally, too, and I saw how beautiful that love could be. When the neighbor boy's parents divorced, and I was worried you might, you sat me on your knee and assured me that you were committed to each other for life. "Real love," you said, "doesn't come and go with emotions."

Because you showed me that love is more than physical chemistry, I was willing to be selective in whom I dated. I was willing to wait for someone who would love me for life.

When I finally found that someone and we were engaged to be married, the temptation was stronger than ever. We both wanted to be obedient to God by waiting, but sometimes the desire to express our love seemed overwhelming. Christian friends didn't help. One told us, "Wouldn't it be easier for your fiancé to sleep at your place instead of finding another spot for him when he visits?"

But you had helped me learn self-control long ago. You told me to choose one hour of TV per day, no more. You set limits on how late I could stay out. You encouraged me to discipline myself in schoolwork and in daily Bible reading. Because I had practiced self-control in the little decisions, I could also exercise self-control in the big choices, such as drugs, alcohol—and sex.

Of course, in some situations none of my past experiences seemed to apply. Then I leaned on something else you also helped me develop: my faith in Christ. You had rejoiced with me when I first gave my heart to Jesus and encouraged me as I grew. You taught me to turn to God's Word when I faced a new situation or difficult decision. You showed me how to trust in God's sovereignty when circumstances were overwhelming. And you taught me never, ever to compromise God's priority in my life by settling for second best.

That faith got me through a thousand gray areas, a hundred times of "What do I do now?"

Because you gave me the resources I needed to make sound sexual choices, I had a rich gift to give my husband on our honeymoon—the same gift my girlfriend Kelsy gave to a guy who thanked her by refusing to return her phone calls.

And now my husband and I enjoy the beauty of God's best for us. *Thank you.*

Your loving daughter.

Myra

Myra Holmes and her husband, Ed, live in Denver, Colorado.

.